PHILOSOPHY AND ORDINARY LANGUAGE

PHILOSOPHY AND
ORDINARY LANGUAGE

edited by Charles E. Caton

University of Illinois Press: Urbana, Chicago, London

Fifth printing, 1970

252 72600 6

INTRODUCTION

The present anthology consists of a selection of essays on language by philosophers of the movement which has come to be known as "ordinary-language" philosophy. This rather heterogeneous group of thinkers form one recent trend in so-called "analytic" philosophy, a still more heterogeneous movement with affinities to the work of many classical philosophers, but flourishing since around the turn of the century. There have been many anthologies of writings by analytic philosophers; but only two of these have been devoted to language[1] and there has been no anthology of writings of ordinary-language philosophers on language, despite the substantial literature, some of it much discussed in philosophical journals. The need seems especially pressing in view of the fact that the distinguishing characteristic of this group of analytic philosophers is their taking special and systematic account of the role played by ordinary language in the genesis and resolution of philosophical problems. It is to the presentation of some of the views on language itself of these thinkers that the present anthology is devoted.

The history and methods of ordinary-language philosophy have been discussed by others and I will not attempt to further their accounts here.[2] Let it suffice to say that the term "ordinary-

[1] *Semantics and the Philosophy of Language,* ed. Leonard Linsky, and *Readings in the Philosophy of Language,* ed. J. Fodor and J. Katz. Full information concerning works cited will be found in the bibliography.

[2] Among the leading sympathetic accounts and discussions may be mentioned Austin's "A Plea for Excuses," Black's introduction to *Philosophical Analysis,* Cavell's "Must We Mean What We Say?", Flew's introductions to his anthologies, Malcolm's "Philosophy for Philosophers" and his review-discussion of Wittgenstein's *Philosophical Investigations,* Ryle's "Ordinary Language" (reprinted here), Weitz's "Oxford Philosophy," Wisdom's *Philosophy and Psychoanalysis* (especially "Philosophical Perplexity" and "Metaphysics and Verification"), and Wittgenstein's *Philosophical Investigations.* The variety of approaches which have come to be referred to as "ordinary-language" philosophy can easily be seen by comparing the writings just mentioned of, e.g., Austin, Ryle, Wisdom, and Wittgenstein.

language philosophers" is ordinarily used to refer to the philosophers whose work is influenced by, similar to, or reminiscent of the later work of G. E. Moore, John Wisdom, and Ludwig Wittgenstein at Cambridge and of the work of Gilbert Ryle and J. L. Austin at Oxford. In the bibliography a list is supplied of the most important anthologies and accounts of the history of this school and of some of their books and articles having to do with language.

Instead of discussing history or method, I would like to discuss a matter which seems to me of special importance in connection with the ways of doing philosophy employed in the essays here reprinted and which, in particular, provides a rationale for the philosophical study of ordinary language.[3] What I wish to emphasize is the fundamental part that ordinary language necessarily plays in our intellectual endeavors. This matter may best be approached via a distinction between ordinary language and technical language. Here I mean by "ordinary" language *everyday* language rather than simply any (part of) language which a group of people shares.[4] Ordinary language in this sense is the language which defines the boundaries of linguistic communities, the boundaries within which people speak the same language or at least the same dialect. It is the language that makes possible their daily dealings with each other. It will be a large part of what a physicist or a carpenter uses in talking or writing to his colleagues, a still larger part of what they use in talking to their wives, and perhaps all they do or could use in talking to each other, or to children, shopkeepers, and policemen. Most adults are able to use and understand some technical language, at least that important in their occupation, special interests, and hobbies. This other part of their language can be used easily and naturally only with their colleagues or fellow fans: physicists with other physicists or people who happen to know some physics, farmers with other farmers or people who know something about farming. Neglecting differences in intelligence, temperament, etc., technical language is as available to anyone as ordinary language is; the difference is that only some people in a given linguistic com-

---

[3] It will be understood that I cannot be sure how far others would agree with what I have to say on this matter.

[4] I do not, then, mean (any) *standard* language in Ryle's sense in his essay "Ordinary Language" reprinted below.

munity know the technical language of, say, physics or farming, while by definition everyone in the linguistic community apart from young children knows what I am calling the ordinary language of that community.[5] It is this latter, what anyone can count on in talking to anyone else in his linguistic community, that I am here referring to as "ordinary language." I do not wish to suggest that ordinary language in this sense comprises a quite definite set of lexical items or syntactical forms; but such a set must be in principle at least vaguely specifiable or there would *be* no linguistic communities.

Consider now the relations between ordinary and technical language. These are, of course, not related as English is to French or Swahili: one could not learn technical language as a native language, neither the technical English language of physics nor the technical French language of farming. Technical language is rather a part of some language like English or French and a part defined only by reference to some particular discipline or occupation or activity among the practitioners of which it is current. I think, further, that the technical language of a discipline consists largely, if not entirely, of vocabulary items, i.e., words and phrases not part of the related ordinary language at all (e.g., 'meson') or not having in ordinary language the senses given them in the discipline in question (e.g., 'ring' in algebra). I know of no case of technical language where the technicality consists in a difference of syntactical form. Further, it seems clear that numerous ubiquitous words and phrases occur in technical contexts in the same senses or used in the same ways in which they are used in everyday contexts: e.g., articles, the verb 'to be', 'all', 'some', 'two', 'at least', 'there is', 'and', 'or', 'if . . . then', 'hardly', 'very', etc. For example, surely the 'are' of 'Canines are vertebrates' is the 'are' of 'Dogs are animals'. Also, most of the kinds of utterances involving technical language appear to be already found in ordinary language — I mean requests, assertions, questions, explanations of what one was referring to, etc.[6] Certainly the kinds of utterances found in

---

[5] For brevity I omit certain qualifications necessary to a completely accurate account, e.g., that a person may "speak the language" while being *so* bad at remembering the names of flowers or trees or animals that he constantly gets them wrong or can't remember them.

[6] I am referring to what Austin in his *How to Do Things with Words* calls "illocutionary acts."

ordinary language are also found in utterances involving technical language; and I think the additions made in technical contexts are not very numerous. They include, perhaps, things like deposing, sentencing a prisoner, and saying 'J'adoube'. Finally, the presuppositions, implications, suggestions, etc., of technical language seem to be of the same sorts and achieved by the same means as in ordinary language. For example, those of 'I don't think neutrinos *have* any charge' with those of 'I don't think elephants *bear* twins' — both imply that one isn't sure of the point and presuppose that someone has said or implied that the thing is so. One might sum these relations up by saying that technical language is always an *adjunct* of ordinary language.

Along with these relations and I think as a consequence of them, there are two further relations between ordinary and technical language which I do not think have been sufficiently emphasized. First, that the clarification of what someone is saying usually is achieved by using devices which are already a part of ordinary language and which are taken over into and used in dealing with technical language. And second, that whatever technical language a person may acquire is and, as things are, has to be acquired against the background of ordinary language.

First, corresponding to these various relations between ordinary and technical language there can occur obscurities and ambiguities. Not to mention the fact that one can fail to *hear* what someone says, for dealing with which there are devices available in ordinary language which are taken over into technical contexts (e.g., 'Huh?'), there are also such devices for use in connection with vocabulary, grammar, kind of utterance, presuppositions, implications, etc. Everyone, as a speaker of ordinary language, has the ability to say what he meant by a certain word or phrase, in what or in which sense he was using a certain word or phrase, what or which one or whom he was or is referring to or meant, whether he was or is implying, suggesting, assuming, or taking for granted this or that, whether he didn't mean this rather than that (when it is suggested that he may have misspoken), that he wasn't *inferring* that at all but rather knows it firsthand, etc. As far as I can see, these various kinds of devices are carried over without exception and without change into contexts in which technical language is being explained or used. It is, indeed, worth emphasizing that this is so. It may be presumed that any clarifying devices in daily use among the general population are fairly serviceable.[7] But what is note-worthy is that physicists and mathematicians, for example — people who necessarily employ large amounts of very technical language — do not find it necessary to devise new kinds of ques-tions in order to cause their colleagues to explain what they are saying: new questions, to be sure, but not new *kinds* of questions. They use the same locutions in the same way they have been accustomed to since childhood and in the way electricians and greengrocers do. 'Do you mean *rings* or *commutative* rings?' differs from 'Do you mean *rings* or *engagement* rings?' only in that the things the person may have meant are different. The 'Do you mean . . . or . . .?' is not different. And the same goes for the answers to the questions. Surely it is worthwhile having a conscious grasp of notions so pervasive and useful as these, in addition to the ability to employ them that we all have and all use everywhere we need to.

Second, given the relations I have mentioned between ordinary and technical language, it is clear that acquiring the use of tech-nical vocabularies can only take place against a background of ordinary language. The facts here tend, I think, to be obscured by the fact (already mentioned) that every adult has some tech-nical language, some language not shared by all or even most other adults. One can't, it seems, any longer grow up without coming to know things and being interested in things and doing things that not everyone or even most people do, and thus not without acquiring the technical language that accompanies know-ing, learning about, and doing those things. It is therefore neither rare nor striking to encounter someone who uses quite naturally and unselfconsciously locutions that one has never

---

[7] Austin was willing to state this presumption more generally: "our common stock of words embodies all the distinctions men have found worth drawing, and the connexions they have found worth marking, in the lifetimes of many generations: these surely are likely to be more numerous, more sound, since they have stood up to the long test of the survival of the fittest, and more subtle, at least in all ordinary and reason-ably practical matters, than any that you or I are likely to think up in our arm-chairs of an afternoon — the most favored alternative method." ("A Plea for Excuses," *Proceedings of the Aristotelian Society,* LVII (1957), p. 8.) Cf. his remarks at pp. 334-335 of *La Philosophie Analytique.*

before run across. But in the case of each of us, when we first came to learn the first linguistic items characteristic of our own special knowledge, special interests, and special skills, we did so on the basis of ordinary language already acquired. I think one has a tendency to forget that technical language is not really like French, say, because one can learn technical items by just picking them up (however exactly this is done) — as one just picked up English in the first place and might just pick up French or Swahili without using though already knowing English.

Now there is, I think, no doubt that technical terms can be and largely are acquired by what might be described as just picking them up from those who already know them. Indeed, if one has a technical term explained to one (by a teacher, say), one still usually needs the other too. To cite just one reason for this, an explanation of a term cannot contain an exact description of how it is used (nor are people facile in its use liable to be able to give such a description) and, even if it did, one probably couldn't keep it all in mind. For example, one may be told that force is the product of mass and acceleration, but one has to learn (to say) that forces in the technical sense, like forces in the ordinary sense and unlike products, can be (said to be) *exerted* on things — and of course what this means — despite the fact that force *is* the product of mass and acceleration and that 'force' is used to mean that product. A student will not usually be informed of such details of usage and will certainly not be given the whole story, but he doesn't need to be given it and probably couldn't use it if he were; whatever mistakes of this sort he may happen to make can be corrected as one goes along. But whether one is given some explanation of the technical locution or just picks it up or, more likely, both has it explained and then later acquires a mastery of it, the things one hears said, asked, requested, etc., involving it or something related to its use will in the great majority of instances involve elements which are also a part of ordinary language. And language which is more technical is learned against a background of language which is less technical and which involves more elements found also in ordinary language; and the less technical language is, in the first instance, learned against the background of ordinary language alone. Thus again whatever conscious awareness of the nature of ordinary language can be acquired appears both useful and desirable.

If what I have said about the relations between ordinary and technical language is along the right lines, the study of ordinary language is recommended for at least the following reasons. First, ordinary language is the basis on which technical language is erected to begin with; second, even when technical language is built on other technical language, certain basic features appear to remain the same (syntax, the kinds and forces of utterances, the use of many frequently occurring expressions); third, utterances involving technical language usually involve nontechnical language used in everyday ways; and, finally, explanations of new locutions and clarification of what one is saying can be and usually are conducted in terms of ordinary clarifying devices. One might say that ordinary language is the basis of all language; and one might almost add that it is therefore the conceptual basis of all inquiry and indeed of all characteristically *human* activities.

I wish to thank the authors, original publishers, copyright holders, and editors of the periodicals in which the essays reprinted originally appeared for their kind permission to reprint them and for their cooperation. I owe a special debt to Mr. G. J. Warnock, who kindly consented to translate Austin's "Performatif-Constatif" together with the discussion from the French, and to my colleague, Leonard Linsky, the larger part of whose essay "Reference and Referents" is published here for the first time. Finally, I have often had the benefit of the advice of Professor Linsky and of Professor Donald Jackson of the University of Illinois Press.

The sources of the articles reprinted are as follows:

J. L. Austin: "The Meaning of a Word," in *Philosophical Papers,* ed. J. O. Urmson and G. J. Warnock, Oxford, 1961, pp. 23-43; reprinted by permission of the Clarendon Press, Oxford.

———: "Performative-Constative," tr. G. J. Warnock from "Performatif-Constatif," in *La Philosophie Analytique,* Paris, 1962, pp. 271-304; by permission of Les Editions de Minuit, Paris.

R. L. Cartwright: "Negative Existentials," *The Journal of Philosophy,* LVII (1960), 629-639.

Roland Hall: "Excluders," *Analysis,* 20 (1959), 1-7; reprinted by permission of the editor.

Leonard Linsky: "Reference and Referents," Sections I-V previously unpublished, Section VI originally published as "Hesperus and Phosphorus," *The Philosophical Review,* LXVIII (1959), 515-518; reprinted by permission of the Editorial Board.

R. Rhees: "Can There Be a Private Language?", *Proceedings of the Aristotelian Society,* supplementary vol. XXVIII (1954), 77-94; reprinted by permission of the editor.

Gilbert Ryle: "Ordinary Language," *The Philosophical Review,* LXII (1953), 167-186; reprinted by permission of the Editorial Board.

———: "The Theory of Meaning," in *British Philosophy in the Mid-Century,* ed. C. A. Mace, London, 1957, pp. 239-264; reprinted by permission of George Allen & Unwin, Ltd., London.

John R. Searle: "Proper Names," *Mind,* LXVII (1958), 166-173; reprinted by permission of the editor and of the publishers, Thomas Nelson and Sons, Ltd., Edinburgh.

P. F. Strawson: "On Referring," originally in *Mind,* LIX (1950), 320-344; reprinted in *Essays in Conceptual Analysis,* ed. Antony Flew, London, 1956, pp. 21-52; reprinted by permission of Macmillan & Co., Ltd., London, and of the editor of *Mind.*

S. E. Toulmin and K. Baier: "On Describing," *Mind,* LXI (1952), 13-38; reprinted by permission of the editor.

J. O. Urmson: "Parenthetical Verbs," originally in *Mind,* LXI (1952), 480-496; reprinted in *Essays in Conceptual Analysis,* pp. 192-212; reprinted by permission of Macmillan & Co., Ltd., London, and of the editor of *Mind.*

CHARLES E. CATON

CONTENTS

1 THE MEANING OF A WORD

by J. L. Austin

SPECIMENS OF SENSE

1. 1.   What-is-the-meaning-of (the word) 'rat'?
1. 11.   What-is-the-meaning-of (the word) 'word'?
1. 21.   What is a 'rat'?
1. 211. What is a 'word'?
1. 22.   What is the 'muzzle' of a rat?
2. 1.   What-is-the-meaning-of (the phrase) 'What-is-the-meaning-of'?
2. 11.   What-is-the-meaning-of (the sentence) 'What-is-the-meaning-of (the word) "x"'??

SPECIMENS OF NONSENSE

1. 1.   What-is-the-meaning-of a word?
1. 11.   What-is-the-meaning-of any word?
1. 12.   What-is-the-meaning-of a word in general?
1. 21.   What is the-meaning-of-a-word?
1. 211. What is the-meaning-of-(the-word)-'rat'?
1. 22.   What is the 'meaning' of a word?
1. 221. What is the 'meaning' of (the word) 'rat'?
2. 1.   What-is-the-meaning-of (the phrase) 'the-meaning-of-a word'?
2. 11.   What-is-the-meaning-of (the sentence) 'What is the-meaning-of-(the-word)-"x"'??
2. 12.   What-is-the-meaning-of (the sentence) 'What is the "meaning" of "the word" "x"'??

THIS paper is about the phrase 'the meaning of a word'. It is divided into three parts, of which the first is the most trite and the second the most muddled: all are too long. In the first, I try to make it clear that the phrase 'the meaning of a word' is, in general, if not always, a dangerous nonsense-phrase. In the other two parts I consider in turn two questions, often asked in philosophy, which clearly need new and careful scrutiny if that facile phrase 'the meaning of a word' is no longer to be permitted to impose upon us.

I

I begin, then, with some remarks about 'the meaning of a word'. I think many persons now see all or part of what I shall say: but not all do, and there is a tendency to forget it, or to get it slightly wrong. In so far as I am merely flogging the converted, I apologize to them.

A preliminary remark. It may justly be urged that, properly speaking, what alone has meaning is a *sentence*. Of course, we can speak quite properly of, for example, 'looking up the meaning of a word' in a dictionary. Nevertheless, it appears that the sense in which a word or a phrase 'has a meaning' is derivative from the sense in which a sentence 'has a meaning': to say a word or a phrase 'has a meaning' is to say that there are sentences in which it occurs which 'have meanings': and to know the meaning which the word or phrase has, is to know the meanings of sentences in which it occurs. All the dictionary can do when we 'look up the meaning of a word' is to suggest aids to the understanding of sentences in which it occurs. Hence it appears correct to say that what 'has meaning' in the primary sense is the sentence. And older philosophers who discussed the problem of 'the meaning of words' tend to fall into *special* errors, avoided by more recent philosophers, who discuss rather the parallel problem of 'the meaning of sentences'. Nevertheless, if we are on our guard, we perhaps need not fall into these special errors, and I propose to overlook them at present.

There are many sorts of sentence in which the words 'the meaning of the word so-and-so' are found, e.g. 'He does not know, or understand, the meaning of the word *handsaw*': 'I shall have to explain to her the meaning of the word *pikestaff*': and so on. I intend to consider primarily the common question, 'What is the meaning of *so-and-so*?' or 'What is the meaning of *the word so-and-so*?'

Suppose that in ordinary life I am asked: 'What is the meaning of the word *racy*?' There are two sorts of thing I may do in response: I may reply *in words*, trying to describe what raciness is and what it is not, to give examples of sentences in which one might use the word *racy*, and of others in which one should not. Let us call this *sort* of thing 'explaining the syntactics' of the word 'racy' in the English language. On the other hand, I might do what we may call 'demonstrating the semantics' of the word, by getting the questioner to *imagine*, or even actually to *experience*, situations which we should describe correctly by means of sentences containing the words 'racy' 'raciness', &c., and again other situations where we should *not* use these words. This is, of course, a simple case: but perhaps the same two *sorts* of procedure would be gone through in the case of at least most ordinary words. And in the same way, if I wished to find out 'whether he understands the meaning of the word *racy*', I should test him at some length in these two ways (which perhaps could not be entirely divorced from each other).

Having asked in this way, and answered, 'What is the meaning of (the word) "rat"?', 'What is the meaning of (the word) "cat"?', 'What is the meaning of (the word) "mat"?', and so on, we then try, being philosophers, to ask the further *general* question, 'What is the meaning of a word?' But there is something spurious about this question. We do not intend to mean by it a certain question which would be perfectly all right, namely, 'What is the meaning of (the word) "word"?': *that* would be no more general than is asking the meaning of the word 'rat', and would be answered in a precisely similar way.

No: we want to ask rather, 'What is the meaning of a-word-in-general?' or 'of *any* word'—not meaning 'any' word *you like to choose*, but rather *no particular* word *at all*, just 'any word'. Now if we pause even for a moment to reflect, this is a perfectly absurd question to be trying to ask. I can only answer a question of the form 'What is the meaning of "*x*"?' if "*x*" is some *particular* word you are asking about. This supposed *general* question is really just a spurious question of a type which commonly arises in philosophy. We may call it the fallacy of asking about 'Nothing-in-particular' which is a practice decried by the plain man, but by the philosopher called 'generalizing' and regarded with some complacency. Many other examples of the fallacy can be found: take, for example, the case of 'reality'—we try to pass from such questions as 'How would you distinguish a real rat from an imaginary rat?' to 'What is a real thing?', a question which merely gives rise to nonsense.

We may expose the error in our present case thus. Instead of asking 'What is the meaning of (the word) "rat"?' we might clearly have asked 'What is a "rat"?' and so on. But if our questions have been put in *that* form, it becomes very difficult to formulate any *general* question which could impose on us for a moment. Perhaps 'What is anything?'? Few philosophers, if perhaps not none, have been foolhardy enough to pose such a question. In the same way, we should not perhaps be tempted to generalize such a question as 'Does he know the meaning of (the word) "rat"?' 'Does he know the meaning of a word?' would be silly.

Faced with the nonsense question 'What is the meaning of a word?', and perhaps dimly recognizing it to be nonsense, we are nevertheless not inclined to give it up. Instead, we transform it in a curious and noteworthy manner. Up to now, we had been asking '*What-is-the-meaning-of* (the word) "rat"?', &c.; and ultimately '*What-is-the-meaning-of* a word?' But now, being baffled, we change so to speak, the hyphenation, and ask 'What is *the-meaning-of-a-word?*' or sometimes, 'What is the "meaning" of a word?' (1. 22): I shall refer, for brevity's sake, only to the other (1. 21). It is easy to see how very different this question is from the other. At once a crowd of traditional and reassuring answers present themselves: 'a concept', 'an idea', 'an image', 'a class of similar sensa', &c. All of which are equally spurious answers to a pseudo-question. Plunging ahead, however, or rather retracing our steps, we now proceed to ask such questions as 'What is the-meaning-of-(the-word) "rat"?' which is as spurious as 'What-is-the-meaning-of (the word) "rat"?' was genuine. And again we answer 'the idea of a rat' and so forth. How quaint this procedure is, may be seen in the following way. Supposing a plain man puzzled, were to ask me 'What is the meaning of (the word) "muggy"?', and I were to answer, 'The idea or concept of "mugginess" ' or 'The class of sensa of which it is correct to say "This is muggy" ': the man would stare at me as at an imbecile. And that is sufficiently unusual for me to conclude that that was not at all the sort of answer he expected: nor, in plain English, *can* that question *ever* require that sort of answer.

To show up this pseudo-question, let us take a parallel case, where perhaps no one has yet been deluded, though they well might be. Suppose that I ask 'What is the point of doing so-and-so?' For example, I ask Old Father William 'What is the point of standing on one's head?' He replies in the way we know. Then I follow this up with 'What is the point of balancing an eel on the end of one's nose?' And he explains. Now suppose I ask as my third question 'What is the point of doing *anything*—not anything *in particular*, but just *anything*?' Old Father William would no doubt kick me downstairs without the option. But lesser men, raising this same question and finding no answer, would very likely commit suicide or join the Church. (Luckily, in the case of 'What is the meaning of a word?' the effects are less serious, amounting only to the writing of books.) On the other hand, more adventurous intellects would no doubt take to asking 'What is the-point-of-doing-a-thing?' or 'What is the "point" of doing a thing?':

and then later 'What is the-point-of-eating-suet?' and so on. Thus we should discover a whole new universe of a kind of entity called 'points', not previously suspected of existence.

To make the matter clearer, let us consider another case which is precisely *unlike* the case of 'What is the meaning of?' I can ask not only the question, 'What is the square root of 4?', of 8, and so on, but also 'What is the square root of a number?': which is either nonsense or equivalent to 'What is the "square root" of a number?' I then give a definition of the 'square root' of a number, such that, for any given number x, 'the square root of x' is a definite description of another number y. This differs from our case in that 'the meaning of p' is not a definite description of any entity.

The general questions which we want to ask about 'meaning' are best phrased as, 'What-is-the-meaning-of (the phrase) "what-is-the-meaning-of (the word) 'x'?"?' The *sort* of answer we should get to these quite sensible questions is that with which I began this discussion: viz. that when I am asked 'What-is-the-meaning-of (the word) "x"?', I naturally reply by explaining its syntactics and demonstrating its semantics.

All this must seem very obvious, but I wish to point out that it is fatally easy to forget it: no doubt I shall do so myself many times in the course of this paper. Even those who see pretty clearly that 'concepts', 'abstract ideas', and so on are fictitious entities, which we owe in part to asking questions about 'the meaning of a word', nevertheless themselves think that there *is something* which is 'the meaning of a word'. Thus Mr. Hampshire[1] attacks to some purpose the theory that there is such a thing as '*the* meaning of a word': what *he* thinks is wrong is the belief that there is a *single* thing called *the* meaning: 'concepts' are nonsense, and no single particular 'image' can be *the* meaning of a general word. So, he goes on to say, the meaning of a word must really be 'a *class* of similar particular ideas'. 'If we are asked "What does this mean?" we point to (!) a class of particular ideas.' But a 'class of particular ideas' is every bit as fictitious an entity as a 'concept' or 'abstract idea'. In the same way Mr. C. W. Morris (in the *Encyclopaedia of Unified Science*) attacks, to some purpose, those who think of 'a meaning' as a definite something which is 'simply located' somewhere: what *he* thinks is wrong is that people think of 'a meaning' as a kind of entity which can be described wholly without reference to the total activity of 'semiosis'. Well and good. Yet he himself makes some of the crudest possible remarks about 'the designatum' of a word: every sign has a designatum, which is not a particular thing but a *kind* of object or *class* of object. Now this is quite as fictitious an entity as any 'Platonic idea': and is due to precisely the same fallacy of looking for 'the meaning (or designatum) of a word'.

Why are we tempted to slip back in this way? Perhaps there are two main reasons. First, there is the curious belief that all words are *names*, i.e. in effect *proper* names, and therefore stand for something or designate it in the way that a proper name does. But this view that general names 'have denotation' in the same way that proper names do, is quite as odd as the view that proper names 'have connotation' in the same way that general names do, which is commonly recognized to lead to error. Secondly, we are afflicted by a more common malady, which is this. When we have given an analysis of a certain sentence, containing a word or phrase '*x*', we often feel inclined to ask, of our analysis, 'What *in it*, *is* "*x*"?' For example, we give an analysis of 'The State owns this land', in sentences about individual men, their relations and transactions: and then at last we feel inclined to ask: well now, *what*, in all that, *is* the State? And we might answer: the State *is* a collection of individual men united in a certain manner. Or again, when we have analysed the statement 'trees can exist unperceived' into statements about sensing sensa, we still tend to feel uneasy unless we can say *something 'really does'* 'exist unperceived': hence theories about 'sensibilia' and what not. So in our present case, having given all that is required, viz. an account of

'What-is-the-meaning-of "What is-the-meaning-of (the word)
'x'?"' we *still* feel tempted, wrongly supposing our original sentence to contain a constituent 'the-meaning-of (the-word)-"x"',
to ask 'Well now, as it turns out, what *is* the meaning of the
word "x", after all?' And we answer, 'a class of similar particular ideas' and what not.

Of course, all my account of our motives in this matter may
be only a convenient didactic schema: I do not think it is—but
I recognize that one should not impute motives, least of all
rational motives. Anyhow, what I claim is clear, is that there is
no simple and handy appendage of a word called 'the meaning
of (the word) "x"'.

II

I now pass on to the first of the two points which need now a
careful scrutiny if we are no longer to be imposed upon by that
convenient phrase 'the meaning of a word'. What I shall say
here is, I know, not as clear as it should be.

Constantly we ask the question, 'Is y the meaning, or *part* of
the meaning, or *contained* in the meaning, of x?—or is it *not*?'
A favourite way of putting the question is to ask, 'Is the judgement "x is y" analytic or synthetic?' Clearly, we suppose,
y *must* be *either* a part of the meaning of x, *or* not any part of it.
And, if y *is* a part of the meaning of x, to say 'x is not y' will
be self-contradictory: while if it is *not* a part of the meaning
of x, to say 'x is not y' will present no difficulty—such a state of
affairs will be readily 'conceivable'. This seems to be the merest
common sense. And no doubt it *would* be the merest common
sense *if* 'meanings' were things in some ordinary sense which
contained parts in some ordinary sense. But they are *not*.
Unfortunately, many philosophers who know they are not,
still speak as though y must either be or not be 'part of the
meaning' of x. But this is the point: *if* 'explaining the meaning
of a word' is really the complicated sort of affair that we have
seen it to be, and *if* there is really nothing to call 'the meaning
of a word'—*then* phrases like 'part of the meaning of the word

x' are completely undefined; it is left hanging in the air, we do not know what it means at all. *We are using a working-model which fails to fit the facts that we really wish to talk about.* When we consider what we really do want to talk about, and not the working-model, what would really be meant at all by a judgement being 'analytic or synthetic'? We simply do not know. Of course, we feel inclined to say 'I can easily produce examples of analytic and synthetic judgements; for instance, I should confidently say "Being a professor is *not* part of the meaning of being a man" and so forth.' 'A is A is analytic.' Yes, but it is when we are required to give a *general definition* of what we mean by 'analytic' or 'synthetic', and when we are required to justify our dogma that *every* judgement is either analytic or synthetic, that we find we have, in fact, nothing to fall back upon *except our working-model.* From the start, it is clear that our working-model fails to do justice, for example, to the distinction between syntactics and semantics: for instance, talking about the contradictory of every sentence having to be either self-contradictory or not so, is to talk as though all sentences which we are prohibited from saying were sentences which offended against *syntactical* rules, and could be formally reduced to verbal self-contradictions. But this overlooks all semantical considerations, which philosophers are sadly prone to do. Let us consider two cases of some things which we simply *cannot say*: although they are *not* 'self-contradictory' and although—and this of course is where many will have axes to grind—we cannot possibly be tempted to say that we have 'synthetic *a priori*' knowledge of their contradictions.

Let us begin with a case which, being about *sentences* rather than *words*, is not quite in point, but which may encourage us. Take the well-known sentence 'The cat is on the mat, and I do not believe it'. That seems absurd. On the other hand 'The cat is on the mat, and I believe it' seems trivial. If we were to adopt a customary dichotomy, and to say *either* a proposition p implies another proposition r, *or p* is perfectly compatible with not-r, we should at once in our present case be tempted to say that 'The cat is on the mat' *implies* 'I believe it': hence both the triviality of adding 'and I believe it' and the absurdity of adding 'and I do not believe it'. But of course 'the cat is on the mat' does *not* imply 'Austin believes the cat is on the mat': nor even 'the speaker believes the cat is on the mat'—for the speaker may be lying. The doctrine which is produced in this case is, that not *p* indeed, but *asserting p* implies 'I (who assert *p*) believe *p*'. And here 'implies' must be given a special sense: for of course it is not that 'I assert *p*' implies (in the ordinary sense) 'I believe *p*', for I may be lying. It is the sort of sense in which by asking a question I 'imply' that I do not know the answer to it. By asserting *p* I *give it to be understood* that I believe *p*.

Now the reason why I cannot say 'The cat is on the mat and I do not believe it' is not that it offends against syntactics in the sense of being in some way 'self-contradictory'. What prevents my saying it, is rather some semantic convention (implicit, of course), about the way we use words *in situations*. What precisely is the account to be given in this case we need not ask. Let us rather notice one significant feature of it. Whereas '*p* and I believe it' is somehow trivial, and '*p* and I do not believe it' is somehow nonsense, a third sentence '*p* and *I might not have* believed it' makes perfectly good sense. Let us call these three sentences Q, not Q, and 'might not Q'. Now what prohibits us from saying '*p*' implies 'I believe *p*' in the ordinary sense of 'implies', is precisely shown by this fact: that although not-Q is (*somehow*) absurd, 'might not Q' is not at all absurd. For in ordinary cases of implication, not merely is not Q absurd, but 'might not Q' is *also* absurd: e.g. 'triangles are figures and triangles have no shape' is no more absurd than 'triangles are figures and triangles might have had no shape'. Consideration of the sentence 'might not Q' will afford a rough test as to whether *p* 'implies' *r* in the *ordinary* sense, or in the special sense, of 'implies'.

Bearing this in mind, let us now consider a sentence which, as I claim, cannot possibly be classified as *either* 'analytic' *or* 'synthetic'. I refer to the sentence, 'This *x* exists', where *x* is a sensum, e.g. 'This noise exists'. In endeavouring to classify it, one party would point to the triviality of 'This noise exists', and to the absurdity of 'This noise does not exist'. They would say, therefore, that *existence* is 'part of the meaning of' *this*. But another party would point out, that 'This noise might not have existed' makes perfectly good sense. *They* would say, therefore, that *existence* cannot be 'part of the meaning of' *this*.

Both parties, as we are now in a position to see, would be correct in their *arguments*, but incorrect in their *conclusions*. What seems to be true is that *using the word 'this'* (not: the word 'this') *gives it to be understood that* the sensum referred to 'exists'.

Perhaps, historically, this fact about the sentence-trio, 'This noise exists', 'This noise does not exist', and 'This noise might not have existed', was pointed out before any philosopher had had time to pronounce that 'This noise exists' is analytic, or is synthetic. But such a pronouncement might well have been made: and *to this day*, even when the fact has been pointed out, many philosophers *worry* about the case, supposing the sentence *must* be one or the other but painfully aware of the difficulties in choosing either. I wish to point out that consideration of the analogy between this case and the other, should cure us once and for all of this bogy, and of insisting on classifying sentences as *either* analytic *or* synthetic. It may encourage us to consider again what the facts in their actual complexity really are. (One thing it suggests is a reconsideration of 'Caesar is bald' and similar propositions: but I cannot go into that.)

So far, however, we have scarcely begun in earnest: we have merely felt that initial trepidation, experienced when the firm ground of prejudice begins to slip away beneath the feet. Perhaps there are other cases, or other sorts of cases, where it will not be possible to say either that *y* is a 'part of the meaning' of *x* or that it is not, without being misleading.

Suppose we take the case of 'being thought good by me' and 'being approved of by me'. Are we to rush at this with the dichotomy: *either* 'being approved of by me' *is* part of the meaning of 'being thought good by me' *or* it is *not*? Is it *obvious* that 'I think *x* good but I do not approve of it' is self-contradictory? Of course it is not *verbally* self-contradictory. That it either is or is not 'really' self-contradictory would seem to be difficult to establish. Of course, we think, it must be one or the other—only 'it's difficult to decide *which*': or 'it depends on how you use the words'. But are those really the difficulties which baffle us? Of course, *if* it were certain that every sentence *must* be either analytic or synthetic, those *must* be the difficulties. But then, it is not certain: no account even of what the distinction means, is given except by reference to our shabby working-model. I suggest that 'I think *x* good but I do not approve of it' may very well be neither self-contradictory nor yet 'perfectly good sense' in the way in which 'I think *x* exciting but I do not approve of it' *is* 'perfectly good sense'.

Perhaps this example does not strike you as awkward. It cannot be expected that all examples will appeal equally to all hearers. Let us take some others. Is 'What is good ought to exist' analytic or synthetic? According to Moore's theory, this must be 'synthetic': yet he constantly in *Principia Ethica* takes its truth for granted. And that illustrates one of the main drawbacks of insisting on saying that a sentence *must* be either analytic or synthetic: you are almost certain to have left on your hands some general sentences which are certainly not analytic but which you find it difficult to conceive being false: i.e. you are landed with 'synthetic *a priori* knowledge'. Take that sentence of ill fame 'Pink is more like red than black'. It is rash to pronounce this 'synthetic *a priori* knowledge' on the ground that 'being more like red than black' is not 'part of the meaning' or 'part of the definition' of 'pink' and that it is not 'conceivable' that pink should be more like black than red: I dare say, so far as those phrases have any clear meaning, that it *is not*: but the question is: *is* the thing therefore 'synthetic' *a priori* knowledge?

Or, again, take some examples from Berkeley: is *extended* 'part of the meaning' of *coloured* or of *shaped*, or *shaped* 'part of the meaning' of *extended*? Is 'est sed non percipitur' self-contradictory (when said of a sensum), or is it not? When we worry thus, is it not worth considering the possibility that we are oversimplifying?

What we are to say in these cases, what even the possibilities are, I do not at present clearly see. (1) Evidently, we must throw away the old working-model as soon as we take account even of the existence of a distinction between syntactics and semantics. (2) But evidently also, our *new* working-model, the supposed 'ideal' language, is in many ways a most inadequate model of any *actual* language: its careful separation of syntactics from semantics, its lists of explicitly formulated rules and conventions, and its careful delimitation of their spheres of operation—all are misleading. An *actual* language has few, if any, explicit conventions, no sharp limits to the spheres of operation of rules, no rigid separation of what is syntactical and what semantical. (3) Finally, I think I can see that there are difficulties about our powers of imagination, and about the curious way in which it is enslaved by words.

To encourage ourselves in the belief that this sort of consideration may play havoc with the distinction 'analytic or synthetic', let us consider a similar and more familiar case. It seems, does it not, perfectly obvious that every proposition must have a contradictory? Yet it does not turn out so. Suppose that I live in harmony and friendship for four years with a cat: and then it delivers a philippic. We ask ourselves, perhaps, 'Is it a real cat? or is it *not* a real cat?' 'Either it *is*, or it *is not*, but we cannot be sure which.' Now actually, that is not so: *neither* 'It is a real cat' *nor* 'it is not a real cat' fits the facts semantically: each is designed for other situations than this one: you could not say the former of something which delivers philippics, nor yet the latter of something which has behaved as this has for four years. There are similar difficulties about choosing between 'This *is* a hallucination' and 'This is *not* a hallucination'. With sound instinct, the plain man turns in such cases to Watson and says 'Well now, *what would you* say?' 'How would you *describe* it? The difficulty is just that: there is *no* short description which is not misleading: the only thing to do, and that can easily be done, is to set out the description of the facts at length. Ordinary language breaks down in extraordinary cases. (In such cases, the cause of the breakdown is semantical.) Now no doubt an *ideal* language would *not* break down, whatever happened. In doing physics, for example, where our language is tightened up in order precisely to describe complicated and unusual cases concisely, we *prepare linguistically for the worst.* In ordinary language we do not: *words fail us.* If we talk as though an ordinary must be like an ideal language, we shall misrepresent the facts.

Consider now 'being extended' and 'being shaped'. In ordinary life we never get into a situation where we learn to say that anything is extended but not shaped nor conversely. We have all learned to use, and have used, the words only in cases where it is correct to use both. Supposing now someone says '*x* is extended but has no shape'. Somehow we cannot see what this 'could mean'—there are no semantic conventions, explicit or implicit, to cover this case: yet it is not prohibited in any way— there are no limiting rules about what we might or might not say *in extraordinary cases.* It is not *merely* the difficulty of imagining or experiencing extraordinary cases, either, which causes worry. There is this too: we can only describe what it is we are trying to imagine, by means of words which precisely describe and evoke the *ordinary* case, which we are trying to think away. Ordinary language *blinkers* the already feeble imagination. It would be difficult, in this way, if I were to say 'Can I think of a case where a man would be neither at home nor not at home?' This is inhibiting, because I think of the *ordinary* case where I ask 'Is he at home?' and get the answer, 'No': when certainly he is not at home. But supposing I happen *first* to think of the situation when I call on him just after he has died: then I see at once it would be wrong to say either. So in our case, the only thing to do is to imagine or experience all kinds of odd situations, and then suddenly round on oneself and ask: there, *now* would I say that, being extended it must be shaped? A new idiom might in odd cases be demanded.

I should like to say, in concluding this section, that in the course of stressing that we must pay attention to the facts of *actual* language, what we can and cannot say, and *precisely* why, another and converse point takes shape. Although it will not do to force actual language to accord with some preconceived model: it *equally* will not do, having discovered the facts about 'ordinary usage' *to rest content* with that, as though there were nothing more to be discussed and discovered. There may be plenty that might happen and does happen which would need new and better language to describe it in. Very often philosophers are only engaged on this task, when they seem to be perversely using words in a way which makes no sense according to 'ordinary usage'. There may be extraordinary facts, even about our everyday experience, which plain men and plain language overlook.

III

The last, and perhaps least unimportant point I have to make is the following: it seems to me that far more *detailed* attention ought to be given to that celebrated question, the posing of which has given birth to, and still keeps alive, so many erroneous theories, namely: why do we call different things by the same name? In reply to this, the philoprogenitive invent theories of 'universals' and what not: some entity or other to be that of which the 'name' is the name. And in reply to *them*, the more cautious (the 'nominalists') have usually been content to reply simply that: the reason why we call different things by the same name is simply that the things are *similar*: there is nothing *identical* present in them. This reply is inadequate in many respects: it does not, for example, attack the misleading form in which the question is posed, nor sufficiently go into the peculiarities of the word 'similar'. But what I wish to object to in it tonight is rather this: that *it is not in the least true* that all the things which I 'call by the same (general) name' *are* in general 'similar', in any ordinary sense of that much abused word.

It is a most strange thing that 'nominalists' should rest content with this answer. Not merely is it untrue to the facts; but further, if they had examined the facts, which are, in themselves, interesting enough, they could have produced with little trouble a far more formidable case against their opponents. So long as they say the things *are similar*, it will always be open to someone to say: 'Ah yes, similar *in a certain respect*: and that can only be explained by means of universals' (or whatever the name may be that they prefer for that well-tried nostrum): or again to maintain that similarity is only 'intelligible' as partial *identity*: and so on. And even those who are not persuaded entirely, may yet go so far as to allow that the 'similarity' and 'identity' languages are *alternatives*, the choice between which is indifferent. But surely, if it were made evident that we often 'call different things by the same name', and for perfectly 'good reasons',[1] when the things are not even in any ordinary sense 'similar', it will become excessively difficult to maintain that there is something 'identical' present in each—and after all, it is in *refuting* that position that the nominalist is really interested. Not, of course, that we can really *refute* it, or hope to cure those incurables who have long since reached the tertiary stage of universals.

Leaving historical disputes aside, it is a matter of urgency that a doctrine should be developed about the various kinds of good reasons for which we 'call different things[2] by the same name'. This is an absorbing question, but habitually neglected, so far as I know, by philologists as well as by philosophers. Lying in the no man's land between them, it falls between two schools, to develop such a doctrine fully would be very complicated and perhaps tedious: but also very useful in many ways. It demands the study of *actual* languages, *not* ideal ones. That the Polish semanticists have discussed such questions I neither know nor believe. Aristotle did to a quite considerable extent, but scrappily and inexactly.

---

[1] We are not interested in mere equivocation, of course.
[2] Strictly, *sorts* of things rather than *particular* things.

I shall proceed forthwith simply to give some of the more obvious cases where the reasons for 'calling different sorts of things by the same name' are not to be dismissed lightly as 'similarity'. And show how consideration of these facts may warn us against errors which are constant in philosophy.

1. A very simple case indeed is one often mentioned by Aristotle: the adjective 'healthy': when I talk of a healthy body and again of a healthy complexion, of healthy exercise: the word is *not* just being used *equivocally*. Aristotle would say it is being used 'paronymously'.[1] In this case there is what we may call a *primary nuclear* sense of 'healthy': the sense in which 'healthy' is used of a healthy body: I call this *nuclear* because it is 'contained as a part' in the other two senses which may be set out as 'productive of healthy bodies' and 'resulting from a healthy body'.

This is a simple case, easily understood. Yet constantly it is forgotten when we start disputing as to whether a certain word *has* 'two senses' or has *not* two senses. I remember myself disputing as to whether 'exist' has two senses (as used of material objects and again of sensa), or only one: actually we were agreed that 'exist' is used paronymously, only he called that 'having two senses', and I did not. Prichard's paper[2] on ἀγαθόν (in Aristotle) contains a classic instance of misunderstanding about paronymity, and so worrying about whether a word really 'has always the same meaning' or 'has several different meanings'.

Now are we to be content to say that the exercise, the complexion, and the body are all called 'healthy' 'because they are similar'? Such a remark cannot fail to be misleading. Why make it? And why not direct attention to the important and actual facts?

2. The next case I shall take is what Aristotle calls 'analogous' terms. When A : B :: X : Y then A and X are often called by

[1] But there are other varieties of paronymity of course.
[2] 'The Meaning of ΑΓΑΘΟΝ in the *Ethics* of Aristotle', by H. A. Prichard. Reprinted in his *Moral Obligation*, Oxford, 1949.

the same name, e.g. the foot of a mountain and the foot of a list. Here there is a good reason for calling the things both 'feet' but are we to say they are 'similar'? Not in any ordinary sense. We may say that the relations in which they stand to B and Y respectively are similar relations. Well and good: but A and X are not the relations in which they stand: and anyone simply told that, in calling A and X both 'feet' I was calling attention to a 'similarity' in them, would probably be misled. Anyhow, it is most necessary to remember that 'similarity' covers such possibilities if it is to do so. (An especially severe case of 'analogy' arises when a term is used, as Aristotle says 'in different categories': e.g. when I talk about 'change' as qualitative change, change of position, place, &c., how far is it true to say these 'changes' are 'similar'?)

3. Another case is where I call B by the same name as A, because it resembles A, C by the same name because it resembles B, D . . . and so on. But ultimately A and, say, D do not resemble each other in any recognizable sense at all. This is a very common case: and the dangers are obvious, when we search for something 'identical' in all of them!

4. Another case which is commonly found is this. Take a word like 'fascist': this originally connotes, say, a great many characteristics at once: say x, y, and z. Now we will use 'fascist' subsequently of things which possess only *one* of these striking characteristics. So that things called 'fascist' in these senses, which we may call 'incomplete' senses, need not be similar at all to each other. This often puzzles us most of all when the original 'complete' sense has been forgotten: compare the various meanings of 'cynicism': we should be puzzled to find the 'similarity' there! Sometimes the 'incompleteness' of the resemblance is coupled with a positive lack of resemblance, so that we invent a phrase to mark it as a warning, e.g. 'cupboard love'.

5. Another better-known case is that of a so-called determinable and its determinates: colour and red, green, blue, &c., or rather 'absolutely specific' reds, greens, blues, &c. Because

this is better known, I shall not discuss it, though I am as a matter of fact rather sceptical about the accounts usually given. Instead, it should be pointed out how common this sort of relationship is and that it should be suspected in cases where we are prone to overlook it. A striking example is the case of 'pleasure': pleasures we may say not merely resemble each other in being pleasant, but also *differ* precisely in the way in which they are pleasant.[1] No greater mistake could be made than the hedonistic mistake (copied by non-hedonists) of thinking that pleasure is always a single similar feeling, somehow isolable from the various activities which 'give rise' to it.

6. Another case which often provides puzzles, is that of words like 'youth' and 'love': which sometimes mean the object loved, or the thing which is youthful, sometimes the passion 'Love' or the quality (?) 'youth'. These cases are of course easy (rather *like* 'healthy'?). But suppose we take the noun 'truth': here is a case where the disagreements between different theorists have largely turned on whether they interpreted this as a name of a substance, of a quality, or of a relation.

7. Lastly, I want to take a specially interesting sort of case, which is perhaps commoner and at the bottom of more muddles than we are aware of. Take the sense in which I talk of a cricket bat and a cricket ball and a cricket umpire. The reason that all are called by the same name is perhaps that each has its part—its *own special* part—to play in the activity called cricketing: it is no good to say that cricket *simply* means 'used in cricket': for we cannot explain what we mean by 'cricket' *except* by explaining the special parts played in cricketing by the bat, ball, &c. Aristotle's suggestion was that the word 'good' might be used in such a way: in which case it is obvious how far astray we should go if we look for a 'definition' of the word 'good' in any ordinary simple sense: or look for the way in which 'good' things are 'similar' to each other, in any ordinary sense. If we tried to find out by such methods what

---

[1] If we say that they are all called 'pleasures' 'because they are similar', we shall overlook this fact.

'cricket' meant, we should very likely conclude that it too was a simple unanalysable supersensible quality.

Another thing that becomes plain from such examples is that the apparently common-sense distinction between 'What is the meaning of the word x' and 'What particular things *are* x and to what degrees?' is not of universal application by any means. The questions cannot be distinguished in such cases. Or a similar case would be some word like 'golfing': it is not sense to ask 'What is the meaning of golfing?' 'What things are golfing?' Though it *is* sense to ask what component activities go to constitute golfing, what implements are used in golfing ('golf' clubs, &c.) and in what ways. Aristotle suggests 'happiness' is a word of this kind: in which case it is evident how far astray we shall go if we treat it as though it were a word like 'whiteness'.

These summarily treated examples are enough to show how essential it is to have a thorough knowledge of the different reasons for which we call different things by the same name, before we can embark confidently on an inquiry. If we rush up with a demand for a definition in the simple manner of Plato or many other philosophers, if we use the rigid dichotomy 'same meaning, different meaning', or 'What x means', as distinguished from 'the things which are x', we shall simply make hashes of things. Perhaps some people are now discussing such questions seriously. All that is to be found in traditional Logics is the mention that there are, besides univocal and equivocal words, 'also analogous words': which, without further explanation, is used to lump together all cases where a word has not always absolutely the same meaning, nor several absolutely different meanings. All that 'similarity' theorists manage is to say that all things called by some one name are similar to some one pattern, or are all more similar to each other than any of them is to anything else; which is *obviously* untrue. Anyone who wishes to see the complexity of the problem, has only got to look in a (good) dictionary under such a word as 'head': the different meanings of the word 'head' will be related to each other in all sorts of different ways at once.

To summarize the contentions of this paper then. Firstly, the phrase 'the meaning of a word' is a spurious phrase. Secondly and consequently, a re-examination is needed of phrases like the two which I discuss, 'being a part of the meaning of' and 'having the same meaning'. On these matters, dogmatists require prodding: although history indeed suggests that it may sometimes be better to let sleeping dogmatists lie.

"The Meaning of a Word" was written in 1940 and never published by Austin, appearing for the first time in his *Philosophical Papers,* published posthumously in 1961. References to his later work may be found in the bibliography.

2 PERFORMATIVE-CONSTATIVE

by J. L. Austin

Translator's Note: "Performative-Constative" is a straightforward translation of Austin's paper "Performatif-Constatif," which he wrote in French and presented at a (predominantly) Anglo-French conference held at Royaumont in March 1958. The case of the discussion which follows it is somewhat more complex. The actual discussion at Royaumont was carried on in both French and English. What appears in the published volume after Austin's text (*Cahiers de Royaumont, Philosophie* No. IV, *La Philosophie Analytique:* Les Editions de Minuit, 1962, pp. 271-304) is a version of this, based on a transcript but substantially cut and edited, in which the contributions originally made in English were translated into French by M. Béra. It might have been possible, for the present publication, to procure copies at least of those portions of the original transcript that were in English. However, it seemed to me preferable simply to translate into English the entire French text, mainly for the reason that it is this edited version, and this only, that all those taking part are known to have seen and approved for publication.

G. J. WARNOCK

One can quite easily get the idea of the performative utterance — though the expression, as I am well aware, does not exist in the French language, or anywhere else. This idea was brought in to mark a contrast with that of the declarative utterance, or rather, as I am going to call it, the constative utterance. And there we have straight off what I want to call in question. Ought we to accept this Performative-Constative antithesis?

The constative utterance, under the name, so dear to philosophers, of *statement*,[1] has the property of being true or false. The performative utterance, by contrast, can never be either: it has its own special job, it is used to perform an action. To issue such an utterance[2] *is* to perform the action — an action, perhaps, which one scarcely could perform, at least with so much precision, in any other way. Here are some examples:

> I name this ship 'Liberté'.
> I apologise.
> I welcome you.
> I advise you to do it.

Utterances of this kind are common enough: we find them, for instance, everywhere in what are called in English the 'operative' clauses of a legal instrument.* Plainly, many of them are not without interest for philosophers: to say 'I promise to . . .' — to issue, as we say, this performative utterance — just *is* the act of making a promise; not, as we see, at all a mysterious act. And it may seem at once quite obvious that an utterance of this kind can't be true or false — notice that I say it can't *be* true or false, because it may very well *imply* that some *other* propositions are true or are false, but that, if I'm not mistaken, is a quite different matter.

However, the performative utterance is not exempt from all criticism: it may very well be criticized, but in a quite different dimension from that of truth and falsity. The performative must be issued in a situation appropriate in all respects for the act in question: if the speaker is not in the conditions required for its performance (and there are many such conditions), then his utterance will be, as we call it in general, 'unhappy'.[3]

First, our performative, like any other ritual or ceremony, may be, as the lawyers say, 'null and void'. If, for example, the speaker is not in a position to perform an act of that kind, or if the object with respect to which he purports to perform it is not suitable for the purpose, then he doesn't manage, simply by issuing his utterance, to carry out the purported act. Thus a bigamist doesn't get married a second time, he only 'goes through the form' of a second marriage; I can't name the ship if I am not the person properly authorized to name it; and I can't quite bring off the baptism of penguins, those creatures being scarcely susceptible of that exploit.

Second, a performative utterance may be, though not void, 'unhappy' in a different way — if, that is, it is issued *insincerely*. If I say 'I promise to . . .' without in the least intending to carry out the promised action, perhaps even not believing that it is in my power to carry it out, the promise is hollow. It is made, certainly; but still, there is an 'unhappiness': I have *abused* the formula.

Let us now suppose that our act has been performed: every-

* The clauses, that is to say, in which the legal act is actually performed, as opposed to those — the 'preamble' — which set out the circumstances of the transaction.

thing has gone off quite normally, and also, if you like, sincerely. In that case, the performative utterance will characteristically 'take effect'. We do not mean by that that such-and-such a future event is or will be brought about as an effect of this action functioning as a cause. We mean rather that, in consequence of the performance of this act, such-and-such a future event, *if* it happens, will be *in order,* and such-and-such other events, *if* they happen, will not be in order. If I have said 'I promise', I shall not be in order if I break my word; if I have said 'I welcome you', I shall not be in order if I proceed to treat you as an enemy or an intruder. Thus we say that, even when the performative has taken effect, there may always crop up a third kind of unhappiness, which we call 'breach of commitment'.[4] We may note also that commitments can be more or less vague, and can bind us in very different degrees.

There we have, then, three kinds of unhappiness associated with the performative utterance. It is possible to make a complete classification of these unhappinesses; but it must be admitted that, as practically goes without saying, the different kinds may not always be sharply distinguishable and may even coincide.[5] Then we must add that our performative is both an *action* and an *utterance*: so that, poor thing, it can't help being liable to be substandard in all the ways in which actions in general can be, as well as those in which utterances in general can be. For example, the performative may be issued under duress, or by accident; it may suffer from defective grammar, or from misunderstanding; it may figure in a context not wholly 'serious', in a play, perhaps, or in a poem. We leave all that on one side — let us simply bear in mind the more specific unhappinesses of the performative, that is, nullity, abuse (insincerity), and breach of commitment.

Well, now that we have before us this idea of the performative, it is very natural to hope that we could proceed to find some criterion, whether of grammar or of vocabulary, which would make it possible for us to answer in every case the question whether a particular utterance is performative or not. But this hope is, alas, exaggerated and, in large measure, vain.

It is true that there exist two 'normal forms', so to speak, in which the performative finds expression. At first sight both of them, curiously enough, have a thoroughly constative look. One of these normal forms is that which I have already made use of in producing my examples: the utterance leads off with a verb in the first person singular of the present indicative active, as in 'I promise you that . . .'. The other form, which comes to exactly the same but is more common in utterances issued in writing, employs by contrast a verb in the *passive* voice and in the *second* or *third* person of the present indicative, as in 'Passengers are requested to cross the line by the footbridge only'. If we ask ourselves, as sometimes we may, whether a given utterance of this form is performative or constative, we may settle the question by asking whether it would be possible to insert in it the word 'hereby' or some equivalent — as, in French, the phrase 'par ces mots-ci'.

By way of putting to the test utterances which one might take to be performative, we make use of a well-known asymmetry, in the case of what we call an 'explicit performative' verb, between the first person singular of the present indicative, and other persons and tenses of the same verb. Thus, 'I promise' is a formula which is used to perform the act of promising; 'I promised', on the other hand, or 'he promises', are expressions which serve simply to describe or report an act of promising, not to perform one.

However, it is not in the least necessary that an utterance, if it is to be performative, should be expressed in one of these so-called normal forms. To say 'Shut the door', plainly enough, is every bit as performative, every bit as much the performance of an act, as to say 'I order you to shut the door'. Even the word 'Dog' by itself can sometimes (at any rate in England, a country more practical than ceremonious) stand in place of an explicit and formal performative; one performs, by this little word, the very same act as by the utterance 'I warn you that the dog is about to attack us', or by 'Strangers are warned that here there is a vicious dog'. To make our utterance performative, and quite unambiguously so, we can make use, in place of the explicit formula, of a whole lot of more primitive devices such as intonation, for instance, or gesture; further, and above all, the very context in which the words are uttered can make it entirely certain how they are to be taken — as a description, for example, or again as a warning. Does this word 'Dog' just give us a bit of detail about the local fauna? In the context — when confronted, that is, with the notice on the gate — we just don't need to ask ourselves that question at all.

All we can really say is that our explicit performative formula ('I promise . . .', 'I order you . . .', etc.) serves to make explicit, and at the same time more precise, what act it is that the speaker purports to perform in issuing his utterance. I say 'to make explicit', and that is not at all the same thing as to *state*.[6] Bending low before you, I remove my hat, or perhaps I say 'Salaam'; then, certainly, I am doing obeisance to you, not just engaging in gymnastics; but the word 'Salaam' does not, any more than does the act of removing my hat, in any way *state* that I am doing obeisance to you. It is in this way that our formula *makes* the issuing of the utterance that action which it is, but does not *state* that it is that action.

The other forms of expression, those that have no explicit performative formula, will be more primitive and less precise, one might almost say more vague. If I say simply 'I will be there', there will be no telling, just by considering the words, whether I am taking on a commitment, or declaring an intention, or making perhaps a fatalistic prediction. One may think of the precise formulae as a relatively recent phenomenon in the evolution of language, and as going together with the evolution of more complex forms of society and science.

We can't, then, expect any purely verbal criterion of the performative. We may hope, all the same, that any utterance which is in fact performative will be reducible (in some sense of that word) to an utterance in one or the other of our normal forms. Then, going on from there, we should be able, with the help of a dictionary, to make a list of all the verbs which can figure in one of our explicit formulae. Thus we will achieve a useful classification of all the varieties of acts that we perform in saying something (in one sense, at least, of that ambiguous phrase).

We have now brought in, then, the ideas of the performative utterance, of its unhappinesses, and of its explicit formulae. But we have been talking all along as if every utterance had to be *either* constative *or* performative, and as if the idea of the constative at any rate was as clear as it is familiar. But it is not.

Let us note in the first place that an utterance which is undoubtedly a statement of fact, therefore constative, can fail to get by[7] in more than one way. It can be untrue, to be sure; but it can also be absurd, and that not necessarily in some gross fashion (by being, for instance, ungrammatical). I would like to take a closer look at three rather more subtle ways of being absurd, two of which have only recently come to light.

(1) Someone says 'All John's children are bald, but [or 'and'] John has no children'; or perhaps he says 'All John's children are bald', when, as a matter of fact, John has no children.

(2) Someone says 'The cat is on the mat, but [or 'and'] I don't believe it is'; or perhaps he says 'The cat is on the mat', when, as a matter of fact, he does not believe it is.

(3) Someone says 'All the guests are French, and some of them aren't'; or perhaps he says 'All the guests are French', and then afterwards says 'Some of the guests are not French'.

In each of these cases one experiences a feeling of outrage, and it's possible each time for us to try to express it in terms of the same word — 'implication', or perhaps that word that we always find so handy, 'contradiction'. But there are more ways of killing the cat than drowning it in butter;* and equally, to do violence to language one does not always need a contradiction.

Let us use the three terms 'presuppose', 'imply', and 'entail'[8] for our three cases respectively. Then:

1. Not only 'John's children are bald', but equally 'John's children are not bald', presupposes that John has children. To talk about those children, or to refer to them, presupposes that they exist. By contrast, 'The cat is not on the mat' does *not,* equally with 'The cat is on the mat', imply that I believe it is; and similarly, 'None of the guests is French' does *not,* equally with 'All the guests are French', entail that it is false that some of the guests are not French.

2. We can quite well say 'It could be the case both that the cat is on the mat and that I do not believe it is'. That is to say, those two propositions are not in the least incompatible: both can be true together. What is impossible is to state both at the same time: his *stating* that the cat is on the mat is what implies that the speaker believes it is. By contrast, we couldn't say 'It could be the case both that John has no children and that his

* English proverb. I am told that this rather refined way of disposing of cats is not found in France.

children are bald'; just as we couldn't say 'It could be the case both that all the guests are French and that some of them are not French'.

3. If 'All the guests are French' entails 'It is not the case that some of the guests are not French', then 'Some of the guests are not French' entails 'It is not the case that all the guests are French'. It's a question here of the compatibility and incompatibility of propositions. By contrast, it isn't like this with presupposition: if 'John's children are bald' presupposes that John has children, it isn't true at all that 'John has no children' presupposes that John's children are not bald. Similarly, if 'The cat is on the mat' implies that I believe it is, it isn't true at all that to say 'I don't believe that the cat is on the mat' implies that the cat is not on the mat (not, at any rate, in the same sense of 'implies'; besides, we have already seen that 'implication', for us, is not a matter of the incompatibility of propositions).

Here then are three ways in which a statement can fail to get by without being untrue, and without being a sheer rigmarole either. I would like to call attention to the fact that these three ways of failing to get by correspond to three of the ways in which a performative utterance may be unhappy. To bring out the comparison, let's first take two performative utterances:

4. 'I bequeath my watch to you, but [or 'and'] I haven't got a watch'; or perhaps someone says 'I bequeath my watch to you' when he hasn't got a watch.

5. 'I promise to be there, but [or 'and'] I have no intention of being there'; or perhaps someone says 'I promise to be there' when he doesn't intend to be there.

We compare case 4 with case 1, the case, that is, of presupposition. For to say either 'I bequeath my watch to you' or 'I don't bequeath my watch to you' presupposes equally that I have a watch; that the watch exists is presupposed by the fact that it is spoken of or referred to, in the performative utterance just as much as in the constative utterance. And just as we can make use here of the term 'presupposition' as employed in the doctrine of the constative, equally we can take over for that doctrine the term 'void' as employed in the doctrine of the unhappinesses of the performative. The statement on the subject of John's children is, we may say, 'void for lack of reference', which is exactly what lawyers would say about the purported bequest of the watch. So here is a first instance in which a trouble that afflicts statements turns out to be identical with one of the unhappinesses typical of the performative utterance.

We compare case 5 with case 2, that is, the case where something is 'implied'. Just as my saying that the cat is on the mat implies that I believe it is, so my saying I promise to be there implies that I intend to be there. The procedure of stating is designed for those who honestly believe what they say, exactly as the procedure of promising is designed for those who have a certain intention, namely, the intention to do whatever it may be that they promise. If we don't hold the belief, or again don't have the intention, appropriate to the content of our utterance, then in each case there is lack of sincerity and abuse of the procedure. If, at the same time as we make the statement or the promise, we announce in the same breath that we don't believe it or we don't intend to, then the utterance is 'self-voiding', as we might call it; and hence our feeling of outrage on hearing it. Another instance, then, where a trouble which afflicts statements is identical with one of the unhappinesses which afflict performative utterances.

Let us look back, next, to case 3, the case of entailment among statements. Can we find, in the case of performatives, some analogue for this as well? When I make the statement, for instance, 'All the guests are French', do I not commit myself in a more or less rigorous fashion to behaving in future in such-and-such a way, in particular with respect to the statements I will make? If, in the sequel, I state things incompatible with my utterance (namely, that all the guests are French), there will be a breach of commitment that one might well compare with that of the case in which I say 'I welcome you', and then proceed to treat you as an enemy or an intruder — and perhaps even better, with that of which one is guilty when one says 'I define the word thus' (a performative utterance) and then proceeds to use the word with a different meaning.

So then, it seems to me that the constative utterance is every bit as liable to unhappinesses as the performative utterance, and indeed to pretty much the same unhappinesses. Furthermore, making use of the key provided by our list of unhappinesses noted for the case of performatives, we can ask ourselves whether there are not still more unhappinesses in the case of statements, besides the three we have just mentioned. For example, it often happens that a performative is void because the utterer is not in a state, or not in a position, to perform the act which he purports to perform; thus, it's no good my saying 'I order you' if I have no authority over you: I can't order you, my utterance is void, my act is only purported. Now people have, I know, the impression that where a statement, a constative utterance, is in question, the case is quite different: anybody at all can state anything at all. What if he's ill-informed? Well then, one can be mistaken, that's all. It's a free country, isn't it? To state what isn't true is one of the Rights of Man. However, this impression can lead us into error. In reality nothing is more common than to find that one can state absolutely nothing on some subject, because one is simply not in a position to state whatever it may be — and this may come about, too, for more than one reason. I *cannot* state at this moment how many people there are in the next room: I haven't been to see, I haven't found out the facts. What if I say, nevertheless, 'At this moment there are fifty people in the next room'? You will allow, perhaps, that in saying that I have made a guess,[9] but you will not allow that I have made a statement, not at any rate without adding 'but he had no right whatever to do so'; and in this case my 'I state . . .' is exactly on a par with our 'I order . . .', said, we remember, without any right to give an order. Here's another example. You confide to me 'I'm bored', and I quite coolly reply 'You're not'. You say 'What do you mean, I'm not? What right have you to say how I feel?' I say 'But what do *you* mean, what right have I? I'm just stating what your feelings are, that's all. I may be mistaken, certainly, but what of that? I suppose one can always make a simple statement, can't one?' But no, one can't always: usually, I can't state what your feelings are, unless you have disclosed them to me.

So far I have called attention to two things: that there is no purely verbal criterion by which to distinguish the performative from the constative utterance, and that the constative is liable to the same unhappinesses as the performative. Now we must ask ourselves whether issuing a constative utterance is not, after all, the performance of an act, the act, namely, of stating. Is stating an act in the same sense as marrying, apologising, betting, etc.? I can't plumb this mystery any further at present. But it is already pretty evident that the formula 'I state that . . .' is closely similar to the formula 'I warn you that . . .' — a formula which, as we put it, serves to make explicit what speech-act[10] it is that we are performing; and also, that one can't issue any utterance whatever without performing some speech-act of this kind.

What we need, perhaps, is a more general theory of these speech-acts, and in this theory our Constative-Performative antithesis will scarcely survive.

Here and now it remains for us to examine, quite briefly, this craze for being either true or false, something which people think is peculiar to statements alone and ought to be set up on a pedestal of its own, above the battle. And this time let's begin with the performative utterance: is it the case that there is nothing here in the least analogous with truth?

To begin with, it is clear that if we establish that a performative utterance is not unhappy, that is, that its author has performed his act happily and in all sincerity, that still does not suffice to set it beyond the reach of all criticism. It may always be criticised in a different dimension.

Let us suppose that I say to you 'I advise you to do it'; and let us allow that all the circumstances are appropriate, the conditions for success are fulfilled. In saying that, I actually do advise you to do it — it is not that I *state*, truly or falsely, *that* I advise you. It is, then, a performative utterance. There does still arise, all the same, a little question: was the advice good or bad? Agreed, I spoke in all sincerity, I believed that to do it would be in your interest; but was I right? Was my belief, in these circumstances, justified? Or again — though perhaps this matters less — was it in fact, or as things turned out, in your interest? There is confrontation of my utterance with the situation in, and the situation with respect to which, it was issued. I was fully justified perhaps, but was I right?

Many other utterances which have an incontestably performative flavour are exposed to this second kind of criticism. Allowing that, in declaring the accused guilty, you have reached your verdict properly and in good faith, it still remains to ask whether the verdict was just, or fair. Allowing that you had the right to reprimand him as you did, and that you have acted without malice, one can still ask whether your reprimand was deserved.

Here again we have confrontation with the facts, including the circumstances of the occasion of utterance.

That not all performative utterances without exception are liable to this quasi-objective evaluation — which for that matter must here be left pretty vague and multifarious — may very well be true.

There is one thing that people will be particularly tempted to bring up as an objection against any comparison between this second kind of criticism and the kind appropriate to statements, and that is this: aren't these questions about something's being good, or just, or fair, or deserved entirely distinct from questions of truth and falsehood? That, surely, is a very simple black-and-white business: either the utterance corresponds to the facts or it doesn't, and that's that.

Well, I for my part don't think it is. Even if there exists a well-defined class of statements and we can restrict ourselves to that, this class will always be pretty wide. In this class we shall have the following statements:

> France is hexagonal.
> Lord Raglan won the battle of Alma.
> Oxford is 60 miles from London.

It's quite true that for each of these statements we can raise the question 'true or false'. But it is only in quite favourable cases that we ought to expect an answer yes or no, once and for all. When the question is raised one understands that the utterance is to be confronted in one way or another with the facts. Very well. So let's confront 'France is hexagonal' with France. What are we to say, is it true or not? The question, plainly, oversimplifies things. Oh well, up to a point if you like, I see what you mean, true perhaps for some purposes or in some contexts, that would do for the man in the street but not for geographers. And so on. It's a rough statement, no denying that, but one can't just say straight out that it's false. Then Alma, a soldier's battle if ever there was one; it's true that Lord Raglan was in command of the allied army, and that this army to some extent won a confused sort of victory; yes, that would be a fair enough judgment, even well deserved, for schoolchildren anyway, though really it's a bit of an exaggeration. And Oxford, well, yes, it's true that that city is 60 miles from London, so long as you want only a certain degree of precision.

Under the heading 'truth' what we in fact have is, not a simple quality nor a relation, not indeed *one* anything, but rather a whole dimension of criticism. We can get some idea, perhaps not a very clear one, of this criticism; what *is* clear is that there is a whole lot of things to be considered and weighed up in this dimension alone — the facts, yes, but also the situation of the speaker, his purpose in speaking, his hearer, questions of precision, etc. If we are content to restrict ourselves to statements of an idiotic or ideal simplicity, we shall never succeed in disentangling the true from the just, fair, deserved, precise, exaggerated, etc., the summary and the detail, the full and the concise, and so on.

From this side also, then, from the side of truth and falsehood, we feel ourselves driven to think again about the Performative-Constative antithesis. What we need, it seems to me, is a new doctrine, both complete and general, of *what one is doing in saying something,* in all the senses of that ambiguous phrase, and of what I call the speech-act, not just in this or that aspect abstracting from all the rest, but taken in its totality.

DISCUSSION

President: W. V. Quine.

Weil: I would like to ask a question. It is genuinely a question, and the very opposite of an objection. It seemed to me, thinking over the later pages of your paper, that one might perhaps sketch out a solution, with regard to the difficulty you bring up, by turning the problem round, and asking oneself whether all, or nearly all, the utterances of ordinary life are not in fact performative. In saying 'of ordinary life' I am of course excluding the examples given by logicians. When a logician gives an example, that example is not performative, though the fact that he gives it *is* performative. What I mean is this: when I say to someone in conversation 'It's a nice day', I 'perform' an act: I make conversation. My remark has often no other force than to introduce myself, and to oblige the other party in his turn to answer me. It does not constitute a serious judgment, true or false, on the state of the weather. If one took the remark at the foot of the letter, one could give some such answer as 'So I see', or 'Of what interest do you suppose that is to me?'; but such an answer would certainly arouse, by its rudeness or aggressiveness, some anxiety as to the state of mind of the person giving it. The same goes for a thousand and one commonplaces of this kind. And conversation is often nothing but a tissue of commonplaces.

I wonder, then, whether it is not necessary to distinguish between 'expressly' performative expressions or formulae, and those which are performative only implicitly, by implication. And there would perhaps be room for analysis of linguistic situations, if I may use that term, and of the performative implications which those situations either produce, or contain.

Austin: I agree entirely on both points. I myself regularly make a distinction between 'explicitly performative formulae' and 'primary' or 'primitive utterances'. That is, I think, the same distinction that you want to bring in.

As for whether we're in a position to say that all utterances of ordinary language are in fact performative, that's a different matter. We would be inclined to think so when we look at things from the point of view I've adopted here. The classic example of a constative utterance is the one where you say 'I state that . . .'. We take off from there, and at once we run into 'I warn you that . . .'. Is that still a statement, or is it perhaps a threat? And if it's still a constative utterance, how shall we distinguish these two acts? There would perhaps be no great harm in not distinguishing them, if by degrees we were brought to see, in every phrase of ordinary language, an implicit performative utterance — which would of course leave no sharp edge at all to the distinction we set out from. This is exactly the kind of difficulty I came up against all through my paper.

All that I would venture to say in answer to your question is that, setting out from a pretty vague distinction between the straightforward utterance (*stating*) and the act (*ordering*), we meet, as we go along, a number of difficulties which lead us appreciably to modify our original analysis, and not to go on seeing inside language just two types of 'speech-acts': and this leads us to reconsider in its entirety our conception of language, which may emerge from the test a good deal the worse for wear, without our yet being in a position to formulate a theory embracing every kind of 'speech-act'.

That said, I agree with you entirely.

Hare: I wonder whether the confusion does not arise, in part, from the fact that the two terms are commonly used to mark two sorts of distinctions. I don't say that Professor Austin confuses them; but I wonder whether certain passages in his paper do not invite this confusion in the minds of his audience.

1. There is, first, the distinction established by logicians between two ways of expressing, or of doing, the same thing: for example, between 'I order you to do so-and-so' and 'Do so-and-so'; or between 'I state that the cat is on the mat' and 'The cat is on the mat'.

2. But there is also the distinction between the different linguistic acts: between what we do when we state something about whatever it may be, and what we do when we promise something to somebody, or what we do when we order someone to do something, and so on.

The two distinctions are liable to be confused, because in certain cases both apply. It is in the name of both that we distinguish, for instance, 'I promise to do so-and-so' from 'The cat is on the mat'.

It seems to me that Austin, particularly towards the end of his paper, would allow some of his hearers to suppose that, *because* we can express a statement of fact, just as we can express an order, for example, or a promise, in the solemn and formal style 'I tell you that . . .', 'I order you to . . .', 'I promise you that . . .', instead of using the indicative, the imperative, or the future (distinction 1), we ought for this reason to conclude that they are not so different from one another as our distinction 2 would lead one to believe. I do not say that this confusion is in his mind, but I think that he would clarify the problem a great deal, for a great many people, by inventing another pair of terms, allowing a distinction to be made between these two distinctions.

Austin: Your question comes quite close to the one that Weil put to me, and I think my answer can only be much the same. The difficulty, if difficulty there is, proceeds from the fact that the distinction between performative utterances and the other class of utterances which one supposedly wants to contrast with them (but which one refrains, very often, from defining in any but very vague terms) was originally arrived at just by rushing bald-headed at the first examples that came to hand — examples which in fact contain, when you look at them a bit more closely, what I call explicit performative formulae of the type of 'I promise you that . . .', 'I warn you that . . .', etc. But one soon sees that, to promise or to threaten, one does not have to use these roundabout methods, and that in a great many cases we don't beat about the bush in this way. This state of affairs leads one to distinguish what I call the explicit from the primary performative, exactly as from the other side we distinguish the explicit constative from the primary constative. As I said in my paper, that doesn't mean that the difference between the performative and the constative is always clear.

So I don't believe there is actual confusion (unless perhaps in the historical order in which these distinctions were brought into philosophy), but rather not enough detailed working out, perhaps, in our discussions of this matter.

But I'm not so sure I understand what kind of philosophical difficulty Mr. Hare thinks the confusion, if confusion there was, could lead us into. If I refer to his notes, that would perhaps refresh my memory, and help to clarify the point under discussion for you as well as for me. He says: 'It seems to me that Austin, towards the end of his paper, might mislead his hearers, by making them suppose that the distinction between, say, 'stating' and 'ordering' (distinction 2) can be whittled away[11] by showing that in both cases we can do what we do by making use of an explicit performative utterance, in the sense of distinction 1.' My comment is that, leaving open the question on what level the distinction is made (1 or 2), what I'm trying to do is not so much to whittle it away as to call it in question, by showing that it is not firmly based enough, and not clear enough. I don't see how the way I adopted of whittling it away (as he says) or of calling it in question (as I think I'm doing) is not a perfectly valid method. As I've already said in my answer to Professor Weil, and I can only say the same now, what bothers me about this distinction that we try to make at the start between performative utterances and constative utterances, what makes me think that this distinction isn't clear, is that the formula 'I state that . . .' appears to me to satisfy all the criteria, doubtless still much too vague, that we make use of to characterize performative utterances. I haven't the least intention of whittling away the difference, if difference there is, between the act of stating and the act of commanding. I simply want to bring out that, insofar as one can apply the very vague notion that we have in mind in speaking of the performative, the distinction is not well founded, since the formula 'I state that . . .' shows all the characteristics by which we thought performative utterances were to be identified.

Hare: If I understand you correctly, you want to say that the criteria one usually employs don't allow us to distinguish 'I state that . . .' from 'I promise you that . . .' or 'I order you to . . .'. But you don't mean that there isn't a difference between these two types of acts in language?

Austin: Certainly not. I suggested, moreover, no doubt much too briefly at the end of my paper, in what direction one could look. It seems to me that we ought to draw up a list of all the formulae of this kind, a complete and general list of what one is doing in saying something, in every sense of that ambiguous phrase, as a preliminary to working out a general doctrine of what I call 'the speech-act' viewed in all its aspects and taken in its totality. Then we could decide, with clearer heads and some sort of plan before us, on the families or classes in which they could be arranged. And we shall not be tempted to accord to just one expression, 'I state that . . .' — which seems to me personally to have very little right to such promotion — the pre-eminent place that we do in practice accord to it. It could very well be that, in drawing up a classification of all speech-acts, we came to set a pretty wide gulf, in one place or another, between the acts of promising, warning, ordering, and a considerable number of other acts among which stating would come in again. One thing seems to me certain, and that is that 'I state that . . .' doesn't occupy the conspicuous position that we want to give it.

All that comes back to saying that the distinction we set out from, between performative and constative, is inadequate. We must get a much more general theory of the speech-act before we can set up a well-founded distinction.

Devaux: I am inclined to hold, with Professor Austin, that our utterances, our statements, are at the same time, or at any rate can be at the same time, what he calls 'performative' and 'indicative'. That does not seem to me incompatible, in fact.

But where I begin to run into difficulties is where commitments are in question, and in particular utterances which involve a moral commitment on the part of one who makes them, to respect his given word. And the question I would like to put to Professor Austin is the following: when I undertake, with regard to myself, and before my moral conscience, a commitment to myself, without witnesses, am I, in that case, confronted with a performative activity? And if I am confronted with a performative activity, can one allow that it is neither true nor false? The absence of truth and falsity seems to me difficult to allow when it is a question of a formal commitment before the tribunal of my conscience, or when it is my loyalty to myself that is at stake.

Austin: The question you raise has many sides to it. And I don't know how I ought to take it. Do you mean to ask me what in fact goes on, when I promise something to myself, without witnesses? Are you asking me whether the act that I perform is, according to me, performative? Are you asking me why, in this case, I don't think any question of truth or falsity comes up? There are three distinct questions there, if not more.

Let's take the first. When you say 'I promise myself to be faithful to my promise', I don't think you mean to refer to all the cases without distinction in which one may say to oneself, without always wanting to say it out loud, 'I promise myself to do such-and-such, or not to do it' — as one can make a promise to oneself to give up smoking. I suppose you mean to refer to that species of mental act which accompanies in general every promise made in good faith to another, and which makes us say *sotto voce* 'I promise myself to keep this promise I've just made' — or conversely, if we are in bad faith, 'I promise myself to do nothing of the kind'.

Devaux: No, I was thinking simply of the case where we commit ourselves, or bind ourselves by a promise to ourselves, with regard to any act that we desire to perform or avoid.

Austin: You don't accept my distinction between 'promising yourself', as one would promise something or other to somebody else, and 'promising yourself to keep the promise you've just made to somebody else'?

Devaux: If you prefer — the case where I promise myself to do something, and where I promise myself to keep this promise I have made to myself.

Austin: It's always a tricky business to talk about the cases in which, as we say, one 'tells oneself', 'promises oneself', 'asks oneself' something. On the other hand, the case of 'I promise myself to keep my promise' looks like a kind of parasitic case in a general series of promises to others. There we already have two aspects which would have to be considered separately. I don't say that we haven't an instance here of a difficulty of a very general sort, that one finds to be involved in all kinds of problems. And you're right to call attention to it.

But I don't know whether that requires me to work out an answer to the question whether 'I promise myself' is different from 'I promise someone else'; or whether 'saying to oneself' can be compared with expressing oneself out loud in someone else's presence. What you're really asking me, if I understand you correctly, is whether 'what I do when I promise myself to keep my promise', whatever we take that to mean, is in my sense performative or not performative. Well, I'm inclined to answer that it can't be anything else. Whatever is meant by saying one promises oneself, and whatever we understand by saying one tells oneself something, I don't see — going by the very rough criteria we've used to characterize performative utterances, and at present, however rough, we haven't got any others — how it could be anything else, because the only alternative would be for them to be statements that one could call true or false. And where would the criterion of truth or falsity have any application?

As for why utterances of this sort aren't true or false, I think it's true by definition, of all acts, that they occur or they don't, but can't be true or false. When we get married, we perform an act. What can be said *about* this act can be true or false: are they married, or aren't they? But about the marriage itself that question just can't come up. I don't see what alternative you have in mind in asking your last question.

Devaux: It is precisely with reference to that last point that I ask it.

Austin: A performative utterance can't be true or false. When I say 'I bet you sixpence it will rain tomorrow', a perfectly natural and ordinary thing to say, the bet that I make can't be said

to be true or false. What can be true or false is that I made the
bet. I could very well have betted you the opposite, or not betted
at all.

Devaux: It can be true or false in two senses: true or false
in what concerns the speaker, true or false in the sense of the bet.

Austin: But the fact of saying 'I bet you . . .' constitutes betting; it really can't be questioned or be said to be true or false.
I don't see how anyone can imagine it could be.

Devaux: We've come to a dead end.

Austin: Well, to get out of it again, let's go back to the marriage ceremony. If, at the moment when the affianced parties, in
answer to the official conducting the ceremony, pronounce the
sacramental 'Yes' which binds them, someone came along and
asked whether this 'Yes' was really *true,* we'd take him for a
lunatic. He can ask whether it's a good marriage, whether
they're made for one another, whether they're sincere in saying
this 'Yes', whether the marriage is valid for one reason or
another; but we can't ask whether this 'Yes' is true or false. To
take a still more familiar example: when I say 'Shut the door',
you can't ask me whether 'Shut the door' is true or false. At best
you could raise the question whether I was right to say it, for
example in the case where the door is already shut. But the
order I give is not, in itself, either true or false. You accept that?

Devaux: I don't agree, but I see the point you want to make.

Austin: 'Shut the door' —

Devaux: No, I was thinking of marriage or any kind of un-
dertaking.

Austin: But let's begin at the beginning: can 'Shut the door'
be true or false?

Devaux: Yes, as an act mentioned in an utterance.

Austin: One can say of an act that it's useful, that it's appropriate, that it's reasonable even. One can't say that it's true or
false. Anyway, all I meant to say is that utterances of this type
are much more numerous and various than people think, and
that many of them have, at first sight, the air of statements.
'Shut the door' doesn't have the air of a statement, because it
uses the imperative; but when I switch to 'I tell you to shut the
door', one can easily go wrong. And if one relied on the grammar

books, it would be counted as an 'indicative sentence' under the same heading as an utterance like 'I tell you it's raining'. All I meant, if you like, is that 'I tell you to shut the door' belongs in the same category as 'Shut the door', and in a different category from 'I tell you the door is shut'. We think we know quite a bit about this latter kind of utterance (though perhaps I may not be quite sure what we mean when we state that the door is shut), and in particular we think we can say that they're capable of being true or false. Which doesn't apply to utterances of the other type.

Wahl: I am going to put my question in a somewhat unsatisfactory form: is philosophy an island, or a promontory? I mean simply that I often have the impression that one shuts oneself up on a narrow strip of linguistic territory, debars oneself from going outside it, but that one knows all the same that there are things outside it. So that, if pressed, I should be obliged to wonder how one could explain this state of affairs; and then I should be offered psychoanalytic explanations, Marxist explanations . . . I do not find the explanations particularly convincing. However, it seems to me all the same that here is a situation where an explanation would be welcome.

I have before me a statement like 'I have a watch'. There are two things here. There is, first, the idea of a watch, and leading on from that idea, there is the idea of measurement of time, there is time, and then there are the categories. On the other side, there is the word 'have'. And I believe that, in each of these directions, one encounters the categories. I believe that even in Oxford people study categories. But for the moment, we wish to restrict ourselves to the study of statements. I would rather, however, that our attention was directed to the idea of 'having', or the idea of 'time'.

And since we are discussing statements, I wonder, about two examples very different from that one, what their status is. Take 'To be or not to be, that is the question'; to what class does that belong? I have no idea. It is, in appearance, constative; but is it really? I have no idea. I am happy to have here, in the next room to mine, as neighbour and friend, and as colleague, Mr. Austin; so that, being his neighbour, I can ask him each morning 'Did you sleep well last night?' If unfortunately he should say, giving me a certain look, 'I slept very badly' — well, that would mean 'Mind you make less noise tonight'. Here again, what is this statement? 'I slept very badly' can be a warning. It can also be a request. Or a complaint. In short, it can be all sorts of things. Just that is my point.

Austin: I shall not try to answer all the points which M. Wahl has brought up. But I shall take first his initial question: is philosophy an island or a promontory? If I were looking for an image of this kind, I think I should say that it's more like the surface of the sun — a pretty fair mess.[12] You disentangle yourself as best you can with the means you have at hand. Psychology, sociology, physiology, physics, grammar, can all be pressed into service.[13] Philosophy is always breaking out of its frontiers and into neighbouring territories. I believe the only clear way of defining the subject matter of philosophy is to say that it deals with what's left over, all the problems that remain still insoluble, after all the other recognized methods have been tried. It's the dumping ground for all the leftovers from other sciences, where everything turns up which we don't know quite how to take. As soon as someone discovers a respectable and reliable method of handling some portion of these residual problems, a new science is set up, which tends to break away from philosophy just as and when its subject matter becomes better defined and its authority made good. So then we give it a name: mathematics (a divorce of long standing), or physics (a more recent separation), or psychology, or mathematical logic, where the breakaway is still quite new; or even, who knows, tomorrow perhaps grammar or linguistics. I think that in this way philosophy will overflow more and more widely from its original channel. Then grammar, linguistics, logic, and psychology will form perhaps a new combination, which will break away from the still considerable mass of problems which philosophy bundles along with it in uneasy suspension.

But this breaking away takes a long time, a very long time. Psychology, the youngest of the sciences sprung from the original matrix, has been being born for a very great many years already, and still isn't entirely out.[14] The same thing will happen with linguistics: a science of language will separate off in the end, and will embrace a great many things which philosophy deals with today. So your question is an entirely natural one. Where is the boundary? Is there one anywhere? You could ask the same question about the four quarters of the horizon. There is no boundary. The field is wide open to anyone who chooses to enter it; first come, first served, and good luck to anyone who is the first to hit on something worthwhile.

Your last question was a more specific one. Can assertions which look so factual, so constative, as 'I slept badly last night', in reality be orders, requests, threats in disguise? My answer is: certainly they can. Besides what we understand by the 'meaning' of an expression — and I'm well aware just how obscure that term can be, even if we restrict it to its ordinary, everyday use — we always have what we may call, for the sake of a name, its 'force'. We shall always be able to assign a meaning — even if it's a question of a cluster of exceedingly complex meanings and significances — to an expression like 'I slept badly last night', without so much as approaching the question which arises on a quite different level: is it a constative utterance? Is it a complaint? Is it a warning? Is it a threat? And so on. We have here a second dimension, so to speak. We could still talk here about 'meaning'; but as we've already used this word at the other level, let's choose a different word, and set ourselves to work out a new doctrine to take account of what one can call the *force* of the expression. These 'forces' are just what we were meeting with as we went along just now, and what I described, or attempted to describe, under the name of 'speech-acts'. In trying to make clear the second kind of 'meaning', or the force, of an expression like 'I slept badly last night', we say: it's a threat, a warning, a complaint, and so on — that is to say, we try to characterize the kind of speech-act which it exemplifies.

So I entirely agree with you: there is a problem here quite distinct from that of meaning, which arises not on the level of the factual content of expressions, but on the level of the 'forces' which show themselves when we speak.

Perelman: I would like to begin with an example of a linguistic expression, which I will present in French — because, in English, I fear it is a different matter. And here perhaps is another reason, which I offer to Mr. Apostel, in favour of comparative analysis.[15]

Suppose that a sergeant gives a soldier an order. The soldier answers 'Je refuse d'obéir'. That is a performative utterance in Professor Austin's sense. The sergeant goes to the captain to

make his report. The captain sends for the soldier, and asks him
'Est-il vrai que vous refusez d'obéir?'. And he replies 'C'est vrai'.
The question and the answer are certainly constative utterances:
'Il est vrai que je refuse d'obéir'. But in English, it would not go
like that at all, for in place of the expression 'I refuse', the
question would be 'Are you refusing?'. One would transform
the present into the present participle active. It would not be
necessary to bring in the expression 'It is true that . . .', for
there is available a particular grammatical form — which in
French is replaced by 'Est-il vrai que . . .' — for effectively distinguishing the two forms. I believe it is true in general that, in
French, one can in this way transform performative into constative utterances, by prefixing 'Il est vrai que . . .', 'Il est faux
que . . .', etc. There are all sorts of expressions of the same kind.

If we take it, then, simply on the level of the current use of
language, if we keep the expression 'Il est vrai . . .' in front of
what follows, we cannot completely eliminate constative utterances. I wonder, also, whether we have any interest in wanting
to reduce all these utterances, and I believe that, on the contrary,
Mr. Austin is trying to safeguard them, and to give them a status.

My second question concerns the use of the [French] word
'ridicule'. No doubt you noticed that, in Mr. Austin's paper, the
word 'absurde' occurred several times. Now, there are cases in
which one would not speak of the notion of absurdity, but would
invoke rather that of the ridiculous. When a child tries to argue
with his elders, the parents would not say 'Il est absurde'; they
would prefer to say 'C'est ridicule'. It is 'ridicule' to give an
order to someone when one has no authority to give orders and
is sure they will not be carried out.

That, I believe, would hold for quite a number of examples
in which Mr. Austin gave prominence to the term 'absurde', and
where we would prefer to employ the term 'ridicule'. In fact
there is a whole family of notions, not just one or two, a whole
spectrum of shades of meaning, which permit us to express our
appraisals of this or that speech-act, and which reveal our attitudes in this or that situation. For me, absurdity has something
more logical about it, the ridiculous something more social. I
wonder whether Mr. Austin accepts this distinction.

Austin: Yes, and many others. There is a whole lot of notions
of this kind that we make use of, or could make use of if we spoke

our language more correctly. The trouble is that for these emotion-charged epithets — they're nearly always pejorative or insulting — we are inclined to use the first term that springs to mind, the one that's uppermost because it's fashionable, rather than trying to pin down exactly the precise nature of our disagreement. But I believe something could in fact be got out of a closer study of epithets of this kind, and so I gladly accept the distinction you make.

I agree on the first point as well. Even in the first stage, where we try to set up — vainly for the most part, as I think I succeeded in showing — a firm distinction between the performative and the constative, one could point out many more snares and pitfalls than I did in my paper. I think that even in English, notwithstanding the distinction you made with reference to your example, you'll find the expressions 'It is true that . . .' or 'It is false that . . .' used to introduce a purely constative utterance, exactly as in French. And to take an everyday case, you can use the expression 'I promise to . . .' as a simple historic present. You say, for instance: 'By Article 37, second sub-section, paragraph 3, I promise to do such-and-such'. Obviously in that case the utterance is constative, can be true or false, in spite of the fact that it contains the formula designed for promising. We're led to say: this is a historic present tense, not the kind of present tense we're interested in.

But I'm not so sure that I agree with you when you invoke an 'extralinguistic' criterion. The distinction we've just agreed on could quite well be found in a work on linguistics, or a properly done grammar. A linguist would be careful to mark the difference between the two uses. And how would he do it? Certainly not by recourse to a *purely* linguistic criterion — understanding by that, I suppose, attentive examination of the order of the words and their functions in the phrase. He would certainly have to appeal to something outside language, in that sense, to appreciate the distinction between two uses of one and the same group of three words, 'I promise to . . .', in the two cases. So I don't see how what he would do would be any more reputable than, or even any different from, what we are trying to do.

However that may be, I agree with you on your first point; and I even go further, because what you spotted in French can occur in the same way in English. But I don't think that we're thereby thrown back on an 'extralinguistic' enquiry, to make a distinction which for one thing is a matter of common sense, and for another is already current among grammarians. I don't think that this will push us out of our little cabbage patch. Those distinctions, and the well-tried method we use for making them, have always existed inside our territory.

Poirier: I should like to say first of all how delighted I was to hear Professor Austin, and how much I feel myself to be, fundamentally, in agreement with him. The questions I would like to ask him relate to logical and philosophical extensions of the analysis of language; and they are surely quite proper questions, insofar as the Oxford school does not seek to restrict itself to a philological or psychological explication of texts. These questions relate to three points: the linguistic expression of performative thoughts, the relation of the performative to the logical, and the nature of a possible logic of performative utterances.

1. First of all, is it possible to characterize declarative and performative utterances linguistically, in such a way as to make possible the eventual construction of a theory, a logic of performative utterances (which would also be a logic of performative thoughts)?

What somewhat complicates the discussion, it seems, is that one naturally begins with utterances which, grammatically, are in the indicative (or the infinitive). And no doubt there are, among these utterances, some which are declarative and derive from material situations; but there are also some which express feelings, states of mind of very diverse kinds — promises, fears, instructions, wishes, desires, hope, confidence, etc. Can we distinguish these and give rules for doing so? The thing is difficult both in fact and in principle,* for usage is often uncertain, and it is not clear how it could be fixed even by stipulation. If it were a question only of ambiguities of language, the case would not be hopeless, but often the ambiguity extends to the thought itself. Thus when I say 'I order . . .', I may express a firm and seriously intended instruction, and that is equivalent to 'Do it, obey!'. But I may also express the knowledge or the certainty that I have of giving an order, making a demand, or, if you like, I describe myself giving an order. Again, I may quite well give

---

* E.g., the case of attempting to construct a logic of imperatives.

an order for the sake of giving it, and be quite unconcerned as to its execution.* Plainly there would be no point in setting out the rules for the expression 'I order' without having determined in what sense one is taking it.

What fixes the sense of utterances in current usage? It is not just vocabulary. The grammatical context, and the psychological or human context, must be taken into account. In the third person, 'He orders . . .' is purely descriptive; in the first, 'I order . . .' can be imperative. But if I add the remark 'Either do it or don't', the formula can scarcely convey a volition, a seriously meant instruction. Attention must also be paid to gesture and tone, as indicating the real intention. If I say 'It was a fine conference', the words may, by the merest shade of emphasis, shift from simple statement to admiration, or again to irony.

Tone and context are not the only devices we can normally make use of. What about putting in (even orally!) inverted commas, or using differently coloured inks to indicate different senses? Then we should have to make sure that *these* were unambiguous in thought!

There is, in fact, one thing we can always do, since we do not move on several different levels of thought at once, and that is to say, at the start of our discourse, on what level we are moving — whether we are taking personal indicatives in a sense fundamentally imperative, optative, etc., or rather in a reflexive and descriptive sense. Then there are quite simply the classical procedures for removing ambiguities, and which consist in, for instance, eliminating the indicative mood, at least in the first person, or again in the active voice. Normally an instruction is expressed by the use of the imperative (or even the active or passive subjunctive) — 'Do it', 'Let him do it', 'Let it be done'. Again one can use positive impersonal forms — 'It is prescribed . . .', 'It is ordered . . .' — which practically eliminate the ambiguities of subjectivity. Similarly, instead of saying 'I wish . . .', which is ambiguous, one may say 'May he come!', 'Let him come!', 'It is to be wished that . . .', etc.

What conclusion follows? That, on the one hand, subjective thoughts are infinitely diverse and subtly distinct, and we our-

* And sometimes, in speaking the words, I do not myself know just what my intention really is.

selves do not always know what we are thinking; and that, on the other hand, their linguistic expression is extremely various, extremely uncertain, and depends on a thousand grammatical and psychological circumstances. Any kind of expression whatever can, depending on the circumstances, convey any kind of thought whatever. This is the famous contention, not easy to disagree with, of Ferdinand Brunot, particularly in his *La Pensée et la Langue*. There are no genuine synonyms, nor any grammatical forms with one unique significance, and no thought has one and only one expression.

All that is not to deny that there are in practice thoughts as to which there is general agreement, which can be considered as definite, more or less rough mental categories, and that these thoughts are almost always capable, besides ambiguous expression, of unambiguous expression, at least in certain languages and for those who speak them correctly.* It is obviously appropriate, in discourse undertaken in good faith, to make use of these unambiguous expressions, after having taken the trouble of determining what one means.

As for what 'the language' means 'in itself', 'objectively', regardless of those who speak it, of circumstances, of the particular context, no doubt that does not mean anything much.

2. A second point, then, is this. Suppose† that by a linguistic and psychological analysis we have managed to classify objectively definite performative utterances, to distinguish those mental and grammatical categories that are genuinely performative — what is the relation of each of these to logic? Must we not say that that deals only with declarative or indicative expressions, and that the performative belongs to individual or group psychology? Is the answer really so simple as that? I do not think so; and I imagine Professor Austin would agree in the view that that would be too good to be true.

To be sure, if logic is by definition merely the study and formal representation of the most general laws of events or groups of events, of their presence and absence, co-presence and co-absence, then performative utterances come in only as the expression of

---

* It is precisely the case, I think, of performative notions that can lead to an appeal to the logician or the philosopher.

† The supposition may perhaps be objected to; but if so, there is no philosophical problem and nothing left to discuss.

particular material facts, with their own relations and laws. One can simply work out the theory of them, in the framework of general logic, as one does the theory of electrostatic attraction, of memory or instinct, or of movements of opinion. But if we take the word 'logic' in a wide sense, taking it to denote (as is also quite common) the study of the general methods and procedures by which we seek to define and to grasp the truth, in the fullest sense of that term, then the problem is much more complicated, the antithesis of logic and psychology vanishes, and performative utterances are perhaps entitled to a place in the realm of logic.

Thus the laws of certainty, of its modalities, of its implications, make up from this point of view a logic which is even, probably, the most fundamental of all and the most deserving of the name of logic (for truth, in the broadest sense, is that which it is necessary to believe, that which it is right to be certain of). Now these laws are those of a privileged experience, in nature fundamentally psychological, and lead on naturally to the hazier laws of belief, of probability, of desire, of hope, of volition — those, in a word, of performative thought.

Furthermore, the notions of truth and falsity themselves, which are the very type of logical notions, are limiting cases of notions that have numerous variants and aspects: one passes by insensible degrees from strictly logical absurdity or necessity to an absurdity and necessity which allow of, and reflect, all the pragmatic and affective *nuances* of performative thought, as Mr. Austin so rightly emphasizes. When I ask myself whether a belief is true, am I on the logical or the affective plane? Is the sincerity of the belief in question, its inner authenticity, its objective validity? The equivocation is not only in the words but at the heart of things. No doubt the logician will say that he considers only the objective validity of the belief and of the judgment which expresses it. But the distinction, so simple when definite physical facts are in question, disappears in many other cases. Not to mention Spinoza and the Adequate Idea which itself bears witness to its truth, we must surely agree that in many instances, and above all in morals, the objective truth of a judgment is defined by a kind of necessity, of inner evidence, which is akin to performative notions. One cannot then, in general, separate the material truth of a judgment from the truth of authenticity of the belief or the corresponding feelings.

3. The third point is this. Under what form can we envisage a logic, and in particular a formal logic, of performative thoughts as such (of performative utterances, if you prefer that notation), and what is the relation of this logic to the logic of declarative utterances, the current logic of truth?

First of all, will it be a matter of a logic of utterances, or a logic of the psychological reality which underlies those utterances — of performative thoughts and intentions? We find here, beside all the similarities and all the divergences of meaning which Mr. Austin analysed with such subtlety and depth, the equivalent of the problem which Professor Quine raised yesterday;[16] that is to say, how far, when we construct such a logic, do we attend to the properties of expressions (which in origin can only be conventional, imposed by the decisions of the axiomatizer, the legislator, or current usage), or rather of the reality, the meaning, which underlies the expressions and determines their use (or their different uses).*

Let us take an example. If I wish to construct a logic of promises, what promises, behind utterances of the type of 'I promise', are at issue here? The inner and sincere promise? Such a mental act, depending on the objects to which it is applied, the situation which produces it, the other promises with which it is combined, has in fact properties which could be studied experimentally. The formulation of a promise, a declaration, in speech or writing, in promissory form? Then the implications of that are settled externally by civil law or by public opinion, and it scarcely matters whether it expresses a deep and sincere intention. Or an ideal entity, a promise *in abstracto,* which moreover is in some peril of being no more than a word? And we must not suppose that the separation of these notions is an easy matter; for a civil promise, to be binding, must have been freely made, though it need not indeed have been sincere. In any case, an expression like 'One is bound by a promise' is quite ambiguous:

* There are evidently no natural laws of expressions. At the most there are formulae which must be accepted if one is to arrive ultimately, by verbal combinations, at certain other formulae and only those. It is thus that symbolic logic can be expected to allow the quasi-mechanical reconstruction of classical mathematics.

is it a question of the natural effects of inner promising, or of the civil consequences of a legal promise? Now how can the study of performative utterances give place to a formal logic within the ambit of ordinary logic — a formal logic in the strong sense, and not just a theory that, like any theory, can be axiomatized?

First — insofar as the notions and operations involved have some resemblance to those of logic in the ordinary sense — truth, falsehood, assertion, negation, entailment, conjunction, disjunction, applied to objects, to things, to utterances.

Next — insofar as one combines these operations directly by applying them either to themselves (iteration) or to others (product in general), and the thought progresses without other intermediaries. If beyond certain limits progress consists in applying, to the results of the immediate logic itself regarded as indicative utterances, the methods of ordinary logic, then we shall get a mixed system, a deductive theory.

Let us consider then, for example, what might be called the 'logic of imperatives'. Then there will be imperative procedures, which can be applied to various objects and combined among themselves. In what form should they be taken? The personal indicative form is fundamentally ambiguous, and besides is very ill adapted to meaningful iteration — what does 'I order that I order' mean? The personal imperative form, e.g., 'Do . . .', is not ambiguous, and one could work out a logic of 'do's'. But what meaning would attach to the iteration of 'Do . . .', or in general to the combination of two imperatives?* What could correspond to an entailment?

The only usable form seems to be the impersonal form† — 'It is prescribed that . . .'; or again, in French, the subjunctive forms. This eliminates the problems of subjective psychology; it lends itself in some degree to composition and iteration. 'It is prescribed that it is prescribed' has a sense (not, it is true, a very natural one) which in certain conditions could be taken as identical with 'It is prescribed'. 'It is prescribed that it is forbidden' can mean 'It is forbidden'. One can even establish a certain isomorphism between the categories of the imperative and those of what I have called elsewhere 'organic' logic — 'proved',

---

* The sentence 'Faites que vous veniez' does not combine two imperatives, either grammatically or semantically.

† A logic, like any science, naturally has an impersonal character.

'excluded', 'not proved', 'not excluded', 'allowed' (corresponding to 'nonexcluded' or 'possible'). But that does not go far, for expressions like 'A prescribes B' do not correspond at all to 'A proves B' — presumably because in the first case A and B cannot be of the same nature and so transitivity has no sense. A schema like 'A is prescribed, and A prescribes B, so B is prescribed' has sense only if 'prescribes' is taken in the sense of 'entails' and it is thus reduced to a schema of ordinary logic.

Can we, then, envisage an independent logic of performative utterances? That seems doubtful, and it would be as well, here again, to feel our way as we go along.

There then, among many others, are some points on which I should be glad to hear Professor Austin's views.

Austin: I can't reply point by point to your contribution — which, I am happy to observe, reveals agreement rather than disagreement with what I said. We agree in particular that, logically and psychologically, there are different levels, and different methods relating to each. So I will just take up your last point: can there be a formal logic of performative utterances?

I would be inclined to say yes. But at the same time with this reservation — that I think we should have to be quite sure we know what we mean by 'performative utterance'; and that calls, to begin with, for a much more minute and detailed inventory than the one I just briefly indicated in my paper. Then, and only then, armed with an inventory and a definition, we could if necessary consider formalizing the logic of performative utterances, at least for certain types or families of expressions of this kind. And then again, there would be a good deal needing to be knocked down, before we achieve anything useful on certain points.

But I would like above all to go back to what seems to me a central point all through your contribution — in the examples you chose, where expressions like 'I wish . . .', 'I know . . .', 'I believe . . .' come in, as well as in the implication which I think is carried by your choice of examples — namely, that these phrases express inner states, what could be called states of the soul, psychic phenomena or inner sentiments, which would be the business of psychologists or of ontology. I'm quite prepared to agree that by my own criteria a lot of examples of the sort you mentioned would be counted as performative utterances, and

I willingly admit too that such utterances, along with many others, express 'states of mind': for example, 'I intend to do so-and-so' certainly expresses my intention to do so-and-so. But shall I go so far as to say that all utterances of this sort are in the same position, or even that the essential job of any of them is to express something about our inner states? The promise is here¯ the guarantee of the intention. But above all, and to my mind this is much the most important point, the words *bind* me by a contract, and *commit* me to doing something. I would not want to make the expressive function of an utterance of this kind, with respect to our mental life, the essential feature, or even a main one, of a performative expression.

And for the matter of that I'm not going to call on the psychologist to help me in interpreting these expressions. It seems to me that on this matter the liar would have a lot more things to teach me than the psychologist.

Translator's Notes

1. The French term is 'assertion'. I am sure that 'statement' is the English term Austin would have used here, and I have so translated 'assertion' throughout.

2. 'Formuler un tel énoncé'. The translation is supplied in a footnote by Austin himself.

3. 'Unhappy' is a term Austin regularly used in this connection, and he supplies it himself in brackets after the French 'malheureux'.

4. 'Rupture d'engagement'. Austin himself supplies the translation.

5. That is to say, a particular case of unhappiness might arguably, or even quite properly, be classifiable under more than one heading.

6. 'Affirmer'. I have translated this verb by 'state' throughout.

7. The French phrase is 'peut ne pas jouer'. Austin himself sometimes used in English the coined term 'non-play' (see, e.g., *How to Do Things with Words,* pp. 18n. and 31), but in a more restricted sense than would be appropriate here.

8. These three English terms are supplied in a footnote by Austin himself.

9. The French text has 'conjoncture' here, but this must surely be a misprint for 'conjecture'.

10. Austin supplies this English term himself. It is in any case the term he regularly used.

11. The French text here has 'peut s'établir'; but this gives exactly the opposite of the required sense, and must surely be an error.

12. This phrase is quoted verbatim in the text, a literal French version being tentatively offered in a footnote.

13. 'On fait flèche de tout bois'.

14. This sentence is quoted verbatim in a footnote to the French text.

15. In an earlier paper presented at the same conference, "Le Champ Sémantique de l'Incertitude", L. Apostel had compared French with German and English expressions and idioms, and advocated such comparative stuay of different languages. In discussion of that paper, Austin agreed that such comparative study was highly desirable, mentioned that, in discussions between philosophers in Oxford, references at least to Greek and Latin were pretty common, but suggested that an excessive attachment to traditional philosophical problems tended to inhibit his colleagues from extensive linguistic researches.

16. The reference is presumably to Quine's paper "Le Mythe de la Signification", presented earlier at the same conference.

3 NEGATIVE EXISTENTIALS*

by Richard L. Cartwright

Sentences of the forms 'There is no such thing (person, place, etc.) as ....' and 'There are no such things (persons, places, etc.) as .... (s)' are characteristically used to make statements which I shall call _negative existentials_. A negative existential which can be formulated in a sentence of the first form is _singular;_ one which takes a sentence of the second form is _general_. Sentences of other forms can also be used to formulate negative existentials, singular or general. Instead of 'There is no such person as Santa Claus' we may have 'Santa Claus does not exist' or 'No such person as Santa Claus really exists'; and instead of 'There are no such things as unicorns' we may have 'There are no unicorns' or 'No such animal as a unicorn exists'. I will not attempt a review of the subtle differences among the various ways in which negative existentials may be formulated. For some purposes, this might be desirable or even necessary; but for my purposes here it is not.

Since ancient times negative existentials have been a source of puzzlement. Although it is plain that among them some are true and some false, it has sometimes appeared on reflection that none can possibly be true. Several lines of argument have seemed to lead to this conclusion, and prominent among them is the following. To deny the existence of something — of unicorns, for example — we must indicate _what_ it is the existence of which is denied; and this requires that unicorns be _referred to,_ or _mentioned:_ the negative existential must be _about_ them. But things which do not exist cannot be referred to or mentioned; no statement can be about them. So, given that we have denied their existence, unicorns must after all exist. The apparently true negative existential is thus either false or not really a statement

* Presented in a symposium on "Reference and Existence" at the fifty-seventh annual meeting of the American Philosophical Association, Eastern Division, December 27, 1960.

at all; and, since the argument applies as well in any other case, we seem forced to conclude that there are no true negative existentials.

Presumably the argument tempts no one to renounce his cherished denials of existence. Nevertheless, as do other such puzzles, it focuses attention on a question of fundamental importance to logical theory. To formulate this question precisely, it is convenient first to state the argument (or rather, a slightly altered version of it) in a standard logical form. Let S be any negative existential, and let a (or K's, where S is general) be what in S is said not to exist. The argument is then as follows:

  (i) S is about a (or, K's);
  (ii) If S is about a (or, K's), there is such a thing as a (or, there are such things as K's);
  (iii) If there is such a thing as a (or, there are such things as K's), S is false;

therefore,

  (iv) S is false.

Clearly, the argument is formally valid; but its conclusion is obviously false. Hence, there must be some defect in the premises — either plain falsity or the sort which gives rise to an informal fallacy. The question is: What is this defect?

Two proposed answers are by now classic. I shall begin by expounding these; then, through commenting on them, I shall make some suggestions of my own.

Proponents of the first answer, whom I shall call Inflationists,[1] regard the argument as involving a fallacy of equivocation. According to them, the words 'there is', and consequently the term 'negative existential', are ambiguous; and it is by surreptitiously trading on this ambiguity that the argument simultaneously enjoys both an appearance of soundness and an air of paradox. Inflationists contend that so-called existential statements, whether positive or negative, are of two quite different kinds. Some are affirmations or denials of *being*, others are affirmations or denials of *existence*. Taken as denials of being, "negative existentials" *are* one and all false. Thus, in a famous passage, Russell wrote:

[1] I have borrowed this term, and also the term 'Deflationist', introduced below, from Isaiah Berlin. See his "Logical Translation," *Aristotelian Society Proceedings*, 1949-50.

Being is that which belongs to every conceivable term, to every possible object of thought. . . . Being belongs to whatever can be counted. If *A* be any term that can be counted as one, it is plain that *A* is something, and therefore that *A* is. "*A* is not" must always be either false or meaningless. For if *A* were nothing, it could not be said not to be; "*A* is not" implies that there is a term *A* whose being is denied, and hence that *A* is. Thus unless "*A* is not" be an empty sound, it must be false — whatever *A* may be, it certainly is. . . . Thus being is a general attribute of everything, and to mention anything is to show that it is.[2]

But, taken as denials of existence, not all "negative existentials" are false; for, as Russell remarked, "*existence* is the prerogative of some only amongst beings."[3] As to *how* existence is to be distinguished from being, there is apparently not much to be said; but it seems that only such things as are in some sense "concrete," or occupy some portion of space or time, enjoy existence as well as being.[4]

As applied to the argument under discussion, the Inflationist distinction between being and existence is said to have this effect. If "negative existentials" are understood as denials of being, and if the words 'there is' are correspondingly interpreted, then each of (i) through (iv) is true. But this need not be viewed as paradoxical. For "negative existentials" are more naturally taken as denials of existence; and, when (i) through (iv) are interpreted accordingly, (ii) — as well as (iv) — is false. In order to be mentionable, a thing need only *be;* it need not exist.

To treat the Inflationists fairly — especially to mitigate the distressingly *ad hoc* character which otherwise attaches to the distinction between being and existence, it is necessary to remark that what I have presented as a solution to a problem more often appears as an independent argument for the necessity of that distinction. The argument is a familiar one: given that some denials of existence are true, that which, in any one of them, is truly said not to exist must nevertheless be; for a denial of existence is about what it says not to exist — which is possible only if

[2] *The Principles of Mathematics,* second edition, p. 449.
[3] *Ibid.*
[4] In *The Principles* Russell said simply that "to exist is to have a specific relation to existence" (p. 449). In the articles on Meinong he remarked: ". . . for my part, inspection would seem to lead to the conclusion that, except space and time themselves, only those objects exist which have to particular parts of space and time the special relation of *occupying* them" ("Meinong's Theory of Complexes and Assumptions," first installment, *Mind,* n.s., Vol. XIII (1904), p. 211).

what it claims not to *exist* nevertheless *is*.) From this argument I have extracted, in an obvious way, the Inflationist solution to the problem before us.

Although classic, the Inflationist solution is not popular. Indeed, it has become a favorite whipping boy of metaphysical economists. They, in turn, propose an alternative which I shall call the Deflationist solution. Expositions of it vary in detail from one author to another, but the central point in each is the contention that (i) is simply false. Negative existentials are *not* about those things the existence of which they deny. They may *seem* to be; but this, Deflationists say, is mere semantic appearance, resulting from the misleading verbal form in which they are cast.

Again, this contention typically appears as the conclusion of an argument, not as an *ad hoc* device for avoiding a paradox. Deflationists argue that no negative existential is about that which it denies to exist; for, if true, there is no such thing for it to be about. Thus Ryle wrote:

Suppose I assert of (apparently) the general subject 'carnivorous cows' that they 'do not exist', and my assertion is true, I cannot really be talking about carnivorous cows, for there are none. So it follows that the expression 'carnivorous cows' is not really being used, though the grammatical appearances are to the contrary, to denote the thing or things of which the predicate is being asserted.[5]

Contrary to what the quotation might suggest, Ryle does not intend to limit the conclusion to true negative existentials. It is easily extended to false ones as well by adding the premise that a false statement is about only what it would be about if true.

Deflationists characteristically proceed to tell us what negative existentials are *really* about; and here the main variations occur. Russell, once he disavowed Inflationism, regarded them as being about *propositional functions*.[6] To say there are no unicorns is, on this view, to say of the function *x is a unicorn* that it is "always false"; and to deny the existence of the present King of France is to say of *x is a present King of France* that it is not uniquely satisfied. Others[7] have said that a negative existential asserts of an *attribute (characteristic, property, concept)* either that it is

---

[5] "Systematically Misleading Expressions," in *Logic and Language*, first series, edited by A. Flew; the quotation is from pp. 15-16.

[6] See, e.g., Part V of "The Philosophy of Logical Atomism."

[7] See, e.g., Ryle, *op. cit.*, and Broad, *Examination of McTaggart's Philosophy*, Vol. I, p. 20.

not exemplified at all or (where the negative existential is singular) that it is not uniquely exemplified. But the variations are less important than the theme; for they would not have been fashioned were it not for the conviction that negative existentials are not about what they seem to be.

The classic answers invite obvious objections. It is a commonplace to point out that the Inflationist peoples the world not only with fictitious, mythical, and imaginary beings but also with such thoroughgoing non-existents as carnivorous cows and such contradictions as round squares. If, in defense, it is said that he grants these "being" but not "existence," it may well be replied that he thereby parries the charge of over-population only by invoking an unexplained concept of being. The result is to dispel a paradox by substituting for it a mystery. The Deflationist, on the other hand, avoids mystery — but only at the cost of creating a new paradox. For if it is paradoxical to say that all negative existentials are false, it is at least disturbing to be told that, when we finally tell our children that Santa Claus does not exist, we say nothing about Santa Claus. Presumably they *expect* to hear something about him — the truth about him, one way or the other; and it is scarcely believable that the hard facts of semantics force us to disappoint them. Nor is it much consolation (to us or to them) to be told that we say nothing about him *in the same sense* as that in which we say something about Caesar when we say he crossed the Rubicon; for it is not clear that 'about' has an appropriately different sense. Perhaps a Deflationist can simply *give* it one; but then it is left open whether he says anything relevant to our problem.

Perhaps these objections are too easy to be decisive. Still, they suggest a need for re-examination of the classical theories. It is convenient to begin by considering the position of the Deflationist. He says, for example, that

(1) Carnivorous cows don't exist

is not about carnivorous cows. In so saying he intends to contrast (1) with, for example,

(2) Barking dogs don't bite,

which obviously *is* about barking dogs.[8] Now, without denying

[8] Some who advocate Deflationism deny that (2) is about barking dogs. But this denial enters at a deeper level than that on which I am moving.

the truth of what the Deflationist says, it may be doubted whether
he thus succeeds in calling attention to the vital point of contrast
between (1) and (2). He says that (1) is not about carnivorous
cows because, if true, there are no carnivorous cows for it to be
about. To say this is to imply that a statement can be about only
such things as exist. But if we are thus led to deny that (1) is
about carnivorous cows, we shall have to deny it also of

(3) Carnivorous cows have horns;

for (1) *is* true, and there are hence no carnivorous cows for (3)
to be about. So the point of contrast between (1) and (2), to
which the Deflationist calls attention, obtains also — and this by
his own principles — between (2) and (3). But, now, I wish
to argue that there is an important respect in which (1) differs
from (2), *in which respect it also differs from (3)*; and I wish
to argue that it is *this* point of contrast between (1), on the one
hand, and (2) and (3), on the other, which must be recognized
if we are to deal adequately with the paradox of negative existentials.

A person who affirms (2) purports to refer to certain things
and to say of or about them that they don't bite. More than this,
he purports to *specify* which things it is he is saying don't bite.
Purported references to things are not always specifying. If
someone says, "*Some* dogs don't bite," he refers certainly to
dogs and possibly to barking dogs; but he does not specify which
dogs are those he alleges don't bite — as is shown by the fact that
a hearer might ask, "Which dogs do you mean?" Of course, one
who affirms (2) does not purport to mention any *individual* dogs;
his purported reference is essentially *plural*, rather than *singular*
— which it would not have been had he said instead that Rover,
Fido, and Spot don't bite. But, though he mentions no barkers
in particular, he leaves no doubt as to which things he claims to
be non-biters. Now, insofar as any proper part of his utterance
can be said to carry the burden of all this, it is clearly the subject
phrase which does so. Thus we may say that the grammatical
subject of this formulation of (2) is so used that it there *purports
to make a plural specifying reference to certain things* — namely,
to barking dogs.

Exactly parallel comments can be made about (3). Its subject phrase is so used that it there purports to make a plural

specifying reference to carnivorous cows. But there is an important difference. Though there are barking dogs, there are no carnivorous cows; and this may lead us to say that although one who affirms (2) refers to barking dogs, one who affirms (3) does not refer to carnivorous cows. The grammatical subject of (3) *purports* to refer, in a plural specifying way, to carnivorous cows; but, it may be said, it does not *actually* do so, since (1) is true. This contrast between (2) and (3) need not be denied, but it is more important in the present context to emphasize the respect in which they are alike; for in *this* respect, *both* stand in contrast to (1). The grammatical subject of (1) is *not* there used the way it is in (3); it does *not*, in (1), purport to refer, in a plural specifying way, to carnivorous cows. It is not that a person who affirms (1) *purports* to refer to carnivorous cows, but — since there are none — fails actually to do so; rather, he does not purport to refer at all. If this is not evident in itself, it becomes so once it is recognized that any purported plural specifying reference to carnivorous cows, though plural, nevertheless presupposes the possibility of singular specifying references to particular carnivorous cows. Thus, anyone who affirms (3) must acknowledge that there is some true statement the making of which consists in actually referring in a singular specifying way to some particular carnivorous cow and saying of or about it that it has horns.[9] But it is surely evident that (1) does not require for its truth that there be a true statement the making of which consists in actually referring in a singular specifying way to some particular carnivorous cow and saying of it that it does not exist; indeed, (1) is properly taken as implying that there is no such true statement. Of course, if (1) is true, so are

(4) The carnivorous cow does not exist

and

(5) The cow that is carnivorous has not yet been found.

But I take it as obvious that in neither of these is the grammatical subject so used that it even purports to make a singular specifying reference to a particular cow.

The vital contrast between (1) and (2) is thus that the grammatical subject of (2), but not that of (1), is so used that it

---

[9] Note that (3) is not to be confused with the statement that there is nothing which is both a carnivorous cow and also hornless.

purports to refer in a plural specifying way. Now, this feature of
(1) is paralleled by a feature found in certain singular negative
existentials. In essentially the same way as (1) contrasts with
(2), so, for example,

(6) The man who can beat Tal does not exist

contrasts with

(7) Botwinnik does not gamble.

The grammatical subject of (7) is so used that it there purports
to refer in a singular specifying way to something. But this is
obviously not true of 'the man who can beat Tal' in (6). One
who affirms (6) does not purport to single out a particular man
and say of him that he does not exist — as is shown by the fact
that it would be absurd to respond with "To whom are you referring?" or "Who *is* the man who can beat Tal?" And to bring
out *this* contrast between (6) and (7) it is not sufficient to say
that whereas (7) is about Botwinnik, (6) is not about the man
who can beat Tal. For neither is

(8) The man who can beat Tal lives in Brooklyn

about the man who can beat Tal, given that (6) is true and that
a statement can't be about what doesn't exist. In (8), 'the man
who can beat Tal' purports to make a singular specifying reference; nor does it necessarily altogether fail to refer: it may there
refer to (though mistakenly describe) Fisher. But in (6) it does
not even purport to refer.

I do not really wish to insist that Deflationists are completely
unaware of all this. Indeed, there is reason for thinking they are
not, since many of them class together (2), (3), (7), and (8), as
subject-predicate statements, while withholding this status from
(1) and (6). Put in these terms all I wish to suggest is that
underlying the classification is the contrast I have drawn. Again,
Deflationists may be expected to say that (1) and (6) *could* not
be about, respectively, carnivorous cows and the man who can
beat Tal, whereas this only *happens* to be true of (3) and (8);
and, with respect to this, I wish to be understood as saying only
what seems to me to be the explanation of the alleged impossibility in the one case and contingency in the other.

Still, if the Deflationist recognizes that (1) and (6) are different from, respectively, (2) and (7), in the way I claim, he fails
to recognize that this cannot be said of all negative existentials.

He incautiously assumes that, in their referential features, all negative existentials are essentially alike; and he is thus led to suppose that what has been seen to be true of (1) and (6) is true of negative existentials generally. Broad, for example, asks us to consider "the two negative propositions *Cats do not bark* and *Dragons do not exist*." And concerning them he says: "It is obvious that the first is about cats. But, if the second be true, it is certain that it cannot be about dragons, for there will be no such things as dragons for it to be about."[10] Now, this is to extend Deflationist reasoning concerning (1) to

(9) Dragons do not exist;

and it is thus to assume that (9) differs in no relevant way from (1). But the questionableness of this assumption is indicated by the linguistic outrage we feel at being told that (9) is not about dragons. Feeling this outrage, the Inflationist is led to affirm the being of dragons. And, though we may hope to avoid this metaphysical conclusion, we cannot afford to ignore the semantic point upon which it is based. For behind the reluctance to concede that (9) is not about dragons is the implicit recognition that it is referentially quite different from (1).

To see this, notice first that whereas (2) is not true if there are no barking dogs, both (9) and

(10) Dragons don't have fur

are true; to deny (10) is to exhibit an ignorance of mythology as pathetic as the ignorance of natural history displayed by denying (9). Some are led by this consideration to say that in neither (9) nor (10) is anything said about dragons. But to compound the paradox in this way is to overlook the referential similarity of (2) and (10). One who affirms (2) says of barking dogs that they don't bite; similarly, one who affirms (10) says of dragons that they don't have fur. In both cases a plural reference is made to those things of which something is said, and in both the reference is specifying: one who affirms (10) specifies *which* things he is claiming have no fur, just as one who affirms (2) specifies which things he alleges don't bite. Anyone who affirms (10) must, of course, grant that there is some true statement the making of which consists in actually referring in a singular specifying way to some particular dragon and saying of or about it that it

[10] *Religion, Philosophy, and Psychical Research,* p. 182.

has no fur. But this he may happily do, since mythology assures us of the truth of

(11) Faffner had no fur

as much as it does of (10).

Doubtless those who say that (10) is not about dragons will also say that (11) is not about Faffner. But how is this to be understood? To the contention that in (11) 'Faffner' only *purports* to refer in a singular specifying way, it may be replied that to say this is to overlook the fact that, in just the way that (7) contrasts with (8), (11) contrasts with

(12) Hamlet's wife was a blonde.

Hamlet had no wife; hence, (12) is not true, and one who affirms it — though perhaps he refers to Ophelia — at best purports to refer to Hamlet's wife. But (11) is not in this way defective; if it were, it would not be true. And this shows also that it will not do to say that in (11) 'Faffner' does not even purport to refer; for this would leave us with, at best, an artificial way of identifying the respect in which it succeeds and (12) fails.

Thus (10) is referentially on all fours with (2); and it differs referentially from (3) only in involving an actual, rather than merely a purported, reference to certain things. Still, whereas (2) is incompatible with there being no barking dogs and (3) is in fact not true because of the truth of (1), both (9) and (10) are true. These facts taken together point to some fundamental difference between (9), on the one hand, and (1) and the denial that there are barking dogs, on the other. Now, there is in any event a striking difference between, for example, (9) and (1). Notice that although (9) is equivalent to

(13) Dragons are not real,

it is not the case that (1) is equivalent to

(14) Carnivorous cows are not real.

To say of certain things that they are not real is to invite the question, What are they? And although one who affirms (13) may respond by saying that dragons are mythical, legendary, imaginary, or whatever, no such answer is available to one who affirms (14). The fact is that it is not of *anything* non-existent that unreality may be correctly predicated: given only that a person has no brothers, we can hardly say that his brothers are unreal. On the other hand, the playmates of a child whose only playmates are imaginary *are* unreal. The question whether something is real or not itself presupposes that the thing has some "status" — imaginary, fictional, or whatever.

Critical readers will have noticed that I just now spoke of "predicating" unreality. This was no parapraxis. For in one sense (philosophical as well as ordinary), to predicate is to say something of or about something to which one refers; and this, I suggest, is precisely what *is* done in affirming (13) — and hence (9). It is, indeed, in this respect that (9) fundamentally differs from (1). To assert (9) is to say of dragons that they are unreal, just as to assert (10) is to say of them that they lack fur. In both cases there is a plural reference to dragons; and in both the reference is specifying. Furthermore, if someone who asserts (9) is challenged to refer in a singular specifying way to a particular dragon, and to say truly of it that it never existed, he may easily do so; for

(15) Faffner did not (really) exist

is among the true statements to which he may have recourse. We *objection* are apt to be told, of course, that in (15) there is not really a singular specifying reference to Faffner. But what can this mean? *reply* Surely, one who affirms (15) *purports* to refer to some one particular thing; he is (or at least should be) prepared to answer such questions as, To whom are you referring? and Who is Faffner? In this respect he differs from one who affirms (6). And it could hardly be said that in (15) there is *only* a purported reference to Faffner. To say this would be to liken (15) to (12) and thus to overlook the fact that whereas nothing can be correctly said to have been Hamlet's wife, something *can* be correctly said to have been Faffner — namely, the dragon Siegfried slew. The familiar doctrine that existence is not a predicate, if understood as implying that *no* negative existentials are (in the sense in question) predicative, thus seems to me to be false. There is admittedly no call to regard negative existentials such as (1) as predicative; but those which, like (9) and (15), are assertions of unreality have as much claim to the subject-predicate classification as do, for example, (2) and (7).

Neither Deflationists nor Inflationists are sufficiently sensitive to the distinction between these two sorts of negative existentials.

I have already argued that the former wrongly take statements like (1) and (6) as typical of negative existentials generally, and that the latter do the same with statements such as (9) and (15) is evident from their admission of such things as carnivorous cows and round squares into the realm of being. But even if the distinction should be granted, it may still be felt that the crux of the philosophical problem of negative existentials remains untouched. If some negative existentials are subject-predicate statements, then, of these, either all are false — which is absurd — or some are about what does not exist. But, it will be asked, How *can* a statement be about what does not exist?

Asked by an Inflationist, the question represents an effort to win a metaphysical consolation prize. Even if the truth of (1) does not require the being of carnivorous cows, does not what I have said about (9) require that dragons *be* even though they don't *exist?* Must not dragons have some *mode of being,* exist in some *universe of discourse?* To these rhetorical questions it is sufficient to reply with another: What, *beyond the fact that it can be referred to,* is said of something when it is said to have some mode of being or to exist in a universe of discourse? The alleged modes and universes are so admirably suited to perform their function that they are not above suspicion of having been invented for the purpose.

Put by a Deflationist, the question registers a residual fear that to give up the Bradleian dictum that "no one ever *means* to assert about anything but reality"[11] is to foster metaphysical excesses. But to remove this fear it is sufficient to recognize that discourse which is not "about reality" is "about unreality"; and unreality is just that: it is not another reality.

[11] *Appearance and Reality,* ninth impression, p. 145.

4 EXCLUDERS

by Roland Hall

The Notion Introduced.

' INSTEAD of asking what "real" means we should try to find out what we mean by "a real so-and-so"', might be regarded as a commonplace in recent philosophy. That is, 'real', and a good many other philosophically troublesome adjectives, are attributive, and cannot be understood until it is known what they are being applied to in a given case.[1] Likewise the suggestion that many (or most) words are systematically ambiguous or multivocal is familiar enough,[2] and even older.

Acting on the first suggestion we find the use of 'real' determined in each case not by a given set of qualities in that case, but by the use of some opposite, which is (in Prof. Austin's picturesque phrase) 'the word that wears the trousers'. Thus real experiences are not dreams (or nightmares), real tigers are not stuffed ones, real silk is not artificial (i.e. manufactured) silk, real estate is not movable property, a real example is not an invented one, and so on. Further, 'real' is not only ambiguous between different types of cases, but often also within the class of comparison,[3] e.g. real tigers may in a particular instance be opposed not to stuffed ones but to cardboard tigers, or electric tigers, or two men in a tiger outfit, and there is no limit *a priori* to this ambiguity. It depends on the context alone which and how many of the possible alternatives are ruled out. This characteristic I call ' *open ambiguity*' on the analogy of ' open texture '.[4]

Adjectives that have these features, i.e. (1) are attributive as opposed to predicative, (2) serve to rule out something without themselves adding anything, and (3) ambiguously rule out different things according to the context, I call ' *excluders* '. What has passed unnoticed about them is the extent to which they pervade the English language. It is mainly to this that I wish to draw attention.

History

Mill is the philosopher who stands out as noting the existence of such words, which he classifies under ' negative names '.[5] He

[1] Geach, ' Good and Evil ', ANALYSIS, Dec. 1956, on p. 33.
[2] Ryle, *CM*, p. 23 (' rising '); Waismann, ' Verifiability ', in *Logic and Language* I, pp. 134–46, applies it to ' real ' *inter alia*.
[3] For the term, see Hare, *The Language of Morals*, p. 96 and passim.
[4] Waismann, *l.c.*, pp. 120–1.   [5] *System of Logic*, I. ii. 6.

points out that 'idle' and 'sober' are respectively equivalent to 'not working' and 'not drunk', or, when used disposition-ally, to 'not disposed to work' and 'not drunken'. These examples are only mildly ambiguous; but in the following section he gives a more telling instance quite by the way: to justify his use of 'non-relative' instead of the excluder 'abso-lute'' 'which does too much hard duty in metaphysics', he says:

> It resembles the word *civil* in the language of juris-prudence, which stands for the opposite of criminal, the opposite of ecclesiastical, the opposite of military, the opposite of political—in short, the opposite of any positive word which wants a negative.

'Civil' is as good a standard excluder as one may hope to find.

However, other philosophers had noticed certain single words as having the features for which I call them 'excluders'. Descartes (*Principles*, II. 17) stressed feature (3) for the word 'empty', in order to say that though a vacuum in the philoso-phical sense was impossible, there could be a vacuum in the ordinary sense, i.e. a space containing no sensible matter. Locke (*Essay* II. 26. 4–5) discussed the attributiveness of various words, such as 'old' and 'big'. Hume (*Treatise* III. 1.2) points out that feature (3) *invalidates* systems using 'natural' or 'nature' as a foundation for ethics, and discusses the ambiguities involved. Mill takes this discussion further, in his *Essay on Nature*, pp. 59–60, where he considers 'the numerous acceptations [of 'natural'], in which it is employed as a distinctive term for certain parts of the constitution of humanity *as contrasted with* other parts' (my italics), and distinguishes five senses, giving examples. This detailed treatment is too long to quote, but worth reading.

'Real' deserves special mention, as it has received so many detailed but misguided treatments,[1] which it is not possible to go into here. Russell's efforts are sufficiently instructive to serve as typical. In discussing the word 'real', Russell falls into several traps. He sees the symptoms: 'The question what properties must belong to an object in order to make it real is one to which an adequate answer is seldom if ever forthcoming'.[2] But he still tries to find properties, not realising the word is negative and attributive in use, and suggests two criteria for

---

[1] E.g. Moore, *Some Main Problems of Philosophy*, ch. xxi; Laird, in *Mind* 1942 (who sees to some extent its excluding features).

[2] *Mysticism and Logic* (Pelican ed.), p. 116.

being real: 'A thing is real if it persists at times when it is not perceived', and if 'it is correlated with other things in a way which experience has led us to expect'. This would have to be discussed on its merits as a proposal for a predicative use of 'real'; it doesn't aid understanding of the existing uses. Elsewhere[1] he puts forward a different theory, that 'real' can be applied to propositions and descriptions, but not to proper names, and for this theory he gives the following argument: 'Words that go in pairs, such as 'real' and 'unreal', 'existent' and 'non-existent', 'valid' and 'invalid', etc., are all derived from the one fundamental pair, 'true' and 'false'. Now 'true' and 'false' are applicable only—except in derivative significations—to *propositions*.' Objections to this are: (a) 'real' does not go in a pair with 'unreal', but corresponds to many words; (b) it is false that 'real' and 'unreal' are derived from 'true' and 'false' in any sense; (c) if the theory were correct, 'real' could only be used predicatively, and as synonymous with 'exists' (which Russell admits on the next page), e.g. 'Are tigers real?' would be an alternative to 'Do tigers exist?', both meaning 'Is there anything to which the description "tiger" correctly applies?' But we couldn't *ask* our usual question, 'Is that a real tiger?' *without* relying on the correctness of the description.

Some Examples

I now mention some typical excluders:

'Ordinary' is one which has given some trouble, as it remains undetermined in the expression 'ordinary language', until it is clear whether what it excludes is the language of the educated, the expert, the symbolic logician, the philosopher, or several of these at once, or something else. E.g. Russell when polemizing[2] misunderstands the phrase as if it always excluded the language of the educated, but uses it himself in his early articles[3] and elsewhere[4] to exclude the language of mathematical logic. Again, whereas the average man has quite definite characteristics (I.Q. about 100, and so on) even when we don't know what they are, 'the ordinary man' is a meaningless expression outside a particular *context*, and many contexts allow it to remain ambiguous enough to be popular among politicians. It leaves the

[1] *Loc. cit.*, p. 166.
[2] 'The Cult of Common Usage', *BJPS*, Vol. III (1952–3), 303–7.
[3] In the reprints in *Logic and Knowledge*, e.g. on pp. 68 and 195.
[4] E.g. in *My Philosophical Development* (1959), on pp. 75, 93, 99; for a different contrast (with jargon) cf. p. 170. Note also 'ordinary written language' in *PM* I(2nd ed.), p. 8.

impression that there is a first-order quality of ' ordinariness '. Here some people are *genuinely* misled by the grammatical forms of the language, because they feel that all adjectives are predicative, whereas no one thinks all nouns are substantial, e.g. that if he goes about in the nude then there is something that he goes about in.

'*Absolute*': absolute music is not programme music, an absolute construction has no relation of syntax to the rest of the sentence, absolute rule is unrestricted by constitutional checks, a verb absolute is not dependent on a following accusative to complete its sense, absolute alcohol is not mixed with water or other fluid; and here the analogy between the different exclusions, viz. that they all exclude some relation to something else, is so simple that the temptation arises to find a subject of which ' absolute ' can be used predicatively, as unambiguously excluding *all* relations to anything else, and to call this ' the Absolute '. Dictionary treatment of this word is instructive: it is either defined by another excluder, such as ' complete ', ' perfect ', ' pure ', or by using overtly negative expressions, beginning ' unrestricted ' ' independent ', ' unqualified ', ' unconditional '.

'*Accidental*': accidental sharps and flats are the signs not in the key signature, while accidental lights (in painting) are lighting effects not resulting from daylight. 'Accidental death ' would require a long definition, but clearly the definition must consist of ruling out other possibilities. (Compare the use of ' act of God ' as an excluder in law: its application is not decided by any theological investigation).

'*Barbarian*' may mean non-Greek, non-Christian, or uncultured. There are other possible meanings, but they are all of this type. Plato (*Politicus* 262d) remarks on how people can be misled by this excluder: ' they separate the Hellenic race from all the rest as one, and to all the other races, which are countless in number and have no relation in blood or language to one another, they give the single name " barbarian "; then, because of this single name, they think it is a single race '.

'*Base*' (adj.) may be used attributively of such various subjects as persons, sounds, tenure, language, birth, metals, and coins, and in all of these attributions it usually serves to rule out something, never to ascribe a quality open to immediate recognition. *Others* are: *plain, pure, normal, simple, standard, regular, perfect, ideal, abstract, bare, barren, empty*; (and possibly) *mental, actual.*

Some further points and explanations

1. *Difference from simple predicates.* It may not be clear why 'bare' is an excluder and 'red' not, since it might be maintained that 'red' could be defined as 'not-green, not-blue, etc.' If someone knows the meaning of the word 'red' he must understand me quite regardless of the context when I say 'That light is red'. But unless he knows from the context or is specially told by me, when I say 'That man's head is bare', he won't understand me even though he knows the meaning of the word, because he won't know what I am intending to rule out. He won't know whether it is covering, camouflage, hair, protective apparatus, or just adornment, that the man lacks. So whereas 'red' would be a genuine predicate even if it *could* be defined negatively, 'bare' is an excluder because it *must* be defined negatively. Excluders must be defined by way of exhaustion, because they are used not to ascribe properties but to exclude them; and this exhaustion can never be completed, in the first place because of the systematic ambiguity of the words in their different applications, and secondly because the class of properties which they are used to exclude is an open class. Consequently, excluders are not amenable to definition in any strict sense: we can only point to where and how they are actually used. A definition would in effect leave us with a new word, that is to say we could certainly not do with the word as defined the most important things we did with the undefined word.

2. *Difference from ambiguous predicates.* It might be felt that the first difference was due just to the unambiguousness of 'red'. If I heard through a closed door the words 'It's certainly acute', I could not know whether they came from a doctor diagnosing a disease, a geometer looking at an angle, or anyone testing a dog's sense of smell, or considering an answer to a problem, or a vast range of other possibilities. Similarly with 'That's the back' (of what?). But systematic ambiguity, though necessary, is not sufficient to make a word an excluder: merely ambiguous words can be genuine predicates in that they may add something instead of merely ruling out, and I can understand them without further ado if I know what they are being applied to. Here again, 'acute' *could* be defined as 'not-obtuse', but it need not be defined negatively in this way; acuteness is an immediately recognisable characteristic of angles.

3. *Difference from simple negative predicates.* There are plenty of adjectives which do not ascribe qualities or relations, but are used to deny them. Since the positive or negative form of the

word can't be used as a criterion for this, as we are inclined to say with Mill e.g. that some 'un'-words express something positive whereas some positive-form words have negative meaning, we may be puzzled which to take as negative out of two incompatibles with positive forms, such as 'light' and 'dark'.[1] Does 'light' mean 'not-dark', or 'dark' mean 'not-light', or are both positive, leaving us to account for the synthetic truth that nothing can be light and dark all over then and there? This question need not be tackled here, for such pairs of terms are *ex hypothesi* not excluders, as they are in a one-one relation with other words, and excluders have a one-many relation to other words. Thus if (defying the dictionary) we regard 'light' (not-heavy) and 'light' (not-dark) as one word, we should be inclined to regard it as an excluder; it seems unnatural to suggest that 'heavy' and 'dark' *both* mean 'not-light', though I find it hard to see reasons for this disinclination, apart from neatness. Similarly, it seems more natural to regard 'old' as meaning 'not young or new or recent' rather than to reverse the procedure. Though here again we might regard them both as positive, using Locke's explanation (*Essay* II. 26.4) that for every sort of thing the usual duration of which we know, we can say whether its present age is nearer to the beginning or the end of that duration, and so call it young or old respectively.

Another kind of negative predicate which is not an excluder is simple, but relational; thus 'anonymous' does not rule out any qualities of a thing, but merely the relation of having a name.

Apart from really simple negative predicates, there are some negative predicates containing an implicit variable, which I do not count as excluders because their ambiguity is merely of the egocentric type: thus 'absent' means 'not *here* (or wherever is in question)'; an alien is a man not belonging to the country of *reference*; a man or thing is alone when not with something else of the *same* general type; and an allotheist *worships* gods who are not those of the country *he inhabits* .

4. *Being an excluder sometimes a matter of degree.* Although there are plenty of indubitable excluders, there might be difficult borderline cases. One word that has developed into an excluder is 'blank', originally meaning just 'white', but coming *via*

---

[1] Is the reason why Locke's examples of negative names seem so unquestionable, that they are far less easily ostensified than what they deny? (In *Essay* II. 8.5. *insipid, silence, nihil*, are said to be negative names signifying the absence of the positive ideas *taste, sound, being*.

' blank paper ' to mean ' not written on or filled in ', so that in time we get ' blank cheque ', ' blank passport ', ' blank verse ', ' blank expression ' (of face). So there must have been a time (probably end of 16th century) when it would have been hard to say whether ' blank ' was an excluder or not, and it is not unreasonable to expect this difficulty with a few words at the present time.

5. *Exclusion not limited to adjectives.* Though the discussion has been restricted to adjectives, and (the notion of an excluder defined as an adjective with certain properties in use, nouns and other parts of speech can be found following the same pattern. Examples would be: *chance, intuition, luck.*)

6. *Whether excluders form a genuine class.* I might be accused of committing the fallacy pointed out by Plato (quoted above), viz. selecting words which have nothing in common, calling them by one name because of three features that they all lack (predicative meaning, ascriptive force, and univocality), and then because of this one name regarding them as forming a genuine class. But the selection of a class is only used here as a convenience for bringing out a certain pattern in language; it is not being inferred that excluders have anything but these negative defining properties in common. If the present article should appear barmecidal to some readers, they would be those who are free from the common and natural inclination to assimilate excluders to a different pattern, that of predicative, positive, univocal words.

5 REFERENCE AND REFERENTS

by Leonard Linsky

I

In discussing the topics of definite descriptions, referring expressions, and proper names, mistakes are made due to a failure to distinguish referring and making a reference, in the ordinary meanings of these terms, from what philosophers call "denoting", and "referring". Of first importance here is the consideration that it is the users of language who refer and make references and not, except in a derivative sense, the expressions which they use in so doing. Ryle, for example, says, "A descriptive phrase is not a proper name, and the way in which the subject of attributes which it denotes is denoted by it is not in that subject's being *called* 'the so-and-so', but in its possessing and being *ipso facto* the sole possessor of the idiosyncratic attribute which is what the descriptive phrase signifies."[1] I do not wish to deny that what Ryle says here is true, in his technical sense of "denote". The example is chosen only to bring out how different this sense is from what we ordinarily understand by referring. I might, for example, refer to someone as "the old man with grey hair". Still, the phrase "the old man with grey hair" does not "signify" an "idiosyncratic attribute", if what is meant by this is an attribute belonging to just *one* person. It is equally obvious that I might refer to a person as "the so-and-so" even though that person did not possess the attribute (idiosyncratic or not) "signified" by that phrase. I might, for example, refer to someone as "the old man with grey hair", even though that person was not old but prematurely grey. In both cases I would be referring to someone not "denoted" (in Ryle's sense) by the expression used in so doing. But these *expressions* do not refer to that person, I do. The question "To whom does the phrase 'the

[1] "Systematically Misleading Expressions", reprinted in *Essays on Logic and Language,* edited by A. Flew, New York, 1951, p. 23.

so-and-so' refer?" is, in general, an odd question. What might be asked is "Who is the president of the United States?", or "To whom are you referring?", not "To whom does the phrase 'the president of the United States' refer?".

The question "To whom (what) does the phrase 'the so-and-so' refer?" is generally odd. It is not always odd. Certainly it sounds odder in some cases than in others. I think one might ask, "To what does the phrase 'the morning star' refer?", or, pointing to a written text, I might ask, "To whom is the author referring with the phrase 'the most influential man in Lincoln's cabinet'?". But, in speaking about referring, philosophers have written as though one might sensibly ask such questions in an unlimited number of cases. What else could have caused Russell to say in "On Denoting", "A phrase may denote ambiguously; e.g., 'a man' denotes not many men, but an ambiguous man."?[2]

It is of course perfectly true that one can ask, "To whom does the pronoun 'he' refer?", if one is oneself referring to a particular passage in a text, or to something which has just been said. But it does not follow that one can ask this question *apart* from such a context. Clearly, the question "To whom does 'he' refer?" is a senseless question unless such a context is indicated. The same is true of Russell's example, "a man". It is senseless to ask, "To whom does 'a man' refer?", or (using Russell's term) "Whom does 'a man' denote?". But even when the context is clearly indicated this question does not *always* make sense. If, for example, I tell you that I need a wife, you can hardly ask me, "To whom are you referring?".

Failure clearly to mark these distinctions leads to confusions about uniqueness of reference. Russell says that a definite description "will only have an application in the event of there being one so-and-so and no more."[3] But can I not refer to someone as "the old madman" even though he is not mad and more than one man is? Does my phrase not have "application" to the one to whom I am referring? Certainly I was speaking of him. What is usually said here is that uniqueness of reference is secured by making the description more determinate, for example by saying, "The old man who lives next door". But this attempt

[2] "On Denoting", reprinted in *Readings in Philosophical Analysis,* edited by H. Feigl and W. Sellars, New York, 1949, p. 103.

[3] *Principia Mathematica,* vol. I, Cambridge, 1910, p. 30.

to secure uniqueness of reference through increased determination of the "referring expression" is otiose, for what secures uniqueness is the user of the expression and the context in which it is used *together* with the expression.

We may now notice Ryle's futile attempt to get uniqueness of reference somehow guaranteed by the words themselves. "Tommy Jones is not the same person as the king of England" means, Ryle says, what is meant by: "(1) Somebody, and — of an unspecified circle — one person only is called Tommy Jones; (2) Somebody, and one person only has royal power in England; and (3) No one both is called Tommy Jones and is king of England." But surely when I say "Tommy Jones is not king of England" I am not claiming that exactly one person of any circle is named "Tommy Jones". What is indeed necessary, if I am to make a definite assertion, is not that one person only be named "Tommy Jones", but that I be referring to just one person, however many others there may be with the same name as his. It is a mistake to think that the "referring expression" itself can secure and guarantee this uniqueness. This is obvious in the case of proper names, for here we cannot appeal to meaning. "Tommy Jones" does not have a meaning, and many people share it. Proper names are usually (rather) common names.

Ryle's account makes it appear that it is an intrinsic characteristic of certain groups of words that they denote something or other. They possess this characteristic in virtue of their "signifying an idiosyncratic attribute". Perhaps he is thinking of such an expression as "the oldest American university". (It is a matter of fact that the oldest American university is Harvard.) But nothing prevents one from referring to another school (by mistake, or in jest) with these words.

Perhaps Ryle has confused referring to something with referring to it correctly as this or that. I might, for example, refer to L. W. in saying, "He is the president of the bank." Still, I would have referred to him incorrectly as the president of the bank, because he is not the president of the bank, but the vice-president. Some of what Ryle says will be correct if we interpret his comments about denoting as giving an account of what it is to refer to something *correctly* as such-and-such. But it is, after all, possible to refer to something incorrectly as such-and-such, and that is still to refer to it. Furthermore, for one to refer correctly to something as "the such-and-such" it is not necessary that the thing referred to be the sole possessor of the "property signified" by the phrase, though it must certainly have that property. Conversely we can say that it is not necessary that the property "signified" by a phrase of the form "the such-and-such" be "idiosyncratic" if one is to refer to something correctly as "the such-and-such".

II

The question "To whom (what) does the phrase 'the so-and-so' refer?" is generally odd. But it is not always odd. I am arguing that the sense in which expressions (as opposed to speakers) can be said to refer to things is derivative. I mean by this that the question "To whom (what) does the phrase 'the so-and-so' refer?" means the same as the question with regard to some person, "To whom (what) is that person referring with the phrase 'the so-and-so'?". Where the question cannot be so rephrased, it cannot be asked at all, for example, "To whom does the pronoun 'he' refer?", "To whom does the phrase 'the old man' refer?".

Much of the philosophical discussion of this topic has assumed that this was not so. Russell says that a denoting phrase is such "solely in virtue of its form". Thus we should be able to ask, "To whom does the phrase 'the tallest man in the prison' refer?", for the denoting phrase here is of the same form as "The Sultan of Swat" and this phrase can be said to refer to someone, namely Babe Ruth. But the first question cannot be asked. The second question, "To whom does the phrase 'The Sultan of Swat' refer?", does not require a special context and is not the same question as the one which asks with regard to some person, "To whom was he referring with that phrase?". For clearly this last question might receive a different answer than the first. This would occur if the speaker in question had erroneously been referring to Mickey Mantle. So the question "To whom does 'the so-and-so' refer?" seems not always to be the same question as the one with regard to some person, "To whom was he referring with the phrase 'the so-and-so'?".

I am claiming that the counter examples are only apparent and that the general thesis is still true. There is a class of expressions which (to use Strawson's happy description) have grown capital letters. Some examples are "The Sultan of Swat", "The Morning Star", "The City of the Angels". One can ask, "To what city does the phrase "The City of Angels" refer?". The answer is, "Los Angeles". Such expressions are on their way to becoming names, for example "The Beast of Belsen". They are what a thing or person is called often and repeatedly, and that is why one can ask to what they refer. Philosophers were perhaps concentrating on such examples as these when they said or implied that the question "To whom (what) does 'the so-and-so' refer?" can always be asked. But it cannot.

Perhaps another source of this mistake derives from a confusion between meaning and referring. One can ask both "What does this phrase mean?" and "Whom do you mean?". Also, "I referred to so-and-so" and "I meant so-and-so" seem very close indeed. But these verbs are radically different, as can be seen from the following considerations. One can ask, "Why did you refer to him?", but not "Why did you mean him?". One can say, "Don't refer to him!", but not "Don't mean him!". "How often did you refer to him?" is a sensible question, but "How often did you mean him?" is not. One can ask, "Why do you refer to him as the such-and-such?", but not "Why do you mean him as the such-and-such?". I can ask why you refer to him at all, but not why you mean him at all. The verb "to mean" has noncontinuous present tense forms, for example, "I mean you", but it lacks the present progressive tense form, "I am meaning you". The verb "to refer" has a present progressive form, "I am referring to you", as well as a noncontinuous present form, "I refer to Adlai Stevenson".

What these grammatical considerations show is that referring to someone is an action; meaning someone is not an action. As an action it can be right or wrong for one to perform. Thus it can be wrong of you to refer to someone, but not wrong of you to mean someone. It can be important or necessary that you should refer to someone, but not important or necessary that you should mean someone. One can intend to refer to someone, but not intend to mean him.

III

In discussions of statements such as "Edward VII is the king of England", it is sometimes said that in making them one is referring to the same person twice. Frege would say that the person is referred to in different ways each time. This way of looking at them leads to their interpretation as identities. But consider the following conversation to see how odd it is to talk of referring twice to the same person in such contexts:

A: He is the king of England.
B: To whom are you referring?
A: That man behind the flag.
B: How many times did you refer to him?

Referring to someone several times during the course of a speech would be a rather different sort of thing. If I mention a man's name, I would not ordinarily be said to have referred to him in so doing. Using a man's name is in some ways opposed to referring to him rather than an instance of it.

If we assume that whenever in an assertion something is mentioned by name by a speaker, he is referring to that thing, certain very paradoxical conclusions can be deduced. It would follow that when I write in my paper "I am not, of course, referring to Ludwig Wittgenstein", I would be referring to Ludwig Wittgenstein. But if someone were asked to show where in my paper I had referred to Ludwig Wittgenstein, it would be absurd for him to point to the statement in which I say, "I am not referring to Ludwig Wittgenstein". The same would be true of the statement in which I say, "I am referring to Ludwig Wittgenstein". If it were asked where in my paper I had referred to Ludwig Wittgenstein, it would be absurd to point to the statement in which I say, "I am referring to Ludwig Wittgenstein". In both cases I would have used Wittgenstein's name. Therefore, to mention someone by name is not necessarily to refer to him. And consider this example. Suppose the porter at Magdalen College asks me whom I am looking for. I answer, "Gilbert Ryle". Would anyone say I had referred to Gilbert Ryle? But if I say, in the course of a talk, "I am not referring to the most important of present-day philosophers", I would then and there be referring to Ludwig Wittgenstein; though in saying, as I just did, "I would then and there be referring to Ludwig Wittgenstein", I could not be said to have referred to Ludwig Wittgenstein. And this is so notwithstanding the fact that Ludwig Wittgenstein is the most important of present-day philosophers. This then is the paradox of reference. In saying "I am referring to Ludwig Wittgenstein" I am not referring to Ludwig Wittgenstein.[4]

Some of the statements which have been counted as identities cannot be interpreted as such. Suppose I explain to my confused son, "Charles de Gaulle is *not* the king of France". That this statement is not an identity can be shown as follows. From $a \neq b$, it follows that $b \neq a$, but from "Charles de Gaulle is *not* the king of France" it does not follow that "The king of France is *not* Charles de Gaulle". The first of these statements is true while the second is neither true nor false. The reason for this is not, as is sometimes said, that I have failed to refer in saying, "The king of France . . .". The reason is that France is not a monarchy and there is no king of France. Just so, and said of a spinster that "Her husband is kind to her" is neither true nor false. But a speaker might very well be referring to someone in using these words, for he may think that someone is the husband of the lady (who in fact is a spinster). Still, the statement is neither true nor false, for it presupposes that the lady has a husband, which she has not. This last refutes Strawson's thesis that if the presupposition of existence is not satisfied, the speaker has failed to refer. For here that presupposition is false, but still the speaker has referred to someone, namely, the man mistakenly taken to be her husband.

Of course a man may "fail to refer", but not as Strawson uses this expression. For example, in your article you may fail to refer to my article.

IV

Now it is, of course, the case that on the analysis of propositions containing descriptive phrases proposed by Russell, the proposition "The king of France is not Charles de Gaulle" is not an identity. The reason he gives for this is entirely different from the reason which I have just given. According to Russell, this proposition is an existential generalization which, however, contains an identity proposition as a part. In fact, on Russell's view, our proposition has two possible interpretations according as the descriptive phrase is considered to have what he calls "primary

[4] Philosophical tradition sanctions the production of such paradoxes. I am thinking of Meinong's paradox about Objects of which it is true to say that no such objects exist; and Frege's paradox that the concept *horse* is not a concept.

occurrence" or "secondary occurrence" in the whole proposition of which it is a part. Another way of putting this is to say that "The king of France is not Charles de Gaulle" has two analyses on Russell's view, depending upon whether the negation in the proposition is viewed as being an inner negation or an outer negation. In the first interpretation it would be of the form:

(1) $\qquad [(\imath x)(\Phi x)]\{\sim\Psi(\imath x)(\Phi x)\}.$

On the second interpretation our proposition would be of the form:

(2) $\qquad \sim\{[(\imath x)(\Phi x)](\Psi(\imath x)(\Phi x))\}.$

On either interpretation, and against Strawson, the proposition "The king of France is not Charles de Gaulle" has a truth-value. On the first interpretation (1) it is false and on the second interpretation (2) it is true.

For this reason I find both interpretations objectionable. But I should now like to present reasons in support of the claim that Russell's analysis of propositions containing definite descriptions is mistaken and that in fact it cannot at all do the job it was designed to do. It does not provide a solution for Russell's famous puzzle about George IV and the author of *Waverley*. What puzzled Russell was why one could not conclude from the premise that George IV wished to know whether Scott was the author of *Waverley* that George IV wished to know whether Scott was Scott, since Scott was the author of *Waverley*. The solution proposed by Russell says that the inference to "George IV wished to know whether Scott was Scott" from "George IV wished to know whether Scott was the author of *Waverley*" is not warranted because this latter proposition, when properly analyzed, contains no constituent definite description for which we may substitute "Scott".

Now there are two ways (and only two ways) in which a descriptive phrase may be eliminated from a proposition and there are good reasons against accepting either of the resulting interpretations. In the first way we interpret "George IV wished to know whether Scott was the author of *Waverley*" as being of the form:

(3) $\qquad [(\imath x)(\Phi x)]\{\Psi(\imath x)(\Phi x)\},$

and the result of the elimination of the descriptive phrase is:

(4) $\qquad (\exists c) [(x)((\Phi x) \equiv (x = c)) \& (\Psi c)].$

In the second way we interpret our proposition as being of the form:

(5) $$X\{\Psi(\imath x)(\Phi x)\},$$

and the result of the elimination is:

(6) $$X\{(\exists c)\,[(x)((\Phi x)\equiv(x=c))\,\&\,(\Psi c)]\}.$$

Interpreted as (4) our proposition would be:

(7) One and only one person wrote *Waverley* and George IV wished to know whether that individual was Scott.

Interpreted as (6) our proposition reads:

(8) George IV wished to know whether one and only one individual wrote *Waverley* and whether that individual was Scott.

And now for the reasons for rejecting *both* interpretations. First let us consider (7). This is the interpretation which accords the definite description a primary occurrence. The trouble with this is that on this interpretation it really does follow from the other premises that George IV wished to know whether Scott was Scott. This last is of the form Ψb. The proposition that Scott is the author of *Waverley* is of the form $b=(\imath x)(\Phi x)$. From these two we get our unwanted conclusion which is of the form Ψb (on the interpretation being considered). The argument on this interpretation becomes a straightforward substitution instance of a theorem of *Principia Mathematica*:

14.15 $$\{(\imath x)(\Phi x)=b\}\rightarrow\{\Psi(\imath x)(\Phi x)\equiv\Psi b\}.$$

Another queer consequence of the interpretation (7) is that if "George IV wished to know whether Scott was the author of *Waverley*" is given that analysis, it follows from it that *Waverley* was not co-authored. But it is obvious that this does not in fact follow and therefore the interpretation (7) is unsatisfactory. But what is the proof that this queer consequence does thus follow from this interpretation? (7) is of the form (4). (4) is an existentially generalized conjunction so that we can distribute the existential quantifier to each of the conjuncts. Now simplifying we get:

(9) $$(\exists c)\{(x)[(\Phi x)\equiv(x=c)]\}.$$

But (9) by the definition 14.02 of *Principia* is:

(10) $$E!(\imath x)(\Phi x).$$

Consistently with the interpretation we have supplied for the variables above, this says,

(11) One and only one person wrote *Waverley*.

From (11) it follows that *Waverley* was not co-authored.

Let us now turn to the alternative interpretation, which accords a secondary occurrence to "the author of *Waverley*" in the proposition "George IV wished to know whether Scott was the author of *Waverley*". This is our (8). But it is obvious that (8) does not mean the same as our proposition, for what (8) says is that George IV wanted to know both whether one and only one individual wrote *Waverley and* whether, if so, Scott was that individual. But surely from the proposition that George IV wished to know whether Scott was the author of *Waverley* it does not follow that George IV wished to know whether or not *Waverley* was either not written at all or written by more than one person. It is entirely possible that George IV knew very well that *Waverley* was written by one and only one man, even though he did not know who that man was. Nor can I see that any other English version of (6) can avoid this unwanted result. It follows that neither (6) nor (4) is a possible form of the proposition in question.

V

Referring does not have the omnipresence accorded to it in the philosophical literature. It sounds odd to say that when I say "Santa Claus lives at the North Pole" I am referring to Santa Claus, or that when I say "The round square does not exist" I am referring to the round square. Must I be referring to something? Philosophers ask, "How is it possible to refer to something which does not exist?". But often the examples produced in which we are supposed to do this ("Hamlet was a prince of Denmark", "Pegasus was captured by Bellerophon", "The golden mountain does not exist") are such that the question "To whom (what) are you referring?" simply cannot sensibly arise in connection with them. In these cases, anyway, there is nothing to be explained.

How is it possible to make a true statement about a nonexistent object? For if a statement is to be about something, that thing must exist, otherwise how could the statement mention *it,* or refer to *it*? One cannot refer to or mention nothing, and if a statement cannot be about nothing it must always be about something. Hence, this ancient line of reasoning concludes, it is not possible to say anything true or false about a nonexistent object. It is not even possible to say that it does not exist.

It is this hoary line of argument which, beginning with Plato, has made the topic of referring a problem for philosophers. Still, ancient or not, the reasoning is outrageously bad. Surely here is a case where philosophers really have been seduced and led astray by misleading analogies. I cannot hang a nonexistent man. I can only hang a man. To hang a nonexistent man is not to do any hanging at all. So, by parity of reasoning, to refer to a nonexistent man is not to refer at all. Hence, I cannot say anything about a nonexistent man. One might as well argue that I cannot hunt for deer in a forest where there are no deer, for that would be to hunt for *nothing*.

It must have been philosophical reflections of this genre which prompted Wittgenstein to say in his *Remarks,* "We pay attention to the expressions we use concerning these things; we do not understand them, however, but misinterpret them. When we do philosophy we are like savages, primitive people, who hear the expressions of civilized men, put a false interpretation on them, and then draw queer conclusions from it."[5]

Let us look a bit closer at what it is to talk about things which do not exist. Of course there are a variety of different cases here. If we stick to the kind of case which has figured prominently in philosophy however, this variety can be reduced. What we now have to consider are characters in fiction like Mr. Pickwick; mythological figures like Pegasus; legendary figures like Paul Bunyan; make-believe figures like Santa Claus, and fairy tale figures like Snow White. (And why not add comic strip figures like Pogo?) And do not these characters really exist? Mr. Pickwick really is a character in fiction; Mr. Ryle is not. There really is a figure in Greek mythology whose name is "Pegasus", but none whose name is "Socrates"; and there really is a comic strip character named "Pogo". In talking about these characters I may say things which are true and I may also say things which are not. If I say, for example, that Pogo is a talking elephant, that is just not true. Neither is Pegasus a duck. In talking about these things there is this matter of getting the facts straight. This is a problem for me; it is not a problem for Dickens or for Walt

---

[5] *Remarks on the Foundations of Mathematics, Oxford,* 1956, p. 39.

Kelly. What Dickens says about Mr. Pickwick in *The Pickwick Papers* cannot be false, though it can be not true to character; and in the comic strip, Walt Kelly does not say anything about his possum Pogo, for Pogo talks for himself. Still, Pogo could say something about Walt Kelly (or Charles de Gaulle) and that might not be true.

There is, however, another group of cases discussed by philosophers, and this group has the important characteristic that in talking about its members there is no such thing as getting the facts straight. Here we find Russell's famous example, the present king of France; and Meinong's equally famous example of the golden mountain. What are they supposed to be examples of? Well, just things that do not exist. But in saying this we must keep in mind how different they are from Mr. Pickwick, Santa Claus, Snow White, etc. Keeping this difference in mind we can see that though it makes perfectly good sense to ask whether Mr. Pickwick ran a bookstore, or whether Santa Claus lives at the North Pole, it makes no sense whatever to ask whether the golden mountain is in California. Similarly, though we can ask whether Mr. Pickwick was married or not, *we* cannot sensibly ask whether the present king of France is bald or not.

If the question is, "How can we talk about objects which do not exist?", then it is wrong to use the examples of the golden mountain and the present king of France. These famous philosophical examples, the round square, the golden mountain, are just things we do *not* talk about (except in telling a story or a fairy tale or something of the kind). Meinong, Russell, and Ryle all puzzle over sentences such as "The golden mountain is in California", as though one just had to make up one's mind whether to put it in the box with all the other true propositions, or into the box with the other false propositions. They fail to see that one would only utter it in the course of telling a story or the like. It does not occur in isolation from some such larger context. If it did so occur, if someone were just to come up to us and say, "The golden mountain is in California," we would not concern ourselves with truth or falsity, but with this man. What is wrong with him? When the sentence occurs in a fairy tale it would never occur to us to raise the question of its truth. And if we are asked to consider whether it is true or false outside of such a context, we can only say that it does not so occur, we just do not say it.

Of course we may sometimes in error, or by mistake, talk about nonexistent things, for example Hemingway's autobiography. So here is *one* way in which it can occur that we speak of nonexistent objects. As a result of a mistake!

VI

It is said to be an astronomical fact of some importance that

(1) the morning star = the evening star.

This was not always known but the identification was early made by the Greeks. Frege said that it was because the two expressions, "the morning star" and "the evening star", had the same reference that (1) was true, and because these two had different senses that (1) was not a trivial thing to say.

Frege's way of putting the matter seems to invite the objection that the two expressions, "the morning star" and "the evening star", do not refer to the same thing. For the first refers to the planet Venus when seen in the morning before sunrise. The second refers to the same planet when it appears in the heavens after sunset. Do they refer then to the same "thing"? Is it, as Carnap says,[6] a matter of "astronomical fact" that they do? One wants to protest that it is a matter of "linguistic fact" that they do not.

Perhaps Frege's view is better put if we think of the two expressions as names, that is, "The Morning Star" and "The Evening Star". Thus Quine,[7] in repeating Frege's example but adding capital letters, speaks of the expressions "Evening Star" and "Morning Star" as names. Quine would say that what the astronomers had discovered was that

(2) The Morning Star = The Evening Star.

This is better, for (1) implies (or presupposes) what (2) does not, that there is only one star in the sky both in the morning and in the evening. Also, a purist might object that it cannot be taken as ground for (1) that Venus is both the morning star and the evening star. Venus is not a star but a planet. It would be wrong to say that what the astronomers discovered was that the morning planet is the evening planet.

[6] *Meaning and Necessity*, Chicago, 1947, p. 119.
[7] *From a Logical Point of View*, Cambridge, Mass., 1953, p. 21.

(2) is free from these criticisms, but still the same protest is in order as was made against (1). The name "The Morning Star" does not refer *simpliciter* to the planet Venus. It does not refer to the planet in the way in which the demonstrative "that" might be used to refer to the planet on some occasion. The names "The Morning Star" and "The Evening Star" are not that sort of "referring expression".

It would be incorrect for me to say to my son as he awakens, "Look to the place where the sun is rising and you will see The Evening Star", for that is not what the star is called when seen in the east before sunrise. Again, the proposal that we stay up until we see The Evening Star is quite a different proposal from the proposal that we stay up until we see The Morning Star. In dealing with failures of substitutivity in some ways like these, Frege developed his concept of "oblique" (*ungerade*) discourse, and Quine has talked about "referential opacity". Names in oblique contexts, according to Frege, do not have their "ordinary" referents but an oblique referent which is the same as their ordinary sense. But it would be absurd to suggest that when I tell my boy that if he looks to the east on arising he will see The Evening Star, I am not referring to a planet but to a "sense", whatever that might be. Using Quine's notion of referential opacity, one might suggest that the reason why the proposal to wait up until we see The Evening Star is a different proposal from the proposal to wait up until we see The Morning Star is that here the context is referentially opaque, so that the two names in these contexts do not refer to anything at all. But surely this result is too paradoxical to be taken seriously, and in any case no one has yet told us how to understand the view that a proposal can be referentially opaque.

Under the entry on "Venus" in the *Encyclopaedia Britannica* we are given the following information: "When seen in the western sky in the evenings, i.e., at its eastern elongations, it was called by the ancients 'Hesperus', and when visible in the mornings, i.e., at its western elongations, 'Phosphorus'." Did the astronomers then discover that

(3) Hesperus = Phosphorus?

In the entry under "Hesperus" in Smith's *Smaller Classical Dictionary* we read, "Hesperus, the evening star, son of Astraeus

and Eos, of Cephalus and Eos, or of Atlas." From this, together
with (3), we are able to get by Leibniz's Law,

(4) Phosphorus is the evening star.

And avoiding unnecessary complications, let us interpret this as
meaning

(5) Phosphorus is The Evening Star.

Any competent classicist knows that this is not true.

Under the entry on "Phosphorus" in Smith's *Smaller Classical
Dictionary* we find, "Lucifer or Phosphorus ('bringer of light'),
is the name of the planet Venus, when seen in the morning before
sunrise. The same planet was called Hesperus, Vespergo, Vesper,
Noctifer, or Nocturnus, when it appeared in the heavens after
sunset. Lucifer as a personification is called a son of Astraeus and
Aurora or Eos; of Cephalus and Aurora, or of Atlas." So the
stars were personified, and it seems to be a matter of mythology
that

(6) Hesperus is not Phosphorus.

Then did the astronomers discover that the mythologists were
wrong?

Of course (3) is false and no astronomical research could have
established it. What could we make of the contention that the
Greeks mistakenly believed that Hesperus was not Phosphorus?
According to the *Encyclopaedia Britannica* (under "Hesperus"),
". . . the two stars were early identified by the Greeks." But
once the identification was made, what was left to be mistaken
about here?

Could not one mistake The Evening Star for The Morning
Star? Certainly one could. This would involve mistaking evening
for morning. One could do this. In the morning it is just getting
light and in the evening it is just getting dark. Imagine someone
awaking from a sleep induced by a soporific. "But there aren't
two stars so how *could* one be mistaken for the other?"

Hence, though it is sometimes made to look as though the
Greeks were victims of a mistaken astronomical belief, this is not
so. And Quine suggests that the true situation was "probably
first established by some observant Babylonian." If that is the
case, a knowing Greek would not have said

(7) The Morning Star is not The Evening Star

unless, of course, he were in the process of teaching his child the *use* of these words. And, drawing on his unwillingness to say (7) (except in special circumstances when he might want to say just that), we might push him into saying that The Morning Star is The Evening Star, and even that Hesperus is Phosphorus, though now he would begin to feel that these sayings were queer.

The moral is that if we allow ourselves no more apparatus than the apparatus of proper names and descriptions, sense and reference, and the propositional function "$x = y$", we just cannot give an undistorted account of what the astronomers discovered, or about Hesperus and Phosphorus. Only the logician's interest in formulas of the kind "$x = y$" could lead him to construct such sentences as "The Morning Star = The Evening Star" or "Hesperus = Phosphorus". Astronomers and mythologists don't put it that way.[8]

[8] The whole of Part VI of this essay has previously been published under the title "Hesperus and Phosphorus", in *The Philosophical Review*, Vol. LXVIII, No. 4, October, 1959.

6 CAN THERE BE A PRIVATE LANGUAGE?

by R. Rhees

THE problem about private languages is the problem of how words mean. This is much the same as the question of what a rule of language is.

When we talk about something, our language does not point to it, nor mirror it. Pointing or mirroring could refer to things only within a convention, anyway: only when there is a way in which pointing is understood and a way in which mirroring is understood. I point for the sake of someone who understands it. Apart from that it were an idle ceremony; as idle as making sounds in front of things.

Our words refer to things by the way they enter in discourse; by their connexions with what people are saying and doing, for instance, and by the way they affect what is said and done. What we say makes a difference. What expressions we use makes a difference. And the notion of a rule goes with that. If it made no difference what sound you made or when, you could not be understood and you would have said nothing. If you have said something, your utterance will be taken in one way and not in another. In many cases you will have committed yourself to saying other things, to answering in certain ways if you are asked, or to doing certain things. That belongs to the regular use of your words, and that is why it would not have been just the same if you had used others instead. That is also why it is possible to learn the language.

When we speak of "use" we may think of general practice and we may think of rules. Sometimes these can be left together, but sometimes there are differences we ought to notice. When I learn the use of an expression, or learn what it means—that is how other people speak. Yet I do not say I have learned what other people do; I have learned what it means. I may learn what it means *by* observing what other people do, and of course if I know what it means I know that others who speak the language will use it in that way. But I have not learned what generally happens. I have learned a rule.

That is in some ways like learning the rules of a game, although in some ways it is very different. It is different from learning the rules of a calculus, too. In fact in some ways it is misleading to talk of rules at all here. But it does make some things clearer—that it is possible to use an expression wrongly, for instance.

A rule is something that is *kept*. That is why we can know what we are talking about. When you have learned how the expression is used, then you can not merely behave as other people do, you can also *say* something. That is not a matter of behaving in a particular way. " This is red " does not mean " Everyone calls this red". If that were all there were to it nothing would mean anything.

And yet, that there should be rules at all does depend on what people do, and on an agreement in what they do. If you teach someone the meaning of a colour word by showing him samples of the colour, then he will probably understand; and if he understands he will go on to use the word in new situations just as you would. If he remembered your instruction all right but differed wildly from you in what he called " the same as " the samples you had shown him, and if this went on no matter how often you repeated your explanation, then he could never learn what that colour word means. And this holds generally, not just with colours. It is a point to which Wittgenstein is referring in *Investigations* 242. Of course that situation practically never arises. And if it were at all general we could not speak.

I am not saying, " People see that their reactions tally, and this makes communication possible". That would assume considerable understanding and language already. The agreement of which I am speaking is something without which it would not be possible for people to " see " that their reactions tallied or that anything else tallied. We see that we understand one another, without noticing whether our reactions tally or not. *Because* we agree in our reactions, it is possible for me to tell you something, and it is possible for you to teach me something.

The consensus of reactions is in this sense prior to language, but the reactions themselves are not languages, nor are they language. Neither does the agreement in reactions come first or anticipate language. It appears as the language does, it is a common way of taking the expressions of the language. They are common reactions within the course of language—not to anything there might have been before language or apart from it.

Because there is this agreement we can understand one another. And since we understand one another we have rules. We might perhaps speak of being " trusted " to go on in the way that is for us the only natural one. But if you have learned the language you take it for granted. If any one did not, we could never understand him.

Because there is this agreement it is possible to say something. When I tell you that the patch on the patient's skin is red, I am not saying that it is called red, but that it *is* red. But I could mean nothing definite by that, and you could not understand me, unless people who have learned the words as we have would agree in calling this red. If people could not be brought to use the word in any regular way, if one man who had been taught as we have should go on to give the name to what we should call the complementary colour, if another used it as we do on Monday but in a different way on Tuesday, and if others did not show even these degrees of regularity—then it would not mean anything to say that someone had used the word mistakenly. There would be no distinction between mistakenly and correctly. And there would be no distinction between saying that it is red and saying anything else.

It is not a statement about what I do or about what people generally do. But unless the words had a regular use I should not know it was red, and I should not know what colour it was, because there would be nothing to know. I know what colour it is because I know red when I see it; I know what red is. A bull may charge at a red flag, and rats may be trained to react in one way to red lights and in another way to blue lights, but neither the bull nor the rat knows what red is, and neither knows that this is red. We might put this by saying that neither of them has the

concept " red " and neither of them has the concept
" colour". No one can get the concept of colour just by
looking at colours, or of red just by looking at red things.
If I have the concept, I know how the word " red " is used.
There must be a use, though; there must be what I have
been calling common reactions. The phrase " the same
colour " must mean something and be generally understood,
and also " a different colour". I must know when it
makes sense to talk about different shades of the same
colour; and so on. Unless I did know what it makes
sense to say, unless I were used to talking about colours
and to understanding people when they did, then I should
not know what red is and I should not know red when
I see it.

Of course the colour red is not the word " red". And I
suppose if a man cannot see he will never know what it is.
But the colour red is not *this*, either. This is red. But if
I say " This is the *colour* red", that is a definition—I am
giving you a definition by showing you a sample. And
the point of that depends upon the definition's being taken
in a particular way; and also on its connexion with other
uses of language. If I had just shown you that sample
without saying anything, and without your asking—what
would you have learned from this ? Not what the colour
red is, anyway.

Someone might say, " I know what *I* mean by ' red'.
It is what I experience when I look at this. Whether I
have this experience under the same circumstances as lead
you to use the word—that is a further question, which may
be important in deciding the description of physical objects.
But I know what colour *I* see in these circumstances". (It
would be hard to keep from asking, " Well, what colour *do*
you see ? ") I suppose the point would be that I know
this independently of having learned the (public) language.
If I know what I mean, in this way—if I know what colour
I am referring to—then apparently I have done something
like giving myself a definition. But I must also have
confused giving a definition and following a definition. It
is this which allows me to evade the difficulty of what I am

going to *call* " following the definition". Which is a real difficulty: what could it mean to say that I had followed the definition—" my " definition—incorrectly ? But if that has no sense, then what on earth is the point of the definition ? And what does the definition *establish* ?

Suppose someone asked " What colour is red ? " and thought it was like asking " What colour is blood ? " This, he might think, is something which I can learn only by my own experience, my immediate experience. And although I can tell you what colour blood is, I cannot tell you what colour red is. I can only suggest things that may enable you to find out for yourself. Well, but in this case what is the sense of " what colour red *is* " ? If it is something nobody can say, then nobody can ask it either. Suppose I ask it only of myself—but whatever is it I am asking ? Something I should like to know ? But if that has no sense, then there is nothing I tell myself either. Perhaps I say " What a colour ! ", but that is all.

I cannot learn the colour unless I can see it; but I cannot learn it without language either. I know it because I know the language. And it is similar with sensations. I know a headache when I feel it, and I know I felt giddy yesterday afternoon, because I know what giddiness is. I can remember the sensation I had, just as I can remember the colour I saw. I feel the same sensation, and that is the same colour. But the identity—the sameness—comes from the language.

A rule is something that is kept. The meaning of a word is something that is kept. It is for this reason that I can say this is the same colour I saw a moment ago. I can see the same colour just because I know red when I see it. And even with shades for which we have no special names, the same thing holds: I know the same colour when I see it.

It is similar, I have said, with sensations. I can say what I felt and I can say what I feel, and I can say it is the same sensation this time—because I know what sensations I am speaking of. It might be said that I can know it is the same only if it *feels* the same; and that is something no language can tell me. Nor can I know whether you are feeling the same as you have felt before. Only you can tell me that, because you are the only one who knows what it feels like. Well I agree that no language can tell me whether this feels the same. No language can tell me whether those two are the same colour, either. And my familiarity with methods of measurement will not tell me whether those two plots have the same area before I have measured them. But without language I could not have told whether this feels the same, either; if only because I could not have asked.

Of course recognizing a sensation is a different sort of thing from recognizing a colour. This holds whether I am speaking of my own or another's. It is different from recognizing what anything looks like or what is going on. When I say the dog is in pain I am not describing what the dog is doing, any more than I describe what I am doing when I give expression to pain. It is more like an expression of pity. At any rate, feeling pity, trying to ease him and so on—or perhaps turning away from the sight—is all part of believing that he is in pain. And to say that I was obviously justified in that—or maybe that I was mistaken— is a different sort of thing from saying that I was justified or mistaken in believing that he had a fracture. " Mistake " means something different here, although it is just as definite. If I made a mistake in thinking the boy was in pain, well he was shamming and my pity was misplaced. The mistake was not that I supposed something was going on in him when nothing was. I may have supposed that too, perhaps that he had a cramp, but that is a different mistake. The dog's pain is not something going on. It is just his *being* in pain. I know for certain that he is in pain, and I know this because I know what pain is and what suffering is. There is an important difference between seeing that he is in pain and being in pain myself, because I do not see that I am in pain, and while it is conceivable that I am mistaken about him, that makes no sense in my own case. But this does not mean that I know something about myself which I cannot know about him.

We do not speak of sensations in the same way as we speak of processes or of colours. The name of a sensation is a different sort of name from the name of a colour. But if it means anything to say I am in pain again or that he is in pain again, this is because the word " pain " has a regular use and because we know this when we know what pain is. If it were something I knew only in myself, then I might say " This is something different now " or " This is the same again " or I might say neither, and in any case it would not make any difference. This is not a question of whether I can trust my memory. It is a question of when it makes sense to speak of remembering; either of a good memory or a faulty one. If I thought I could not trust my memory, then of course I might look for confirmation. But there cannot be any question of confirmation here, nor any question of doubting either. There is just no rule for what is the same and what is not the same; there is no distinction between correct and incorrect; and it is for that reason that it does not make any difference what I say. Which means, of course, that I say nothing.

I cannot say anything unless I know the language. But I cannot know the language—any language—privately. I may have a secret code, but that is not the point here. It is a question of whether I can have a private understanding; whether I can understand something which *could* not be said in a language anyone else could understand. ("He may understand the language I speak, but he will not understand what I understand.") I say I cannot know a language privately, for what would there be to *know*? In language it makes a difference what you say. But how can it make any difference what you say privately? (I do not mean talking to yourself.) It seems that in a private language everything would have to be at once a statement and a definition. I suppose I may define a mark in any way I wish. And if every use of the mark is also a definition—if there is no way of discovering that I am wrong, in fact no sense in suggesting that I might be wrong—then it does not matter what mark I use or when I use it.

One might ask, " Why can I not give myself a definition and decide for myself what following the definition is going to be?" But when? Each time? If I decide once and for all, that only renews the problem: what is " according to my decision " ? But what would the decision be anyway? In ordinary language I may decide to use an expression in a particular way, and I know how to keep to this. I do this in connexion with established usages and rules. That is why " in a particular way " means something. That is also why I can decide to use the expressions of a secret language or the signs of a code in a particular way. For I am dealing with expressions that can be understood, and I know how the matter could be said in ordinary language. I know whether I am saying the same as I said before, and I know what I am deciding. But not when it is something which *could* not be said in ordinary language. Here there would be no point in saying, for instance, " I am going to use S to mean that", because I do not know what " meaning that " could be.

The reason is not that others must see what my words refer to. It is just that if my words are to refer to anything they must be understood. They cannot refer at all except in connexion with a use, a use which you learn when you learn what the word means. They cannot refer to anything unless there is a way in which the language is spoken. That is why there cannot be a private understanding. If it makes no difference what is said, nothing is understood.

There is of course no reason why I should not give an account of something which only I can see. Or of something which only I can feel: as when I tell a doctor what I feel in my abdomen. He does not feel my sensations (if that means anything), but he knows what I am talking about; he knows what sensations they are.

Ayer asks why Crusoe should not invent names for his sensations. (He actually says " names to *describe* his sensations", but I do not understand this.) *I* can invent names for my sensations. But that is because I speak a language in which there are names for sensations. I know what the name of a sensation is. Inventing a name or giving it a name is something that belongs to the language as we speak it.

It is possible, certainly, to invent new expressions, and even in one sense new languages. But it is a different question whether anyone could have invented language. If language were a device or a method which people might adopt, then perhaps he could. But it is not that. And you could as easily speak of someone's inventing commerce; more easily, in fact. For he would have to invent what we call use and meaning. And I do not say so much that this would be beyond anyone's powers as rather that it is unintelligible.

The expressions of a language get their significance and their force from their application, from their extensive uses. Many of them enter in almost everything we do. And this gives them the force and obviousness they have in new contexts. So even if someone dreamed of a language before there was any, how could he put that forward as " a practical proposition "? Or *what* would he put forward? Marks and sounds would be so much gibberish. To invent a vocabulary he would have at least to invent ways of using these sounds in various circumstances—in circumstances of a social life which has in fact grown up *with* language and could no more be invented than language could. And people would have to understand them. They would have to see not just that this sign occurs here and that there; they would have to see the difference it makes if you use the one or the other. And once again the difficulty is that there would be nothing to understand; because there would be no established use, and nothing we should call " the difference it makes".

Wittgenstein did not say that the ascription of meaning to a sign is something that needs justification. That would generally be as meaningless as it would if you said that language needs justification. What Wittgenstein did hold was that if a sign has meaning it can be used wrongly. On the other hand, if anyone had tried to invent language and teach it to others, then you might say the language and the use of expressions did stand in need of justification.

But why could not a dominant individual have brought people to behave as the people in one of Wittgenstein's primitive language games do? Why could he not force them to that as we train animals? Why could he not train them to respond in regular ways when ordered, and perhaps to answer?

Well, no animals have been trained to do even the primitive things that are done in those language games. Those people are not just going through a complicated trick; what they say depends upon what they need and what they find. They are not just carrying out orders. They use the expressions they do because they have something to say, and because that use is understood by all parties. Whereas although you may train animals to make the " correct " responses to different words or signs, the animals themselves do not *use* different words. A dog may respond in one way to " Slippers ! " and in another way to " Basket ! ", but he does not himself have one sound for the one and a different sound for the other; neither does he do anything like always giving two barks when he wants food and one bark when he wants a drink. No training has brought an animal to speak, even in a primitive way. This is not a question of the capacities of animals. If any animals do learn to speak, they will not learn it just as they learn tricks. A dog " knows what you want him to do " when you utter the word, but he does not know what it means.

If people merely carried out orders and made certain utterances when they were ordered—if this were " making the signs they were supposed to make when they were supposed to make them "—they would not be speaking. I suppose people might be trained to do that with Greek sentences without knowing Greek. And the people in our example would not understand what they were saying. They could not do that unless they used the expressions themselves, and using them is not just doing what you are told with them. What we call following a rule in language is not following orders. That is why we talk about " taking part in " a language—the language is not any one man's doing more than another's, and the rules, if they are rules of language, are not one man's rules. This is essential for understanding.

It might be that when people had been trained as we imagined they would eventually begin to speak. But that would not be what was invented, and it would not have come about by invention. It would have grown up through the initiative and spontaneous reactions of varous people, none of whom was inventing language.

We might ask for *whom* would anyone invent language ? Or for what ? For animals, for instance ? Or for people who have a social life as we have ? If it is the latter, he need not trouble, for we have it. But unless it is for those who have the kind of social life people with languages do have—then what is the point and what is he inventing ? What would a " language " for a flock of parrots be, for instance ? Can you get anywhere except by absurdly imagining them to live as human beings do, as in children's stories ?

The point is that no one could invent just *language*. Language goes with a way of living. An invented language would be a wallpaper pattern; nothing more.

A man might invent marks to go with various objects. That is not language. And when Ayer's Crusoe invents *names* to *describe* flora and fauna, he is taking over more than he has invented. He is supposed to keep a diary, too. Ayer thinks that if he could do that when Friday was present he could surely have done it when he was still alone. But what would that be—keeping a diary ? Not just making marks on paper, I suppose (or on a stone or what it might be). You might ask, " Well what is it when *I* do it ? And why should it not be the same for him, only a bit more primitive ? " But it cannot be that. My marks are either marks I use in communication with other people, or they stand for expressions I use with other people. " What difference does that make ? He can *use* them just as I do." No, because I use them in their various meanings. He cannot do that.

What is it he cannot do ? What is it that I can do and

he cannot ? There seems to be nothing logically absurd in supposing that he behaves just as I do. To a large extent I agree. But it is absurd to suppose that the marks he uses mean anything; even if we might want to say that he goes through all the motions of meaning something by them.

I should agree that if " meaning something " were something psychological, he might conceivably do that. If it were a question of what is put into my mind by my association with other people, then there is nothing logically absurd in supposing this to come into someone's mind without that association.

" What is it that I can do . . . ? " To say that meaning something must be something *I* do is rather like saying it is something that happens at the moment. The point is that I speak a language that is spoken. What I say has significance in that language, not otherwise. Or in other words, if I *say* anything I must say it in some language. If there were no more than my behaviour, the marks I make and so on, then I should not mean anything either.

If I say there is " more " than that—it is that I use the expressions in the meanings they have. If Crusoe used the same expressions he would not do that. Nor can he use different expressions but in these meanings. He does not use expressions in any meanings at all.

Using them in their meanings is what we call following a rule. For language there must be " the way the expressions are used", and this goes with the way people live. I need not live that way myself when I use them. Defoe's Crusoe could have kept a diary, but Ayer's could not. Defoe's Crusoe's diary need never be read by anyone, and the meaning of what he writes does not depend on that. What he writes down may never play a part in the lives of other people. But the language in which he has written it does. And for that reason he can understand what he writes, he knows what he is saying. He knows the use or application of the expressions he uses, and it is from that they get the significance they have for him. He knows what he is talking about. Ayer's Crusoe does not and cannot.

Ayer's Crusoe may use marks for particular purposes—
to show where he has hidden something, perhaps—and
with as great regularity as we care to think. This is not
what we mean by the regular use of an expression in a language. If he should suddenly do something which *we*
should call using these marks entirely differently, it would
have no sense to say that he had done anything wrong or
anything inconsistent with what he had done before.
We could not speak of his using them in the same meaning
or in a different meaning. If he always uses them for the
same purpose—as he might always gather wood for the
same purpose—this is not what we mean by using an expression in the same way. *Using an expression in the same way
does not mean using it for the same purpose.* (What I said
about identity is connected with this.)   And if there is any
sort of discrepancy between what I said at one time and
what I say at another—this does not mean that what I do
with a mark or sound at one time is different from what I
did with it before. If I have always done this with the
mark, there is nothing of a rule of language in that.

"But if he uses them just *as* they would be used by
someone who spoke the language, so that they *could* be
understood, what is the trouble with saying that he uses
them in their meanings?"   The first trouble is that he
does not understand them. And this really means that
he does *not* use them just as someone who spoke the language
would. For he cannot be guided by his signs in just the
way in which you and I may be guided by words.

This is not a question of something beyond his powers.
If we ask whether a machine could follow words, or whether
a machine might speak, we are not asking what a machine
might be designed to do. It is not a question of capacity
or performance at all.

If you say something to me I understand you. If a
tape recorder plays back what you have said, I understand
what I hear but I do not understand the tape recorder.
Which is a grammatical statement: I do not fail to understand either. If I say that you have said something but
the tape recorder has not, I am not saying that something

has happened in your case which did not happen in the other. But I do have an entirely different attitude towards you and towards what I hear from you, and I behave towards you in a host of ways as I should never behave towards a machine—for instance I may answer you, and I should never answer the recorder. I should not try to answer you either, nor should I suppose you had said anything, unless I assumed you knew the language; or unless I thought you said something in a language I did not understand. And I take it for granted you are speaking the language as it is spoken.

I am hardly ever in doubt whether you said something, if I have heard you. But I should begin to doubt if I found that you did not follow my answer, and that you did not seem to know anything about the matters to which your words referred. What I should be doubtful about, in that case, would not be whether something went on in you. I should be doubtful whether you knew what you were saying. But for all I know you may have " done " all that you would have done if you had. The trouble is that your utterance was not a move you were making in the conversation or in the language at all.

If I doubt whether you know the language, or if I doubt whether you ever know what you are saying, then in many ways I must regard you more as I should regard the tape recorder. This is not because you do not do anything that other people do. It is because you do not take part in what they do. You do not speak the language they speak. And *speaking* the language they speak is not just uttering the words; any more than understanding the language is just " recognizing " the words. It is carrying on a conversation, for instance; or it may be writing reports, or listening to a play in a theatre. It is being someone to whom the rest of us can speak and get an answer; to whom we can tell something and with whom we can make a joke and whom we can deceive. All this, and of course immeasurably more, belongs to speaking the language. And it belongs to being able to follow words. You can follow words because you know how to speak. And for the same reason a machine cannot follow words. This has nothing to do with any question of what physics and engineering may achieve. It is just that it makes no sense to say that a machine might follow words.

One can say that absolutely of a machine, but not of Crusoe, because Crusoe might learn a language. But so long as he never has learned a language, in the sense of taking part in a language, it is as meaningless to say of him that he follows words as it would be to say this of an electronic computor.

I cannot ask whether a machine has made a mistake or whether it meant what it said. A machine may be out of order, and then you cannot rely on it. But it is not making a mistake. (And when I make a mistake myself there is nothing out of order.) A machine may " correct mistakes " in connexion with the operation of negative feed-back. But there is nothing there like a mistake in understanding; nor like a mistake in calculation either. This is one reason why a machine cannot follow words—why that makes no sense. I can follow words only where a mistake or a misunderstanding is at least conceivable. (" Yes, of *course* that's what it means.") Otherwise there would be nothing like what we call understanding them.

I may react to words, rightly or wrongly, when I do not understand them. They may be words in a language I do not know, but I may have been taught to obey the orders of someone who shouts them. Maybe no one else would use them in these orders as he does, and that is of no consequence to me. It would have been exactly the same if he had used sounds of his own instead of words. I may react wrongly, as an animal might. But if I call this making a mistake, it is not like mistaking the meaning of the words he uses; any more than I have shown I understand the words if I make no mistake. I know what he wants, that is all. (I know enough to get out of the way of a barking dog, too.) If I had understood the words I should probably know what they would mean in other situations; and at any rate I should know what they would mean if somebody else used them too. The latter is the important point.

It is connected with the fact that if I understand the words I should be able to use them, at least in some measure, myself. That is essential if I am guided by the words or if I follow them. But if that is necessary for understanding the words, it is also necessary for misunderstanding them; by which I mean again that it makes no sense to talk about misunderstanding apart from that. Misunderstanding or mistaking the meaning belongs to taking part in the language. You cannot speak of it otherwise.

Ayer's Crusoe may make the kind of mistakes animals do. He may mistake a bird which he does not like to eat for one which he likes. This is not like a mistake in understanding the meaning of an expression, or a mistake in following what was said.

" Why not ? He calls the edible bird *ba*, and when he sees the inedible one he says ' ba ' and kills it."

That is not a mistake in following the meanings of words. He could have made the same mistake without using words at all. (Perhaps it is roughly the kind of mistake that is corrected through negative feed-back.) You cannot ask whether he made the other kind of mistake; any more than you could ask this of a machine.[1]

I can mistake the meanings of the words you use, because I might use those words myself. If different people can use the same words, then the meanings are independent. I may also take your words in the wrong way. That is rather different, but it is connected with this. He said, " I wonder how long it can last", and she thought he was finding their affair intolerable, whereas he meant the opposite. She knew the meanings of the words he was using, and she could not have misunderstood him in that way unless she had. He might have used the same words to mean what she thought he meant. But he could not have meant either the one or the other unless his words had meant what they do independently; unless they had

---

[1] Ayer says Crusoe may think that a bird is " of the same type as one which he had previously named, when in fact it is of a different type, *sufficiently different for him to have* given it a different name if he had observed it more closely". What do the words I have italicized mean here?

been the words of a language. I call their meanings "independent", partly because they have to be learned. That is characteristic of language.

Unless the meanings of words were independent—unless they had to be learned—they could not be misunderstood. You do not misunderstand just a sound. You mistake the cry of an animal for the cry of a bird. You may mistake the call of an enemy for the call of a friend. That is not misunderstanding, not in the present sense. If one spoke of learning the meaning of a sound, that would not be like learning the meaning of a word. Perhaps it would not be nonsense to say that he " knew instinctively " that it was the cry of an animal. But it is nonsense to say that he knew instinctively the meaning of a word.

You can misunderstand what you can learn. And you are misunderstanding a rule—not a matter of fact. Mistaking the cry of a bird for an animal cry is not misunderstanding a rule.

If one spoke of the independent existence of a tree, this might mean partly that I could think there was no tree there and be wrong. But the meanings of words are not quite comparable with that, and by their independence I do not mean quite the same. If I am wrong about the tree, I may run into it. If I am wrong about the meaning of a word, it is not like that. It is just that I use the word incorrectly, or understand it incorrectly. And that seems almost like saying that if I am wrong I am wrong. Which in a sense is just what I do mean. That is why it is better in this case to say that " the meanings are independent" means just that they have to be learned; as a rule has to be learned. And that is why it is natural to speak of *misunderstanding* here; as it is not, so much, when you are speaking of a mistake in fact.

If anyone did not undersand what kind of mistake it is, he would not understand the difference between correct and incorrect; and vice versa. But then he would not understand what words are.

Now since you have learned the meanings of the expressions you use, it may happen that you do not mean what you say.   At least it makes sense to ask of anyone who has spoken whether he meant it.   If he does not mean what he says, this is familiar and definite enough, but you cannot describe it by describing what he is doing.   You can describe it only by taking into account his relation to other people.   In this case it is not simply that various people use the same words, although that is a large part of it. What is important is the special rôle or part played by the person in saying them.   That is what his " not meaning them " is.   And it is as characteristic and essential for language as independent meanings are.   I have said it is essential that different people may use the same words. But if those people were all doing the same thing, it would not be language.   There must be something more like an organisation, in which different people are, as we may put it, playing different rôles.   (The simile limps, but it has something important too.   It must serve here.)   That belongs to the use of language.   Without it there would not be words and there would not be meaning.

Language is something that is spoken.

7 ORDINARY LANGUAGE

by Gilbert Ryle

PHILOSOPHERS' arguments have frequently turned on references to what we do and do not say or, more strongly, on what we can and cannot say. Such arguments are present in the writings of Plato and are common in those of Aristotle.

In recent years, some philosophers, having become feverishly exercised about the nature and methodology of their calling, have made much of arguments of this kind. Other philosophers have repudiated them. Their disputes on the merits of these arguments have not been edifying, since both sides have been apt to garble the question. I want to ungarble it.

"ORDINARY"

There is one phrase which recurs in this dispute, the phrase 'the use of ordinary language'. It is often, quite erroneously, taken to be paraphrased by 'ordinary linguistic usage'. Some of the partisans assert that all philosophical questions are questions about the use of ordinary language, or that all philosophical questions are solved or are about to be solved by considering ordinary linguistic usage.

Postponing the examination of the notion of *linguistic usage,* I want to begin by contrasting the phrase 'the use of ordinary language' with the similar-seeming but totally different phrase 'the ordinary use of the expression "..." '. When people speak of the use of ordinary language, the word 'ordinary' is in implicit or explicit contrast with 'out-of-the-way', 'esoteric', 'technical', 'poetical', 'notational' or, sometimes, 'archaic'. 'Ordinary' means 'common', 'current', 'colloquial', 'vernacular', 'natural', 'prosaic', 'non-notational', 'on the tongue of Everyman', and is usually in contrast with dictions which only a few people know how to use, such as the technical terms or artificial symbolisms of lawyers, theologians, economists, philosophers, cartographers, mathematicians, symbolic logicians and players of Royal Tennis. There is no sharp boundary between 'common' and 'uncommon', 'technical' and 'untechnical' or 'old-fashioned' and 'current'. Is 'carburettor' a word in common use or only in rather uncommon use? Is 'purl' on the lips of Everyman, or on the lips only of Everywoman? What of 'manslaughter', 'inflation', 'quotient' and 'off-side'? On the other hand, no one would hesitate on which side of this no-man's-land to locate 'isotope' or 'bread', 'material implication' or 'if', 'transfinite cardinal' or 'eleven', 'ween' or 'suppose'. The edges of 'ordinary' are blurred, but usually we are in no doubt whether a diction does or does not belong to ordinary parlance.

But in the other phrase, 'the ordinary use of the expression "..."', 'ordinary' is not in contrast with 'esoteric', 'archaic' or 'specialist', etc. It is in contrast with 'non-stock' or 'non-standard'. We can contrast the stock or standard use of a fish-knife or sphygmomanometer with some non-regulation use of it. The stock use of a fish-knife is to cut up fish with; but it might be used for cutting seed-potatoes or as a heliograph. A sphygmomanometer might, for all I know, be used for checking tyre pressures; but this is not its standard use. Whether an implement or instrument is a common or a specialist one, there remains the distinction between its stock use and non-stock uses of it. If a term is a highly technical term, or a non-technical term, there remains the distinction between its stock use and non-stock uses of it. If a term is a highly technical term, most people will not know its stock use or, *a fortiori,* any non-stock uses of it either, if it has any. If it is a vernacular term, then nearly everyone will know its stock use, and most people will also know some non-stock uses of it, if it has any. There are lots of words, like 'of', 'have' and 'object', which have no one stock use, any more than string, paper, brass and pocket-knives have just one stock use. Lots of words have not got any non-stock uses. 'Sixteen' has, I think, none; nor has 'daffodil'. Nor, maybe, have collar-studs. Non-stock uses of a word are, e.g., metaphorical, hyperbolical, poetical, stretched and deliberately restricted uses of it. Besides contrasting the stock use with certain non-stock uses, we often want to contrast the stock use of an expression with certain alleged, suggested, or recommended uses of it. This is a contrast not between the regular use and irregular uses, but between the regular use and what the regular use is alleged to be or what it is recommended that it should be.

When we speak of the ordinary or stock use of a word we need not be characterising it in any further way, e.g., applauding or recommending it or giving it any testimonial. We need not be appealing to or basing anything on its stock-ness. The words 'ordinary', 'standard' and 'stock' can serve merely to refer to a use, without describing it. They are philosophically colourless and can be easily dispensed with. When we speak of the regular night-watchman, we are merely indicating the night-watchman whom we know independently to be the one usually on the job; we are not yet giving any information about him or paying any tribute to his regularity. When we speak of the standard spelling of a word or the standard gauge of British railway tracks, we are not describing or recommending or countenancing this spelling or this gauge; we are giving a reference to it which we expect our hearers to get without hesitation. Sometimes, naturally, this indication does not work. Sometimes the stock use in one place is different from its stock use in another, as with 'suspenders'. Sometimes, its stock use at one period differs from its stock use at another, as with 'nice'. A dispute about which of two or five uses is the stock use is not a philosophical dispute about any one of those uses. It is therefore philosophically uninteresting, though settlement of it is sometimes requisite for communication between philosophers.

If I want to talk about a non-stock use of a word or fish-knife, it is not enough to try to refer to it by the phrase 'the non-stock use of it', for there may be any number of such non-stock uses. To call my hearer's attention to a particular non-stock use of it, I have to give some description of it, for example, to cite a special context in which the word is known to be used in a non-stock way.

This, though always possible, is not often necessary for the stock use of an expression, although in philosophical debates one is sometimes required to do it, since one's fellow-philosophers are at such pains to pretend that they cannot think what its stock use is—a difficulty which, of course, they forget all about when they are teaching children or foreigners how to use it, and when they are consulting dictionaries.

It is easy now to see that learning or teaching the ordinary or stock use of an expression need not be, though it may be, learning or teaching the use of an ordinary or vernacular expression, just as learning or teaching the standard use of an instrument need not be, though it can be, learning or teaching the use of a household utensil. Most words and instruments, whether out-of-the-way or common, have their stock uses and may or may not also have non-stock uses as well.

A philosopher who maintained that certain philosophical questions are questions about the ordinary or stock uses of certain expressions would not therefore be committing himself to the view that they are questions about the uses of ordinary or colloquial expressions. He could admit that the noun 'infinitesimals' is not on the lips of Everyman and still maintain that Berkeley was examining the ordinary or stock use of 'infinitesimals', namely the standard way, if not the only way, in which this word was employed by mathematical specialists. Berkeley was not examining the use of a colloquial word; he was examining the regular or standard use of a relatively esoteric word. We are not contradicting ourselves if we say that he was examining the ordinary use of an unordinary expression.

Clearly a lot of philosophical discussions are of this type. In the philosophy of law, biology, physics, mathematics, formal logic, theology, psychology and grammar, technical concepts have to be examined, and these concepts are what are expressed by more or less recherché dictions. Doubtless this examination embodies attempts to elucidate in untechnical terms the technical terms of this or that specialist theory, but this very attempt involves discussing the ordinary or stock uses of these technical terms.

Doubtless, too, study by philosophers of the stock uses of expressions which we all employ has a certain primacy over their study of the stock uses of expressions which only, e.g., scientific or legal specialists employ. These specialists explain to novices the stock uses of their terms of art partly by talking to them in non-esoteric terms; they do not also have to explain to them the stock uses of these non-esoteric terms. Untechnical terminology is, in this way, basic to technical terminologies. Hard cash has this sort of primacy over cheques and bills of exchange—as well as the same inconveniences when large and complex transactions are afoot.

Doubtless, finally, some of the cardinal problems of philosophy are set by the existence of logical tangles not in this as opposed to that branch of specialist theory, but in the thought and the discourse of everyone, specialists and non-specialists alike. The concepts of *cause, evidence, knowledge, mistake, ought, can*, etc., are not the perquisites of any particular groups of people. We employ them before we begin to develop or follow specialist theories; and we could not follow or develop such theories unless we could already employ these concepts. They belong to the rudiments of all thinking, including specialist thinking. But it does not follow from this that all philosophical questions are questions about such rudimentary concepts. The architect must indeed be careful about the materials of his building; but it is not only about these that he must be careful.

"USE"

But now for a further point. The phrase 'the ordinary (i.e., stock) use of the expression " . . . " ' is often so spoken that the stress is made to fall on the word 'expression' or else on the word 'ordinary' and the word 'use' is slurred over. The reverse ought to be the case. The operative word is *'use'*.

Hume's question was not about the word 'cause'; it was about the *use* of 'cause'. It was just as much about the *use* of 'Ursache'. For the use of 'cause' is the same as the use of 'Ursache', though 'cause' is not the same word as 'Ursache'. Hume's question was not a question about a bit of the English language in any way in which it was not a question about a bit of the German language. The job done with the English word 'cause' is not an English job, or a continental job. What I do with my Nottingham-made boots— namely walk in them—is not Nottingham-made; but nor is it Leicester-made or Derby-made. The transactions I perform with a sixpenny-bit have neither milled nor unmilled edges; they have no edges at all. We might discuss what I can and cannot do with a sixpenny-bit, namely what I can and cannot buy with it, what change I should and should not give or take for it, and so on; but such a discussion would not be a discussion about the date, ingredients, shape, colour or provenance of the coin. It is a discussion about the purchasing power of this coin, or of any other coin of the same value, and not about *this coin*. It is not a numismatic discussion, but a commercial or financial discussion. Putting the stress on the word 'use' helps to bring out the important fact that the enquiry is an enquiry not into the other features or properties of the word or coin or pair of boots, but only into what is done with it, or with anything else with which we do the same thing. That is why it is so misleading to classify philosophical questions as linguistic questions—or as non-linguistic questions.

It is, I think, only in fairly recent years that philosophers have picked up the trick of talking about the use of expressions, and even made a virtue of so talking. Our forefathers, at one time, talked instead of the *concepts* or *ideas* corresponding to expressions. This was in many ways a very convenient idiom, and one which in most situations we do well to retain. It had the drawback, though, that it encouraged people to start Platonic or Lockean hares about the status and provenance of these concepts or ideas. The impression was given that a philosopher who wanted to discuss, say, the concept of *cause* or *infinitesimal* or *remorse* was under some obligation to start by deciding whether concepts have a supra-mundane, or only a psychological existence; whether they are transcendent intuitables or only private introspectibles.

Later on, when philosophers were in revolt against psychologism in logic, there was a vogue for another idiom, the idiom of talking about the *meanings* of expressions, and the phrase 'the concept of cause' was replaced by the phrase "the meaning of the word 'cause' or of any other with the same meaning". This new idiom was also subject to anti-Platonic and anti-Lockean cavils; but its biggest drawback was a different one. Philosophers and logicians were at that time the victims of a special and erroneous theory about meaning. They construed the verb 'to mean' as standing for a relation between an expression and some other entity. The meaning of an expression was taken to be an entity which had that expression for its name. So studying the meaning of the phrase 'the solar system' was supposed or half-supposed to be the same thing as studying the solar system. It was partly in reaction against this erroneous view that philosophers came to prefer the idiom "the use of the expressions '. . . caused . . .' and '. . . the solar system' ". We are accustomed to talking of the use of safety-pins, bannisters, table-knives, badges and gestures; and this familiar idiom neither connotes nor seems to connote any queer relations to any queer entities. It draws our attention to the teachable procedures and techniques of handling or employing things, without suggesting unwanted correlates.

Learning how to manage a canoe-paddle, a traveller's cheque or a postage-stamp, is not being introduced to an extra entity. Nor is learning how to manage the words 'if', 'ought' and 'limit'.

There is another merit in this idiom. Where we can speak of managing, handling and employing we can speak of mismanaging, mishandling and misemploying. There are rules to keep or break, codes to observe or flout. Learning to use expressions, like learning to use coins, stamps, cheques and hockey-sticks, involves learning to do certain things with them and not others; when to do certain things with them, and when not to do them. Among the things that we learn in the process of learning to use linguistic expressions are what we may vaguely call 'rules of logic'; for example, that though Mother and Father can both be tall, they cannot both be taller than one another; or that though uncles can be rich or poor, fat or thin, they cannot be male or female, but only male. Where it would sound unplausible to say that concepts or ideas or meanings might be meaningless or absurd, there is no such unplausibility in asserting that someone might use a certain expression absurdly. An attempted or suggested way of operating with an expression may be logically illegitimate or impossible, but a universal or a state of consciousness or a meaning cannot be logically legitimate or illegitimate.

"USE" AND "UTILITY"

On the other hand there are inconveniences in talking much of the *uses* of expressions. People are liable to construe 'use' in one of the ways which English certainly does permit, namely as a synonym of 'utility' or 'usefulness'. They then suppose that to discuss the use of an expression is to discuss what it is useful for or how useful it is. Sometimes such considerations are philosophically profitable. But it is easy to see that discussing the use (*versus* uselessness) of something is quite different from discussing the use (*versus* misuse) of it, i.e., the way, method or manner of using it. The female driver may learn what is the utility of a sparking-plug, but learning this is not learning how to operate with a sparking-plug. She does not have or lack skills or competences with sparking-plugs, as she does with steering-wheels, coins, words and knives. Her sparking-plugs manage themselves; or, rather, they are not managed at all. They just function automatically, until they cease to function. They are useful, even indispensable to her. But she does not manage or mismanage them.

Conversely, a person who has learned how to whistle tunes may not find the whistling of tunes at all useful or even pleasant to others or to himself. He manages, or sometimes mismanages his lips, tongue and breath; and, more indirectly, manages or mismanages the notes he produces. He has got the trick of it; he can show us and perhaps even tell us how the trick is performed. But it is a useless trick. The question, How do you use your breath or your lips in whistling? has a positive and complicated answer. The question, What is the use, or utility of whistling? has a negative and simple one. The former is a request for the details of a technique; the latter is not. Questions about the use of an expression are often, though not always, questions about the way to operate with it; not questions about what the employer of it needs it for. They are How-questions, not What-for-questions. This latter sort of question can be asked, but it is seldom necessary to ask it, since the answer is usually obvious. In a foreign country, I do not ask what a centime or a peseta is for; what I do ask is how many of them I have to give for a certain article, or how many of them I am to expect to get in exchange for a half-crown. I want to know what its purchasing power is; not that it is for making purchases with.

"USE" AND "USAGE"

Much more insidious than this confusion between the way of operating with something and its usefulness, is the confusion between a 'use', i.e., a way of operating with something, and a 'usage'. Lots of philosophers, whose dominant good resolution is to discern logico-linguistic differences, talk without qualms as if 'use' and 'usage' were synonyms. This is just a howler; for which there is little excuse except that in the archaic phrase 'use and wont', 'use' could, perhaps, be replaced by 'usage'; that 'used to' does mean 'accustomed to'; and that to be hardly used is to suffer hard usage.

A usage is a custom, practice, fashion or vogue. It can be local or widespread, obsolete or current, rural or urban, vulgar or academic. There cannot be a misusage any more than there can be a miscustom or a misvogue. The methods of discovering linguistic usages are the methods of philologists.

By contrast, a way of operating with a razor blade, a word, a traveller's cheque or a canoe-paddle is a technique, knack or method. Learning it is learning how to do the thing; it is not finding out sociological generalities, not even sociological generalities about other people who do similar or different things with razor blades, words, travellers' cheques or canoe-paddles. Robinson Crusoe might find out for himself how to make and how to throw boomerangs; but this discovery would tell him nothing about those Australian aborigines who do in fact make and use them in the same way. The description of a conjuring-trick is not the description of all the conjurors who perform or have performed that trick. On the contrary, in order to describe the possessors of the trick, we should have already to be able to give some sort of description of the trick itself. Mrs. Beeton tells us how to make omelets; but she gives us no information about Parisian chefs. Baedeker might tell us about Parisian chefs, and tell us which of them make omelets; but if he wanted to tell us how they make omelets, he would have to describe their techniques in the way that Mrs. Beeton describes the technique of making omelets. Descriptions of usages presuppose descriptions of uses, i.e., ways or techniques of doing the thing, the more or less widely prevailing practice of doing which constitutes the usage.

There is an important difference between the employment of boomerangs, bows and arrows, and canoe-paddles on the one hand and the employment of tennis rackets, tug-of-war ropes, coins, stamps and words on the other hand. The latter are instruments of inter-personal, i.e., concerted or competitive actions. Robinson Crusoe might play some games of patience; but he could not play tennis or cricket. So a person who learns to use a tennis racket, a stroke-side oar, a coin or a word is inevitably in a position to notice other people using these things. He cannot master the tricks of such inter-personal transactions without at the same time finding out facts about some other people's employment and misemployment of them; and normally he will learn a good many of the tricks from noticing other people employing them. Even so, learning the knacks is not and does not require making a sociological study. A child may learn in the home and the village shop how to use pennies, shillings and pound notes; and his mastery of these slightly complex knacks is not improved by hearing how many people in other places and years have managed and now manage or mismanage their pennies, shillings and pound notes. Perfectly mastering a use is not getting to know everything, or even much, about a usage, even when mastering that use does causally involve finding out a bit about a few other people's practices. We were taught in the nursery how to handle a lot of words; but we were not being taught any historical or sociological generalities about employers of these words. That came later, if it came at all.

Before passing on we should notice one big difference between using canoe-paddles or tennis rackets on the one hand and using postage stamps, safety-pins, coins and words on the other. Tennis rackets are wielded with greater or less skill; even the tennis-champion studies to improve. But, with some unimportant reservations, it is true to say that coins, cheques, stamps, separate words, buttons and shoelaces offer no scope for talent. Either a person knows or he does not know how to use and how not to misuse them. Of course literary composition and argumentation can be more or less skilful; but the essayist or lawyer does not know the meaning of 'rabbit' or 'and' better than Everyman. There is no room here for 'better'. Similarly, the champion chess-player manoeuvres more skilfully than the amateur; but he does not know the permitted moves of the pieces better. They both know them perfectly, or rather they just know them.

Certainly, the cultured chess-player may describe the permitted moves better than does the uncultured chess-player. But he does not make these moves any better. I give change for a half-crown no better than you do. We both just give the correct change. Yet I may describe such transactions more effectively than you can describe them. Knowing how to operate is not knowing how to tell how to operate. This point becomes important when we are discussing, say, the stock way (supposing there is one) of employing the word 'cause'. The doctor knows how to make this use of it as well as anyone, but he may not be able to answer any of the philosopher's enquiries about this way of using it.

In order to avoid these two big confusions, the confusion of 'use'

with 'usefulness' and the confusion of 'use' with 'usage', I try nowadays to use, *inter alia*, 'employ' and 'employment' instead of the
verb and noun 'use'. So I say this. Philosophers often have to try
to describe the stock (or, more rarely, some non-stock) manner or
way of employing an expression. Sometimes such an expression belongs to the vernacular; sometimes to some technical vocabulary;
sometimes it is betwixt and between. Describing the mode of employment of an expression does not require and is not usually
helped by information about the prevalence or unprevalence of
this way of employing it. For the philosopher, like other folk, has
long since learned how to employ or handle it, and what he is trying to describe is what he himself has learned.

Techniques are not vogues—but they may have vogues. Some
of them must have vogues or be current in some other way. For it
is no accident that ways of employing words, as of employing coins,
stamps and chessmen, *tend* to be identical through a whole community and over a long stretch of time. We want to understand and
be understood; and we learn our native tongue from our elders.
Even without the pressure of legislation and dictionaries, our vocabularies tend towards uniformity. Fads and idiosyncrasies in these
matters impair communication. Fads and idiosyncrasies in matters
of postage stamps, coins and the moves of chessmen are ruled out
by explicit legislation, and partly analogous conformities are imposed upon many technical vocabularies by such things as drill-
manuals and text-books. Notoriously these tendencies towards uniformity have their exceptions. However, as there naturally do exist
many pretty widespread and pretty long enduring vocabulary
usages, it is sometimes condonable for a philosopher to remind his
readers of a mode of employing an expression by alluding to 'what
everyone says' or 'what no one says'. The reader considers the
mode of employment that he has long since learned and feels
strengthened, when told that big battalions are on his side. In fact,
of course, this appeal to prevalence is philosophically pointless, besides being philologically risky. What is wanted is, perhaps, the
extraction of the logical rules implicitly governing a concept, i.e.,
a way of operating with an expression (or any other expression that
does the same work). It is probable that the use of this expression,
to perform this job, is widely current; but whether it is so or not,

is of no philosophical interest. Job-analysis is not Mass Observation. Nor is it helped by Mass Observation. But Mass Observation sometimes needs the aid of job-analysis.

Before terminating this discussion of the use of the expression 'the use of the expression " . . . " ', I want to draw attention to an interesting point. We can ask whether a person knows how to use and how not misuse a certain word. But we cannot ask whether he knows how to use a certain *sentence*. When a block of words has congealed into a phrase we can ask whether he knows how to use the phrase. But when a sequence of words has not yet congealed into a phrase, while we can ask whether he knows how to use its ingredient words, we cannot easily ask whether he knows how to use that sequence. Why can we not even ask whether he knows how to use a certain sentence? For we talk about the meanings of sentences, seemingly just as we talk of the meanings of the words in it; so, if knowing the meaning of a word is knowing how to use it, we might have expected that knowing the meaning of a sentence was knowing how to use the sentence. Yet this glaringly does not go.

A cook uses salt, sugar, flour, beans and bacon in making a pie. She uses, and perhaps misuses, the ingredients. But she does not, in this way, use the pie. Her pie is not an ingredient. In a somewhat different way, the cook uses, and perhaps misuses, a rolling-pin, a fork, a frying-pan and an oven. These are the utensils with which she makes her pie. But the pie is not another utensil. The pie is (well or badly) composed out of the ingredients, by means of the utensils. It is what she used them for; but it cannot be listed in either class of them. Somewhat, but only somewhat, similarly a sentence is (well or badly) constructed out of words. It is what the speaker or writer uses them for. He composes it out of them. His sentence is not itself something which, in this way, he either uses or misuses, either uses or does not use. His composition is not a component of his composition. We can tell a person to say something (e.g., ask a question, give a command or narrate an anecdote), using a specified word or phrase; and he will know what he is being told to do. But if we just tell him to pronounce or write down, by itself, that specified word or phrase, he will see the difference between this order and the other one. For he is not now being told to use, i.e., *incorporate* the word or phrase, but only to pronounce it or write it down. Sentences are things that we say. Words and phrases are what we say things *with*.

There can be dictionaries of words and dictionaries of phrases. But there cannot be dictionaries of sentences. This is not because such dictionaries would have to be infinitely and therefore impracticably long. On the contrary, it is because they could not even begin. Words and phrases are there, in the bin, for people to avail themselves of when they want to say things. But the sayings of these things are not some more things which are there in the bin for people to avail themselves of, when they want to say these things. This fact that words and phrases can, while sentences cannot be misused, since sentences cannot be, in this way, used at all, is quite consistent with the important fact that sentences can be well or ill constructed. We can say things awkwardly or ungrammatically and we can say things which are grammatically proper, but do not make sense.

It follows that there are some radical differences between what is meant by 'the meaning of a word or phrase' and what is meant by 'the meaning of a sentence'. Understanding a word or phrase is knowing how to use it, i.e., make it perform its rôle in a wide range of sentences. But understanding a sentence is not knowing how to make it perform its rôle. The play has not got a rôle.

We are tempted to suppose that the question, How are word-meanings related to sentence-meanings? is a tricky but genuine question, a question, perhaps, rather like, How is the purchasing power of my shilling related to the purchasing power of the contents of my pay-envelope? But this model puts things awry from the start.

If I know the meaning of a word or phrase I know something like a body of unwritten rules, or something like an unwritten code or general recipe. I have learned to use the word correctly in an unlimited variety of different settings. What I know is, in this respect, somewhat like what I know when I know how to use a knight or a pawn at chess. I have learned to put it to its work anywhen and anywhere, if there is work for it to do. But the idea of putting a sentence to its work anywhen and anywhere is fantastic.

It has not got a rôle which it can perform again and again in different plays. It has not got a rôle at all, any more than a play has a rôle. Knowing what it means is not knowing anything like a code or a body of rules, though it requires knowing the codes or rules governing the use of the words or phrases that make it up. There are general rules and recipes for constructing sentences of certain kinds; but not general rules or recipes for constructing the particular sentence 'Today is Monday'. Knowing the meaning of 'Today is Monday' is not knowing general rules, codes or recipes governing the use of this sentence, since there is no such thing as the utilisation or, therefore, the re-utilisation of this sentence. I expect that this ties up with the fact that sentences and clauses make sense or make no sense, where words neither do nor do not make sense, but only have meanings; and that pretence-sentences can be absurd or nonsensical, where pretence-words are neither absurd nor nonsensical, but only meaningless. I can say stupid things, but words can be neither stupid nor not stupid.

PHILOSOPHY AND ORDINARY LANGUAGE

The vogue of the phrase 'the use of ordinary language' seems to suggest to some people the idea that there exists a philosophical doctrine according to which (a) all philosophical enquiries are concerned with vernacular, as opposed to more or less technical, academic or esoteric terms; and (b) in consequence, all philosophical discussions ought themselves to be couched entirely in vernacular dictions. The inference is fallacious, though its conclusion has some truth in it. Even if it were true, which it is not, that all philosophical problems are concerned with non-technical concepts, i.e., with the mode of employment of vernacular expressions, it would not follow from this (false) premiss that the discussions of these problems must or had better be in jurymen's English, French or German.

From the fact that a philologist studies those English words which stem from Celtic roots, it does not follow that he must or had better say what he has to say about them in words of Celtic origin. From the fact that a psychologist is discussing the psychology of witticisms, it does not follow that he ought to write wittily all or any of the time. Clearly he ought not to write wittily most of the time.

Most philosophers have in fact employed a good number of the technical terms of past or contemporary logical theory. We may sometimes wish that they had taken a few more pinches of salt, but we do not reproach them for availing themselves of these technical expedients; we should have deplored their long-windedness if they had tried to do without them.

But enslavement to jargon, whether inherited or invented, is, certainly, a bad quality in any writer, whether he be a philosopher or not. It curtails the number of people who can understand and criticise his writings; so it tends to make his own thinking run in a private groove. The use of avoidable jargons is bad literary manners and bad pedagogic policy, as well as being detrimental to the thinker's own wits.

But this is not peculiar to philosophy. Bureaucrats, judges, theologians, literary critics, bankers and, perhaps above all, psychologists and sociologists would all be well advised to try very hard to write in plain and blunt words. None the less, Hobbes who had this virtue of writing plainly and bluntly was a lesser philosopher than Kant who lacked it; and Plato's later dialogues, though harder to translate, have powers which his early dialogues are without. Nor is the simplicity of his diction in Mill's account of mathematics enough to make us prefer it to the account given by Frege, whose diction is more esoteric.

In short, there is no *a priori* or peculiar obligation laid upon philosophers to refrain from talking esoterically; but there is a general obligation upon all thinkers and writers to try to think and write both as powerfully and as plainly as possible. But plainness of diction and power of thought can vary independently, though it is not common for them to do so.

Incidentally it would be silly to require the language of professional journals to be as exoteric as the language of books. Colleagues can be expected to use and understand one another's terms of art. But books are not written only for colleagues. The judge should not address the jury in the language in which he may address his brother judges. Sometimes, but only sometimes, he may be well advised to address even his brother judges, and himself, in the language in which he should address the jury. It all depends on whether his technical terms are proving to be a help or a hindrance.

They are likely to be a hindrance when they are legacies from a period in which today's questions were not even envisaged. This is what justifies the regular and salutary rebellions of philosophers against the philosophical jargons of their fathers.

There is another reason why philosophers ought sometimes to eschew other people's technical terms. Even when a philosopher is interesting himself in some of the cardinal concepts of, say, physical theory, he is usually partly concerned to state the logical cross-bearings between the concepts of this theory and the concepts of mathematical, theological, biological or psychological theory. Very often his radical puzzle is that of determining these cross-bearings. When trying to solve puzzles of this sort, he cannot naïvely employ the dictions of either theory. He has to stand back from both theories, and discuss the concepts of both in terms which are proprietary to neither. He may coin neutral dictions of his own, but for ease of understanding he may prefer the dictions of Everyman. These have this required neutrality, even if they lack that semi-codification which disciplines the terms of art of professionalised thought. Barter-terms are not as well regimented as the terms of the counting-house; but when we have to determine rates of exchange between different currencies, it is to barter-terms that we may have to turn. Inter-theory negotiations can be and may have to be conducted in pre-theory dictions.

So far I have, I hope, been mollifying rather than provoking. I now want to say two philosophically contentious things.

(a) There is a special reason why philosophers, unlike other professionals and specialists, are constantly jettisoning *in toto* all the technical terms of their own predecessors (save some of the technical terms of formal logic); i.e., why the jargon words of epistemology, ethics, aesthetics, etc., seem to be half-hardy annuals rather than hardy perennials. The reason is this. The experts who use the technical terms of bridge, law, chemistry and plumbing learn to employ these terms partly from official instructions but largely by directly engaging in the special techniques and by directly dealing with the special materials or objects of their specialism. They familiarise themselves with the harness by having to drive their (to us unfamiliar) horses.

But the terms of art of philosophy itself (save for those of formal logic), are not like this. There is no peculiar field of knowledge or adeptness in which philosophers *ex officio* make themselves the experts—except of course the business of philosophising itself. We know by what special sorts of work mastery is acquired of the concepts of *finesse, tort, sulphanilamide* and *valve-seating*. But by what corresponding special sorts of work do philosophers get their supposed corresponding mastery of the concepts of *Cognition, Sensation, Secondary Qualities* and *Essences?* What exercises and predicaments have forced them to learn just how to use and how not to misuse these terms?

Philosopher's arguments which turn on these terms are apt, sooner or later, to start to rotate idly. There is nothing to make them point north rather than nor'-nor'-east. The bridge-player cannot play fast and loose with the concepts of *finesse* and *revoke*. If he tries to make them work in a way palatable to him, they jib. The unofficial terms of everyday discourse are like the official terms of specialisms in this important respect. They too jib, if maltreated. It is no more possible to say that someone knows something to be the case which is not so than it is possible to say that the player of the first card in a game of bridge has revoked. We have had to learn in the hard school of daily life how to deploy the verb 'know'; and we have had to learn at the bridge-table how to deploy the verb 'revoke'. There is no such hard school in which to learn how to deploy the verbs 'cognize' and 'sense'. These go through what motions we care to require of them, which means that they have acquired no discipline of their own at all. So the philosophical arguments, which are supposed to deploy these units, win and lose no fights, since these units have no fight in them. Hence, the appeal from philosophical jargon to the expressions which we have all had to learn to use properly (as the chess-player has had to learn the moves of his pieces) is often one well worth making; where a corresponding appeal to the vocabulary of Everyman from the official parlance of a science, of a game or of law would often, not always, be ridiculous. One contrast of 'ordinary' (in the phrase 'ordinary language') is with 'philosophers' jargon'.

(b) But now for quite a different point and one of considerable contemporary importance. The appeal to what we do and do not say, or can and cannot say, is often stoutly resisted by the protagonists of one special doctrine, and stoutly pressed by its antagonists. This doctrine is the doctrine that philosophical disputes can and should be settled by formalising the warring theses. A theory is formalised when it is translated out of the natural language (untechnical, technical or semi-technical), in which it was originally excogitated, into a deliberately constructed notation, the notation, perhaps of *Principia Mathematica*. The logic of a theoretical position can, it is claimed, be regularised by stretching its non-formal concepts between the topic-neutral logical constants whose conduct in inferences is regulated by set drills. Formalisation will replace logical perplexities by logical problems amenable to known and teachable procedures of calculation. Thus one contrast of 'ordinary' (in the phrase 'ordinary language') is with 'notational'.

Of those to whom this, the formaliser's dream, appears a mere dream (I am one of them), some maintain that the logic of everyday statements and even the logic of the statements of scientists, lawyers, historians and bridge-players cannot in principle be adequately represented by the formulae of formal logic. The so-called logical constants do indeed have, partly by deliberate prescription, their scheduled logical powers; but the non-formal expressions both of everyday discourse and of technical discourse have their own unscheduled logical powers, and these are not reducible without remainder to those of the carefully wired marionettes of formal logic. The title of a novel by A. E. W. Mason 'They Wouldn't be Chessmen' applies well to both the technical and the untechnical expressions of professional and daily life. This is not to say that the examination of the logical behaviour of the terms of non-notational discourse is not assisted by studies in formal logic. Of course it is. So may chess-playing assist generals, though waging campaigns cannot be replaced by playing games of chess.

I do not want here to thrash out this important issue. I want only to show that resistance to one sort of appeal to ordinary language ought to involve championing the programme of formalisation. 'Back to ordinary language' can be (but often is not) the slogan of those who have awoken from the formaliser's dream. This slogan, so used, should be repudiated only by those who hope to replace philosophising by reckoning.

VERDICT

Well, then, has philosophy got something to do with the use of expressions or hasn't it? To ask this is simply to ask whether conceptual discussions, i.e., discussions about the concept of, say, *voluntariness, infinitesimals, number* or *cause,* come under the heading of philosophical discussions. Of course they do. They always have done, and they have not stopped doing so now.

Whether we gain more than we lose by sedulously advertising the fact that what we are investigating is the stock way of operating with, say, the word 'cause', depends a good deal on the context of the discussions and the intellectual habits of the people with whom we are discussing it. It is certainly a long-winded way of announcing what we are doing; and inverted commas are certainly vexatious to the eye. But, more important than these nuisances, preoccupation with questions about methods tends to distract us from prosecuting the methods themselves. We run, as a rule, worse, not better, if we think a lot about our feet. So let us, at least on alternate days, speak instead of investigating the concept of *causation.* Or, better still, let us, on those days, not speak of it at all but just do it.

But the more longwinded idiom has some big compensating advantages. If we are enquiring into problems of perception, i.e., discussing questions about the concepts of seeing, hearing and smelling, we may be taken to be tackling the questions of opticians, neuro-physiologists or psychologists, and even fall into this mistake ourselves. It is then salutary to keep on reminding ourselves and one another that what we are after is accounts of how certain words work, namely words like 'see', 'look', 'overlook', 'blind', 'visualise' and lots of other affiliated expressions.

One last point. I have talked in general terms about learning and describing the modes of employment of expressions. But there are many different dimensions of these modes, only some of which are of interest to philosophers. Differences of stylistic elegance, rhetorical persuasiveness, and social propriety need to be considered, but not, save *per accidens,* by philosophers. Churchill would have made a rhetorical blunder if he had said, instead of 'We shall fight them on the beaches . . .', 'We shall fight them on the sands . . .'. 'Sands' would have raised thoughts of children's holidays at Skegness. But this kind of misemployment of 'sands' is not the kind of mishandling that interests us. We are interested in the informal logic of the employment of expressions, the nature of the logical howlers that people do or might commit if they strung their words together in certain ways, or, more positively, in the logical force that expressions have as components of theories and as pivots of concrete arguments. That is why, in our discussions, we argue *with* expressions and *about* those expressions in one and the same breath. We are trying to register what we are exhibiting; to codify the very logical codes which we are then and there observing.

8 THE THEORY OF MEANING

by Gilbert Ryle

WE can all use the notion of *meaning*. From the moment we begin to learn to translate English into French and French into English, we realize that one expression does or does not mean the same as another. But we use the notion of meaning even earlier than that. When we read or hear something in our own language which we do not understand, we wonder what it means and ask to have its meaning explained to us. The ideas of understanding, misunderstanding and failing to understand what is said already contain the notion of expressions having and lacking specifiable meanings.

It is, however, one thing to ask, as a child might ask, What, if anything, is meant by 'vitamin', or 'abracadabra' or '$(a+b)^2 = a^2 + b^2 + 2ab$'? It is quite another sort of thing to ask What are meanings? It is, in the same way, one thing to ask, as a child might ask, What can I buy for this shilling?, and quite another sort of thing to ask What is purchasing-power? or What are exchange-values?

Now answers to this highly abstract question, What are meanings? have, in recent decades, bulked large in philosophical and logical discussions. Preoccupation with the theory of meaning could be described as the occupational disease of twentieth-century Anglo-Saxon and Austrian philosophy. We need not worry whether or not it is a disease. But it might be useful to survey the motives and the major results of this preoccupation.

Incidentally it is worth noticing that many of these issues were explicitly canvassed — and some of them conclusively settled — in certain of Plato's later Dialogues, and in the logical and other works of Aristotle. Some of them, again, were dominant issues in the late Middle Ages and later still with Hobbes; and some of them, thickly or thinly veiled in the psychological terminology of 'ideas', stirred uneasily inside British epistemology between Locke and John Stuart Mill. But I shall not, save for one or two back-references, discuss the early history of these issues.

The shopkeeper, the customer, the banker and the merchant are ordinarily under no intellectual pressure to answer or even ask the abstract questions What is purchasing-power? and What are exchange-values? They are interested in the prices of things, but not yet in the abstract question What is the real nature of that which is common to two articles of the same price? Similarly, the child who tries to follow a conversation on an unfamiliar topic, and the translator who tries to render Thucydides into English are interested in what certain expressions mean. But they are not necessarily interested in the abstract questions What is it for an expression to have a meaning? or What is the nature and status of that which an expression and its translation or paraphrase are both the vehicles? From what sort of interests, then, do we come to ask this sort of question? Doubtless there are many answers. I shall concentrate on two of them which I shall call 'the Theory of Logic' and 'the Theory of Philosophy'. I shall spend a good long time on the first; not so long on the second.

(1) *The Theory of Logic.* The logician, in studying the rules of inference has to talk of the components of arguments, namely their premisses and conclusions and to talk of them in perfectly general terms. Even when he adduces concrete premisses and conclusions, he does so only to illustrate the generalities which are his proper concern. In the same way, he has to discuss the types of separable components or the types of distinguishable features of these premiss-types and conclusion-types, since it is sometimes on such components or features of premisses and conclusions that the inferences from and to them pivot.

Now the same argument may be expressed in English or in French or in any other language; and if it is expressed in English, there may still be hosts of different ways of wording it. What the logician is exploring is intended to be indifferent to these differences of wording. He is concerned with what is said by a premiss-sentence or a conclusion-sentence, not with how it is worded.

So, if not in the prosecution of his inquiry, at least in his explanations of what he is doing, he has to declare that his subject-matter consist not of the sentences and their ingredient words in which arguments are expressed, but of the propositions or judgments and their constituent terms, ideas or concepts of which the sentences and words are the vehicles. Sometimes he may say that his subject matter consists of sentence-meanings and their constituent word-meanings or phrase-meanings, though this idiom is interestingly repellent. Why it is repellent we shall, I hope, see later on. So in giving this sort of explanation of his business, he is talking *about* meanings, where in the prosecution of that business he is just operating *upon* them.

For our purposes it is near enough true to say that the first influential discussion of the notion of meaning given by a modern logician was that with which John Stuart Mill opens his *System of Logic* (1843). He acknowledges debts both to Hobbes and to the Schoolmen, but we need not trace these borrowings in detail.

Mill's contributions to Formal or Symbolic Logic were negligible. It was not he but his exact contemporaries, Boole and de Morgan, and his immediate successors, Jevons, Venn, Carroll, McColl and Peirce who, in the English-speaking world, paved the way for Russell. On the other hand, it is difficult to exaggerate the influence which he exercised, for good and for ill, upon British and Continental philosophers; and we must include among these philosophers the Symbolic Logicians as well, in so far as they have philosophized about their technical business. In particular, Mill's theory of meaning set the questions, and in large measure, determined their answers for thinkers as different as Brentano, in Austria; Meinong and Husserl, who were pupils of Brentano; Bradley, Jevons, Venn, Frege, James, Peirce, Moore and Russell. This extraordinary achievement was due chiefly to the fact that Mill was original in producing a doctrine of meaning at all. The doctrine that he produced was immediately influential, partly because a doctrine was needed and partly because its inconsistencies were transparent. Nearly all of the thinkers whom I have listed were in vehement opposition to certain parts of Mill's doctrine, and it was the other parts of it from which they often drew their most effective weapons.

Mill, following Hobbes's lead, starts off his account of the notion of meaning by considering single words. As we have to learn the alphabet before we can begin to spell, so it seemed natural to suppose that the meanings of sentences are compounds of the components, which are the meanings of their ingredient words. Word-meanings are atoms, sentence-meanings are molecules. I say that it seemed natural, but I hope soon to satisfy you that it was a tragically false start. Next Mill, again following Hobbes's lead, takes it for granted that all words, or nearly all words, are names, and this, at first, sounds very tempting. We know what it is for 'Fido' to be the name of a particular dog, and for 'London' to be the name of a particular town. There, in front of us, is the dog or the town which has the name, so here, one feels, there is no mystery. We have just the familiar relation between a thing and its name. The assimilation of all or most other single words to names gives us, accordingly, a cosy feeling. We fancy that we know where we are. The dog in front of us is what the word 'Fido' stands for, the town we visited yesterday is what the word 'London' stands for. So the classification of all or most single words as names makes us feel that what a word means is in all cases some manageable thing that that word is the name of. Meanings, at least word-meanings, are nothing abstruse or remote, they are, *prima facie*, ordinary things and happenings like dogs and towns and battles.

Mill goes further. Sometimes the grammatical subject of a sentence is not a single word but a many-worded phrase, like 'the present Prime Minister' or 'the first man to stand on the summit of Mt. Everest'. Mill has no qualms in classifying complex expressions like these also as names, what he calls 'many-worded names'. There do not exist proper names for everything we want to talk about; and sometimes we want to talk about something or somebody whose proper name, though it exists, is unknown to us. So descriptive phrases are coined by us to do duty for proper names. But they are still, according to Mill, names, though the tempting and in fact prevailing interpretation of this assertion differs importantly from what Mill usually wanted to convey. For, when Mill calls a word or phrase a 'name', he is using 'name' not, or not always, quite in the ordinary way. Sometimes he says that for an expression to be a name it must be able to be used as the subject or the predicate of a subject-predicate sentence — which lets in, e.g. adjectives as names. Sometimes his requirements are more stringent. A name is an expression which can be the subject of a subject-predicate sentence — which leaves only nouns, pronouns and substantival phrases. 'Name', for him, does not mean merely 'proper name'. He often resisted temptations to which he subjected his successors.

Before going any further, I want to make you at least suspect that this initially congenial equation of words and descriptive phrases with names is from the outset a monstrous howler — if, like some of Mill's successors, though unlike Mill himself, we do systematically construe 'name' on the model of 'proper name'. The assumption of the truth of this equation has been responsible for a large number of radical absurdities in philosophy in general and the philosophy of logic in particular. It was a fetter round the ankles of Meinong, from which he never freed himself. It was a fetter round the ankles of Frege, Moore and Russell, who all, sooner or later, saw that without some big emendations, the assumption led inevitably to fatal impasses. It was, as he himself says in his new book, a fetter round the ankles of Wittgenstein in the *Tractatus*, though in that same book he had found not only the need but the way to cut himself partially loose from it.

I am still not quite sure why it seems so natural to assume that all words are names, and even that every possible grammatical subject of a sentence, one-worded or many-worded, stands to something as the proper name 'Fido' stands to the dog Fido, and, what is a further point, that the thing it stands for is what the expression means. Even Plato had had to fight his way out of the same assumption. But he at least had a special excuse. The Greek language had only the one word ὄνομα where we have the three words 'word', 'name' and 'noun'. It was hard in Greek even to say that the Greek counterpart to our verb 'is' was a word but not a noun. Greek provided Plato with no label for verbs, or for adverbs, conjunctions etc. That 'is' is a word, but is not a name or even a noun was a tricky thing to say in Greek where ὄνομα did duty both for our word 'word', for our word 'name' and, eventually, for our word 'noun'. But even without this excuse people still find it natural to assimilate all words to names, and the meanings of words to the bearers of those alleged names. Yet the assumption is easy to demolish.

First, if every single word were a name, then a sentence composed of five words, say 'three is a prime number' would be a list of the five objects named by those five words. But a list, like 'Plato, Aristotle, Aquinas, Locke, Berkeley' is not a sentence. It says nothing, true or false. A sentence, on the contrary, may say something — some one thing — which is true or false. So the words combined into a sentence at least do something jointly which is different from their severally naming the several things that they name if they do name any things. What a sentence means is not decomposable into the set of things which the words in it stand for, if they do stand for things. So the notion of *having meaning* is at least partly different from the notion of *standing for*.

More than this. I can use the two descriptive phrases 'the Morning Star' and 'the Evening Star', as different ways of referring to Venus. But it is quite clear that the two phrases are different in meaning. It would be incorrect to translate into French the phrase 'the Morning Star' by 'l'Étoile du Soir'. But if the two phrases have different meanings, then Venus, the planet which we describe by these two different descriptions, cannot be what these descriptive phrases mean. For she, Venus, is one and the same, but what the two phrases signify are different. As we shall see in a moment Mill candidly acknowledges this point and makes an important allowance for it.

Moreover it is easy to coin descriptive phrases to which nothing at all answers. The phrase 'the third man to stand on the top of Mt. Everest' cannot, at present, be used to refer to anybody. There exists as yet no one whom it fits and perhaps there never will. Yet it is certainly a significant phrase, and could be translated into French or German. We know, we have to know, what it means when we say that it fits no living mountaineer. It means *something*, but it does not designate *somebody*. What it means cannot, therefore, be equated with a particular mountaineer. Nor can the meaning conveyed by the phrase 'the first person to stand on the top of

Mt. Everest' be equated with Hillary, though, we gather, it fits him and does not fit anyone else. We can understand the question, and even entertain Nepalese doubts about the answer to the question 'Is Hillary the first person to conquer Mt. Everest?' where we could not understand the question 'Is Hillary Hillary?'

We could reach the same conclusion even more directly. If Hillary was, *per impossibile*, identified with what is meant by the phrase 'the first man to stand on the top of Mt. Everest', it would follow that the meaning of at least one phrase was born in New Zealand, has breathed through an oxygen-mask and has been decorated by Her Majesty. But this is patent nonsense. Meanings of phrases are not New Zealand citizens; what is expressed by a particular English phrase, as well as by any paraphrase or translation of it, is not something with lungs, a surname, long legs and a sunburnt face. People are born and die and sometimes wear boots; meanings are not born and do not die and they never wear boots — or go barefoot either. The Queen does not decorate meanings. The phrase 'the first man to stand on the top of Mt. Everest' will not lose its meaning when Hillary dies. Nor was it meaningless before he reached the summit.

Finally, we should notice that most words are not nouns; they are, e.g. adverbs, or verbs, or adjectives or prepositions or conjunctions or pronouns. But to classify as a name a word which is not even a noun strikes one as intolerable the moment one considers the point. How could 'ran' or 'often' or 'and' or 'pretty' be the name of anything? It could not even be the grammatical subject of a sentence. I may ask what a certain economic condition, moral quality or day of the week is called and get the answer 'inflation', 'punctiliousness' or 'Saturday'. We do use the word 'name' for what something is called, whether it be what a person or river is called, or what a species, a quality, an action or a condition is called. But the answer to the question 'What is it called?' must be a noun or have the grammar of a noun. No such question could be answered by giving the tense of a verb, an adverb, a conjunction or an adjective.

Mill himself allowed that some words like 'is', 'often', 'not', 'of', and 'the' are not names, even in his hospitable use of 'name'. They cannot by themselves function as the grammatical subjects of sentences. Their function, as he erroneously described it, is to subserve, in one way or another, the construction of many-worded names. They do not name extra things but are ancillaries to the multi-verbal naming of things. Yet they certainly have meanings. 'And' and 'or' have different meanings, and 'or' and the Latin 'aut' have the same meaning. Mill realized that it is not always the case that for a word to mean something, it must denote somebody or some thing. But most of his successors did not notice how important this point was.

Even more to Mill's credit was the fact that he noticed and did partial justice to the point, which I made a little while back, that two different descriptive phrases may both fit the same thing or person, so that the thing or person which they both fit or which, in his unhappy parlance, they both name is not to be equated with either (or of course both) of the significations of the two descriptions. The two phrases 'the previous Prime Minister' and 'the father of Randolph Churchill' both fit Sir Winston Churchill, and fit only him; but they do not have the same meaning. A French translation of the one would not be a translation of the other. One might know or believe that the one description fitted Sir Winston Churchill while still questioning whether the other did so too. From just knowing that Sir Winston was Prime Minister one could not infer that Randolph Churchill is his son, or *vice versa*. Either might have been true without the other being true. The two phrases cannot, therefore, carry the same information.

Mill, in effect, met this point with his famous theory of denotation and connotation. Most words and descriptive phrases, according to him, do two things at once. They *denote* the things or persons that they are, as he unhappily puts it, all the names of. But they also *connote* or signify the simple or complex attributes by possessing which the thing or person denoted is fitted by the description. Mill's word 'connote' was a very unhappily chosen word and has misled not only Mill's successors but Mill himself. His word 'denote' was used by him in a far from uniform way, which left him uncommitted to consequences from which some of his successors, who used it less equivocally, could not extricate themselves. For Mill, proper names denote their bearers, but predicate-expressions also denote what they are truly predicable of. Fido is denoted by 'Fido' and by 'dog' and by 'four-legged'.

So to ask for the function of an expression is, on Mill's showing, to ask a double question. It is to ask Which person or persons, thing or things the expression denotes? in one or other of Mill's uses of this verb — Sir Winston Churchill, perhaps — ; but it is also to ask What are the properties or characteristics by which the thing or person is described? — say that of having begotten Randolph Churchill. As a thing or person can be described in various ways, the various descriptions given will differ in connotation, while still being identical in denotation. They characterize in different ways, even though their denotation is identical. They carry different bits of information or misinformation about the same thing, person or event.

Mill himself virtually says that according to our ordinary natural notion of meaning, it would not be proper to say that, e.g. Sir Winston Churchill is the meaning of a word or phrase. We ordinarily understand by 'meaning' not the thing denoted but only what is connoted. That is, Mill virtually reaches the correct conclusions that the meaning of an expression is never the thing or person referred to by means of it; and that descriptive phrases and, with one exception, single words are never names, in the sense of 'proper names'. The exception is just those relatively few words which really are proper names, i.e. words like 'Fido', and 'London', the words which do not appear in dictionaries.

Mill got a further important point right about these genuine proper names. He said that while most words and descriptive phrases both denote or name and connote, proper names only denote and do not connote. A dog may be called 'Fido', but the word 'Fido' conveys no information or misinformation about the dog's qualities, career or whereabouts, etc. There is, to enlarge this point, no question of the word 'Fido' being paraphrased, or correctly or incorrectly translated into French. Dictionaries do not tell us what proper names mean — for the simple reason that they do not mean anything. The word 'Fido' names or denotes a particular dog, since it is what he is called. But there is no room for

anyone who hears the word 'Fido' to understand it or misunderstand it or fail to understand it. There is nothing for which he can
require an elucidation or a definition. From the information that
Sir Winston Churchill was Prime Minister, a number of consequences follow, such as that he was the leader of the majority party
in Parliament. But from the fact that yonder dog is Fido, no other
truth about him follows at all. No information is provided for anything to follow from. Using a proper name is not committing oneself to any further assertions whatsoever. Proper names are appellations and not descriptions; and descriptions are descriptions and
not appellations. Sir Winston Churchill *is* the father of Randolph
Churchill. He is not *called* and was not christened 'the father of
Randolph Churchill'. He is called 'Winston Churchill'. The Lady
Mayoress of Liverpool can give the name *Mauretania* to a ship
which thenceforward has that name. But if she called Sir Winston
Churchill 'the father of Sir Herbert Morrison' this would be a
funny sort of christening, but it would not make it true that Morrison is the son of Sir Winston Churchill. Descriptions carry truths
or falsehoods and are not just arbitrary bestowals. Proper names
are arbitrary bestowals, and convey nothing true and nothing
false, for they convey nothing at all.

Chinese astronomers give the planets, stars and constellations
names quite different from those we give. But it does not follow
that a single proposition of Western astronomy is rejected by
them, or that a single astronomical proposition rejected by us is
accepted by them. Stellar nomenclature carries with it no astronomical truths or falsehoods. Calling a star by a certain name is not
saying anything about it, and saying something true or false
about a star is not naming it. Saying is not naming and naming is
not saying.

This brings out a most important fact. Considering the meaning (or Mill's 'connotation') of an expression is considering what
can be said with it, i.e. said truly or said falsely, as well as asked,
commanded, advised or any other sort of saying. In this, which is
the normal sense of 'meaning', the meaning of a sub-expression
like a word or phrase, is a functional factor of a range of possible
assertions, questions, commands and the rest. It is tributary to say-

ings. It is a distinguishable common locus of a range of possible tellings, askings, advisings, etc. This precisely inverts the natural assumption with which, as I said earlier, Mill and most of us start, the assumption namely that the meanings of words and phrases can be learned, discussed and classified before consideration begins of entire sayings, such as sentences. Word-meanings do not stand to sentence-meanings as atoms to molecules or as letters of the alphabet to the spellings of words, but more nearly as the tennis-racket stands to the strokes which are or may be made with it. This point, which Mill's successors and predecessors half-recognized to hold for such little words as 'if', 'or', 'all', 'the' and 'not', holds good for all significant words alike. Their significances are their rôles inside actual and possible sayings. Mill's two-way doctrine, that nearly all words and phrases both denote, or are names, and connote, i.e. have significance, was therefore, in effect, though unwittingly, a coalition between an atomistic and a functionalist view of words. By the irony of fate, it was his atomistic view which was, in most quarters, accepted as gospel truth for the next fifty or seventy years. Indeed, it was more than accepted, it was accepted without the important safeguard which Mill himself provided when he said that the thing or person denoted by a name was not to be identified with what that name meant. Mill said that to mean is to connote. His successors said that to mean is to denote, or, more rarely, both to denote and to connote. Frege was for a long time alone in seeing the crucial importance of Mill's argument that two or more descriptive phrases with different senses may apply to the same planet or person. This person or planet is not, therefore, what those phrases mean. Their different senses are not their common denotation. Russell early realized the point which Mill did not very explicitly make, though Plato had made it, that a sentence is not a list. It says one thing; it is not just an inventory of a lot of things. But only much later, if at all, did Russell see the full implications of this.

I surmise that the reason why Mill's doctrine of denotation, without its safeguards, caught on, while his truths about connotation failed to do so, were two. First, the word 'connote' naturally suggests what we express by 'imply', which is not what is wanted.

What the phrase 'the previous Prime Minister of the United Kingdom' signifies is not to be equated with any or all of the consequences which can be inferred from the statement that Churchill is the previous Prime Minister. Deducing is not translating. But more important was the fact that Mill himself rapidly diluted his doctrine of connotation with such a mass of irrelevant and false sensationalist and associationist psychology, that his successors felt forced to ignore the doctrine in order to keep clear of its accretions.

Let me briefly mention some of the consequences which successors of Mill actually drew from the view, which was not Mill's, that to mean is to denote, in the toughest sense, namely that all significant expressions are proper names, and what they are the names of are what the expressions signify.

First, it is obvious that the vast majority of words are unlike the words 'Fido' and 'London' in this respect, namely, that they are general. 'Fido' stands for a particular dog, but the noun 'dog' covers this dog Fido, and all other dogs past, present and future, dogs in novels, dogs in dog breeders' plans for the future, and so on indefinitely. So the word 'dog', if assumed to denote in the way in which 'Fido' denotes Fido, must denote something which we do not hear barking, namely either the set or class of all actual and imaginable dogs, or the set of canine properties which they all share. Either would be a very out-of-the-way sort of entity. Next, most words are not even nouns, but adjectives, verbs, prepositions, conjunctions and so on. If these are assumed to denote in the way in which 'Fido' denotes Fido, we shall have a still larger and queerer set of nominees or *denotata* on our hands, namely nominees whose names could not even function as the grammatical subjects of sentences. (Incidentally it is not true even that all ordinary general nouns can function by themselves as subjects of sentences. I can talk about *this* dog, or *a* dog, or *the* dog which . . .; or about *dogs*, *all* dogs, or *most* dogs, and so on. But I cannot make the singular noun 'dog' by itself the grammatical subject of a sentence, save inside quotes, though I can do this with nouns like 'grass', 'hydrogen' and 'Man'.) Finally, since complexes of words, like descriptive and other phrases, and entire clauses and sentences have unitary meanings, then these too will have to be construed as denoting complex entities of very surprising sorts. Now Meinong in Austria and Frege in Germany, as well as Moore and Russell in this country, in their early days, accepted some or most of these consequences. Consistently with the assumed equation of signifying with naming, they maintained the objective existence or being of all sorts of abstract and fictional *entia rationis.*

Whenever we construct a sentence, in which we can distinguish a grammatical subject and a verb, the grammatical subject, be it a single word or a more or less complex phrase, must be significant if the sentence is to say something true or false. But if this nominative word or phrase is significant, it must, according to the assumption, denote something which is there to be named. So not only Fido and London, but also centaurs, round squares, the present King of France, the class of albino Cypriots, the first moment of time, and the non-existence of a first moment of time must all be credited with some sort of reality. They must *be*, else we could not say true or false things of them. We could not truly say that round squares do not exist, unless in some sense of 'exist' there exist round squares for us, in another sense, to deny existence of. Sentences can begin with abstract nouns like 'equality' or 'justice' or 'murder' so all Plato's Forms or Universals must be accepted as entities. Sentences can contain mentions of creatures of fiction, like centaurs and Mr. Pickwick, so all conceivable creatures of fiction must be genuine entities too. Next, we can say that propositions are true or false, or that they entail or are incompatible with other propositions, so any significant 'that'-clause, like 'that three is a prime number' or 'that four is a prime number', must also denote existent or subsistent objects. It was accordingly, for a time, supposed that if I know or believe that three is a prime number, my knowing or believing this is a special relation holding between me on the one hand and the truth or fact, on the other, denoted by the sentence 'three is a prime number'. If I weave or follow a romance, my imagining centaurs or Mr. Pickwick is a special relation holding between me and these centaurs or that portly old gentleman. I could not imagine him unless he had enough being to stand as the correlate-term in this postulated relation of being imagined by me.

Lastly, to consider briefly what turned out, unexpectedly, to be a crucial case, there must exist or subsist classes, namely appropriate *denotata* for such collectively employed plural descriptive phrases as 'the elephants in Burma' or 'the men in the moon'. It is just of such classes or sets that we say that they number 3000, say, in the one case, and 0 in the other. For the results of counting to be true or false, there must be entities submitting to numerical predicates; and for the propositions of arithmetic to be true or false there must exist or subsist an infinite range of such classes.

At the very beginning of this century Russell was detecting some local unplausibilities in the full-fledged doctrine that to every significant grammatical subject there must correspond an appropriate *denotatum* in the way in which Fido answers to the name 'Fido'. The true proposition 'round squares do not exist' surely cannot require us to assert that there really do subsist round squares. The proposition that it is false that four is a prime number is a true one, but its truth surely cannot force us to fill the Universe up with an endless population of objectively existing falsehoods.

But it was classes that first engendered not mere unplausibilities but seemingly disastrous logical contradictions — not merely peripheral logical contradictions but contradictions at the heart of the very principles on which Russell and Frege had taken mathematics to depend. We can collect into classes not only ordinary objects like playing-cards and bachelors, but also such things as classes themselves. I can ask how many shoes there are in a room and also how many pairs of shoes, and a pair of shoes is already a class. So now suppose I construct a class of all the classes that are not, as anyhow most classes are not, members of themselves. Will this class be one of its own members or not? If it embraces itself, this disqualifies it from being one of the things it is characterized as embracing; if it is not one of the things it embraces, this is just what qualifies it to be one among its own members.

So simple logic itself forbids certain ostensibly denoting expressions to denote. It is at least unplausible to say that there exist objects denoted by the phrase 'round squares'; there is self-contra-diction in saying that there exists a class which is a member of itself on condition that it is not, and *vice versa*.

Russell had already found himself forced to say of some expres-sions which had previously been supposed to name or denote, that they had to be given exceptional treatment. They were not names but what he called 'incomplete symbols', expressions, that is, which have no meaning, in the sense of denotation, by themselves; their business was to be auxiliary to expressions which do, as a whole, denote. (This was what Mill had said of the syncategorematic words.) The very treatment which had since the Middle Ages been given to such little words as 'and', 'not', 'the', 'some' and 'is' was now given to some other kinds of expressions as well. In effect, though not explicitly, Russell was saying that, e.g. descriptive phrases were as syncategorematic as 'not', 'and' and 'is' had always been allowed to be. Here Russell was on the brink of allowing that the meanings or significations of many kinds of expressions are matters not of *naming* things, but of *saying* things. But he was, I think, still held up by the idea that saying is itself just another variety of naming, i.e. naming a complex or an 'objective' or a proposition or a fact — some sort of postulated *Fido rationis*.

He took a new and most important further step to cope with the paradoxes, like that of the class of classes that are not members of themselves. For he now wielded a distinction, which Mill had seen but left inert, the distinction between sentences which are either true or false on the one hand, and on the other hand sentences which, though proper in vocabulary and syntax, are none the less nonsensical, meaningless or absurd; and therefore neither true nor false. To assert them and to deny them are to assert and deny nothing. For reasons of a sort which are the proper concern of logic, certain sorts of concatenations of words and phrases into sentences produce things which cannot be significantly said. For example, the very question Is the class of all classes which are not members of themselves a member of itself or not? has no answer. Russell's famous 'Theory of Types' was an attempt to formulate the reasons of logic which make it an improper question. We need not consider whether he was successful. What matters for us, and what made the big difference to subsequent philosophy, is the fact that at long last the notion of meaning was realized to be, at least in certain crucial contexts, the obverse of the notion of the nonsensical — what can be said, truly or falsely, is at last contrasted with what cannot be significantly said. The notion of meaning had been, at long last, partly detached from the notion of naming and re-attached to the notion of saying. It was recognized to belong to, or even to constitute the domain which had always been the province of logic; and as it is at least part of the official business of logic to establish and codify rules, the notion of meaning came now to be seen as somehow compact of rules. To know what an expression means involves knowing what can (logically) be said with it and what cannot (logically) be said with it. It involves knowing a set of bans, fiats and obligations, or, in a word, it is to know the rules of the employment of that expression.

It was, however, not Russell but Wittgenstein who first generalized or half-generalized this crucial point. In the *Tractatus Logico-Philosophicus*, which could be described as the first book to be written on the philosophy of logic, Wittgenstein still had one foot in the denotationist camp, but his other foot was already free. He saw and said, not only what had been said before, that the little words, the so-called logical constants, 'not', 'is', 'and' and the rest do not stand for objects, but also, what Plato had also said before, that sentences are not names. Saying is not naming. He realized, as Frege had done, that logicians' questions are not questions about the properties or relations of the *denotata*, if any, of the expressions which enter into the sentences whose logic is under examination. He saw, too, that all the words and phrases that can enter into sentences are governed by the rules of what he called, slightly metaphorically, 'logical syntax' or 'logical grammar'. These rules are what are broken by such concatenations of words and phrases as result in nonsense. Logic is or includes the study of these rules. Husserl had at the beginning of the century employed much the same notion of 'logical grammar.'

It was only later still that Wittgenstein consciously and deliberately withdrew his remaining foot from the denotationist camp. When he said 'Don't ask for the meaning, ask for the use', he was imparting a lesson which he had had to teach to himself after he had finished with the *Tractatus*. The use of an expression, or the concept it expresses, is the rôle it is employed to perform, not any thing or person or event for which it might be supposed to stand. Nor is the purchasing power of a coin to be equated with this book or that car-ride which might be bought with it. The purchasing power of a coin has not got pages or a terminus. Even more instructive is the analogy which Wittgenstein now came to draw between significant expressions and the pieces with which are played games like chess. The significance of an expression and the powers or functions in chess of a pawn, a knight or the queen have much in common. To know what the knight can and cannot do, one must know the rules of chess, as well as be familiar with various kinds of chess-situations which may arise. What the knight may do cannot be read out of the material or shape of the piece of ivory or boxwood or tin of which this knight may be made. Similarly to know what an expression means is to know how it may and may not be employed, and the rules governing its employment can be the same for expressions of very different physical compositions. The word 'horse' is not a bit like the word 'cheval'; but the way of wielding them is the same. They have the same rôle, the same sense. Each is a translation of the other. Certainly the rules of the uses of expressions are unlike the rules of games in some important respects. We can be taught the rules of chess up to a point before we begin to play. There are manuals of chess, where there are not manuals of significance. The rules of chess, again, are completely definite and inelastic. Questions of whether a rule has been broken or not are decidable without debate. Moreover we opt to play chess and can stop when we like, where we do not opt to talk and think and cannot opt to break off. Chess is a diversion. Speech and thought are not only diversions. But still the partial assimilation of the meanings of expressions to the powers or the values of the pieces with which a game is played is enormously revealing. There is no temptation to suppose that a knight is proxy for anything, or that learning what a knight may or may not do is learning that it is a deputy for some ulterior entity. We could not learn to play the knight correctly without having learned to play the other pieces, nor can we learn to play a word by itself, but only in combination with other words and phrases.

Besides this, there is a further point which the assimilation brings out. There are six different kinds of chess-pieces, with their six different kinds of rôles in the game. We can imagine more complex games involving twenty or two hundred kinds of pieces. So it is with languages. In contrast with the denotationist assumption that almost all words, all phrases and even all sentences are alike in having the one rôle of naming, the assimilation of language to chess reminds us of what we knew *ambulando* all along, the fact that there are indefinitely many kinds of words, kinds of phrases, and kinds of sentences — that there is an indefinitely large variety of kinds of rôles performed by the expressions we use in saying things. Adjectives do not do what adverbs do, nor do all adjectives do the same sort of thing as one another. Some nouns are proper names, but most are not. The sorts of things that we do with sentences are different from the sorts of things that we do with most single words — and some sorts of things that we can significantly do with some sorts of sentences, we cannot significantly do with others. And so on.

There is not one basic mould, such as the 'Fido'-Fido mould, into which all significant expressions are to be forced. On the contrary, there is an endless variety of categories of sense or meaning. Even the *prima facie* simple notion of naming or denoting itself turns out on examination to be full of internal variegations. Pronouns are used to denote people and things, but not in the way in which proper names do so. No one is *called* 'he' or 'she'. 'Saturday' is a proper name, but not in the same way as 'Fido' is a proper name — and neither is used in the way in which the fictional proper name 'Mr. Pickwick' is used. The notion of denotation, so far from providing the final explanation of the notion of meaning, turns out itself to be just one special branch or twig on the tree of signification. Expressions do not mean because they denote things; some expressions denote things, in one or another of several different manners, because they are significant. Meanings are not things, not even very queer things. Learning the meaning of an expression is more like learning a piece of drill than like coming across a previously unencountered object. It is learning to operate correctly with an expression and with any other expression equivalent to it.

(2) *The Theory of Philosophy.* I now want to trace, rather more cursorily, the other main motive from which thinkers have posed the abstract question What are meanings? or What is it for an expression to have a certain sense?

Until fairly recently philosophers have not often stepped back from their easels to consider what philosophy is, or how doing philosophy differs from doing science, or doing theology, or doing mathematics. Kant was the first modern thinker to see or try to answer this question — and a very good beginning of an answer he gave; but I shall not expound his answer here.

This question did not begin seriously to worry the general run of philosophers until maybe sixty years ago. It began to become obsessive only after the publication of the *Tractatus.* Why did the philosophy of philosophy start so late, and how did it come to start when and as it did?

It is often not realized that the words 'philosophy' and 'philosopher' and their equivalents in French and German had for a long time much less specific meanings than they now possess. During the seventeenth, the eighteenth and most of the nineteenth centuries a 'philosopher' was almost any sort of a *savant.* Astronomers, chemists and botanists were called 'philosophers' just as much as were Locke, Berkeley or Hume. Descartes's philosophy covered his contributions to optics just as much as his contributions to epistemology. In English there existed for a long time no special word for the people we now call 'scientists'. This noun was deliberately coined only in 1840, and even then it took some time to catch on. His contemporaries could not call Newton a 'scientist', since there was no such word. When a distinction had to be made, it was made by distinguishing 'natural philosophy' from 'moral' and 'metaphysical philosophy'. As late as 1887, Conan Doyle, within two or three pages of one story, describes Sherlock Holmes as being totally ignorant of philosophy, as we use the word now, and yet as having his room full of philosophical, i.e. scientific, instruments, like test-tubes, retorts and balances. A not very ancient Oxford Chair of Physics still retains its old label, the Chair of Experimental Philosophy.

Different from this quite important piece of etymological history is the fact that both in Scotland and in England there existed from perhaps the time of Hartley to that of Sidgwick and Bradley a strong tendency to suppose that the distinction between natural philosophy, i.e. physical and biological science on the one hand and metaphysical and moral philosophy, perhaps including logic, on the other, was that the latter were concerned with internal, mental phenomena, where the former were concerned with external, physical phenomena. Much of what we now label 'philosophy', *sans phrase*, was for a long time and by many thinkers confidently, but quite wrongly equated with what we now call 'psychology'. John Stuart Mill sometimes, but not always, uses even the grand word 'metaphysics' for the empirical study of the workings of men's minds. Protests were made against this equation particularly on behalf of philosophical theology, but for a long time the anti-theologians had it their own way. A philosopher, *sans phrase*, was a Mental and Moral Scientist — a scientist who was exempted from working in the laboratory or the observatory only because his specimens were collected at home by introspection. Even Mansel, himself a philosophical theologian with a good Kantian equipment, maintained that the science of mental phenomena, what we call 'psychology', was the real basis of even ontological or theological speculations.

So not only did the wide coverage of the word 'philosophy' encourage people not to look for any important differences between what scientists, as we now call them, do and what philosophers, as we now call them, do; but even when such differences were looked for, they were apt to be found in the differences between the investigation of physical phenomena by the laboratory scientist and the investigation of psychological phenomena by the introspecting psychologist.

As I see it, three influences were chiefly responsible for the collapse of the assumption that doing philosophy, in our sense, is of a piece with doing natural science or at least of a piece with doing mental science or psychology.

First, champions of mathematics like Frege, Husserl and Russell had to save mathematics from the combined empiricism and psychologism of the school of John Stuart Mill. Mathematical truths are not mere psychological generalizations; equations are not mere records of deeply rutted associations of ideas; the objects of geometry are not of the stuff of which mental images are made. Pure mathematics is a non-inductive and a non-introspective science. Its proofs are rigorous, its terms are exact, and its theorems are universal and not merely highly general truths. The proofs and the theorems of Formal or Symbolic Logic share these dignities with the proofs and theorems of mathematics. So, as logic was certainly a part of philosophy, not all of philosophy could be ranked as 'mental science'. There must, then, be a field or realm besides those of the material and the mental; and at least part of philosophy is concerned with this third realm, the realm of non-material and also non-mental 'logical objects' — such objects as concepts, truths, falsehoods, classes, numbers and implications.

Next, armchair mental science or introspective psychology itself began to yield ground to experimental, laboratory psychology. Psychologists like James began to put themselves to school under the physiologists and the statisticians. Scientific psychology began first to rival and then to oust both *à priori* and introspective psychology, and the tacit claim of epistemologists, moral philosophers and logicians to be mental scientists had to be surrendered to those who used the methods and the tools of the reputable sciences. So the question raised its head What then were the objects of the inquiries of epistemologists, moral philosophers and logicians, if they were not, as had been supposed, psychological states and processes? It is only in our own days that, anyhow in most British Universities, psychologists have established a Faculty of their own separate from the Faculty of Philosophy.

Thirdly, Brentano, reinforcing from medieval sources a point made and swiftly forgotten by Mill, maintained as an *a priori* principle of psychology itself, that it is of the essence of mental states and processes that they are *of* objects or contents. Somewhat as in grammar a transitive verb requires an accusative, so in the field of ideas, thoughts and feelings, acts of consciousness are directed upon their own metaphorical accusatives. To see is to see something, to regret is to regret something, to conclude or suppose is to conclude or suppose that something is the case. Imagining is one thing, the thing imagined, a centaur, say, is another. The centaur has the body of a horse and does not exist. An act of imagining a centaur does exist and does not have the body of a horse. Your act of supposing that Napoleon defeated Wellington is different from my act of supposing it; but what we suppose is the same and is what is expressed by our common expression 'that Napoleon defeated Wellington'. What is true of mental acts is, in general, false of their accusatives or 'intentional objects', and *vice versa.*

Brentano's two pupils, Meinong and Husserl, happened, for different reasons, to be especially, though not exclusively, interested in applying this principle of intentionality or transitivity to the intellectual, as distinct from the sensitive, volitional or affective acts of consciousness. They set out, that is, to rectify the Locke-Hume-Mill accounts of abstraction, conception, memory, judgment, supposal, inference and the rest, by distinguishing in each case, the various private, momentary and repeatable acts of conceiving, remembering, judging, supposing and inferring from their public, non-momentary accusatives, namely, the concepts, the propositions and the implications which constituted their objective correlates. Where Frege attacked psychologistic accounts of thinking from the outside, they attacked them from the inside. Where Frege argued, for instance, that numbers have nothing psychological or, of course, physical about them, Husserl and Meinong argued that for the mental processes of counting and calculating to be what they are, they must have accusatives or objects numerically and qualitatively other than those processes themselves. Frege said that Mill's account of mathematical entities was false because psychological; Husserl and Meinong, in effect, said that the psychology itself was false because non-'intentional' psychology. The upshot, however, was much the same. With different axes to grind, all three came to what I may crudely dub 'Platonistic' conclusions. All three maintained the doctrine of a third realm of non-physical, non-psychological entities, in which realm

dwelled such things as concepts, numbers, classes and propositions.

Husserl and Meinong were both ready to lump together all
these accusatives of thinking alike under the comprehensive title
of Meanings (*Bedeutungen*), since what I think is what is conveyed by the words, phrases or sentences in which I express what
I think. The 'accusatives' of my ideas and my judgings are the
meanings of my words and my sentences. It easily followed from
this that both Husserl and Meinong, proud of their newly segre-
gated third realm, found that it was this realm which provided a
desiderated subject-matter peculiar to logic and philosophy and
necessarily ignored by the natural sciences, physical and psychological. Mental acts and states are the subject-matter of psychology.
Physical objects and events are the subject-matter of the physical
and biological sciences. It is left to philosophy to be the science of
this third domain which consists largely, though not entirely, of
thought-objects or Meanings — the novel and impressive entities
which had been newly isolated for separate investigation by the
application of Brentano's principle of intentionality to the specifically intellectual or cognitive acts of consciousness.

Thus, by the first decade of this century it was dawning upon
philosophers and logicians that their business was not that of one
science among others, e.g. that of psychology; and even that it was
not an inductive, experimental or observational business of any
sort. It was intimately concerned with, among other things, the
fundamental concepts and principles of mathematics; and it
seemed to have to do with a special domain which was not be-
spoken by any other discipline, namely the so-called third realm of
logical objects or Meanings. At the same time, and in some degree
affected by these influences, Moore consistently and Russell spas-
modically were prosecuting their obviously philosophical and
logical inquiries with a special *modus operandi*. They, and not they
alone, were deliberately and explicitly trying to give analyses of
concepts and propositions — asking What does it really mean to
say, for example, that this is good? or that that is true? or that centaurs do not exist? or that I see an inkpot? or What are the differences between the distinguishable senses of the verb 'to know' and

the verb 'to be'? Moore's regular practice and Russell's frequent practice seemed to exemplify beautifully what, for example, Husserl and Meinong had declared in general terms to be the peculiar business of philosophy and logic, namely to explore the third realm of Meanings. Thus philosophy had acquired a right to live its own life, neither as a discredited pretender to the status of the science of mind, nor yet as a superannuated handmaiden of *démodé* theology. It was responsible for a special field of facts, facts of impressively Platonized kinds.

Before the first world war discussions of the status and rôle of philosophy *vis-à-vis* the mathematical and empirical sciences were generally cursory and incidental to discussions of other matters. Wittgenstein's *Tractatus* was a complete treatise dedicated to fixing the position mainly of Formal Logic but also, as a necessary corollary, the position of general philosophy. It was this book which made dominant issues of the theory of logic and the theory of philosophy. In Vienna some of its teachings were applied polemically, namely to demolishing the pretensions of philosophy to be the science of transcendent realities. In England, on the whole, others of its teachings were applied more constructively, namely to stating the positive functions which philosophical propositions perform, and scientific propositions do not perform. In England, on the whole, interest was concentrated on Wittgenstein's description of philosophy as an activity of clarifying or elucidating the meanings of the expressions used, e.g. by scientists; that is, on the medicinal virtues of his account of the nonsensical. In Vienna, on the whole, interest was concentrated on the lethal potentialities of Wittgenstein's account of nonsense. In both places, it was realized that the criteria between the significant and the nonsensical needed to be systematically surveyed, and that it was for the philosopher and not the scientist to survey them.

At this point, the collapse of the denotationist theory of meaning began to influence the theory of philosophy as the science of Platonized Meanings. If the meaning of an expression is not an entity denoted by it, but a style of operation performed with it, not a nominee but a rôle, then it is not only repellent but positively misleading to speak as if there existed a Third Realm whose denizens are Meanings. We can distinguish this knight, as a piece of ivory, from the part it or any proxy for it may play in a game of chess; but the part it may play is not an extra entity, made of some mysterious non-ivory. There is not one box housing the ivory chessmen and another queerer box housing their functions in chess games. Similarly we can distinguish an expression as a set of syllables from its employment. A quite different set of syllables may have the same employment. But its use or sense is not an additional substance or subject of predication. It is not a non-physical, non-mental object — but not because it is either a physical or a mental object, but because it is not an object. As it is not an object, it is not a denizen of a Platonic realm of objects. To say, therefore, that philosophy is the science of Meanings, though not altogether wrong, is liable to mislead in the same way as it might mislead to say that economics is the science of exchange-values. This, too, is true enough, but to word this truth in this way is liable to make people suppose that the Universe houses, under different roofs, commodities and coins here and exchange-values over there.

Hence, following Wittgenstein's lead, it has become customary to say, instead, that philosophical problems are linguistic problems — only linguistic problems quite unlike any of the problems of philology, grammar, phonetics, rhetoric, prosody, etc., since they are problems about the logic of the functionings of expressions. Such problems are so widely different from, e.g. philological problems, that speaking of them as linguistic problems is, at the moment, as Wittgenstein foresaw, misleading people as far in one direction, as speaking of them as problems about Meanings or Concepts or Propositions had been misleading in the other direction. The difficulty is to steer between the Scylla of a Platonistic and the Charybdis of a lexicographical account of the business of philosophy and logic.

There has been and perhaps still is something of a vogue for saying that doing philosophy consists in analysing meanings, or analysing the employments of expressions. Indeed, from Transatlantic journals I gather that at this very moment British philosophy is dominated by some people called 'linguistic analysts'. The word 'analysis' has, indeed, a good laboratory or Scotland to a particular object by using its name.   How, for example, do we learn and teach the use of proper names ?   This seems quite simple—we identify the object, and, assuming that our student understands the general conventions governing proper names, we explain that this word is the name of that object.   But unless our student already knows another proper name of the object, we can only *identify* the object (the necessary preliminary to teaching the name) by ostension or description ; and, in both cases, we identify the object in virtue of certain of its character-istics.   So now it seems as if the rules for a proper name must somehow be logically tied to particular characteristics of the object in such a way that the name has a sense as well as a reference ; indeed, it seems it could not have a reference unless it did have a sense, for how, unless the name has a sense, is it to be correlated with the object ?

Suppose someone answers this argument as follows : "The characteristics located in teaching the name are not the rules for using the proper name : they are simply pedagogic devices employed in teaching the name to someone who does not know how to use it.   Once our student has identified the object to which the name applies he can forget or ignore these various descriptions by means of which he identified the object, for they are not part of the sense of the name ; the name does not have a *sense*. Suppose, for example, that we teach the name ' Aristotle ' by explaining that it refers to a Greek philosopher born in Stagira, and suppose that our student continues to use the name correctly, that he gathers more information about Aristotle, and so on.   Let us suppose it is discovered later on that Aristotle was not born in Stagira at all, but in Thebes.   We will not now say that the meaning of the name has changed, or that Aristotle did not really exist at all.   In short, explaining the use of a name by citing characteristics of the object is not giving the rules for the name, for the rules contain no descriptive content at all. They simply correlate the name to the object independently of any descriptions of it."

But is the argument convincing ? Suppose most or even all of our present factual knowledge of Aristotle proved to be true of no one at all, or of several people living in scattered countries and in different centuries ? Would we not say for this reason that Aristotle did not exist after all, and that the name, though it has a conventional sense, refers to no one at all ? On the above account, if anyone said that Aristotle did not exist, this must simply be another way of saying that " Aristotle " denoted no objects, and nothing more ; but if anyone did say that Aristotle

Yard ring about it; it contrasts well with such expressions as 'spec-ulation', 'hypothesis', 'system-building' and even 'preaching' and 'writing poetry'. On the other hand it is a hopelessly misleading word in some important respects. It falsely suggests, for one thing, that any sort of careful elucidation of any sorts of complex or subtle ideas will be a piece of philosophizing; as if the judge, in explaining to the members of the jury the differences between man-slaughter and murder, was helping them out of a philosophical quandary. But, even worse, it suggests that philosophical pro-blems are like the chemist's or the detective's problems in this respect, namely that they can and should be tackled piecemeal. Finish problem A this morning, file the answer, and go on to pro-blem B this afternoon. This suggestion does violence to the vital fact that philosophical problems inevitably interlock in all sorts of ways. It would be patently absurd to tell someone to finish the problem of the nature of truth this morning, file the answer and go on this afternoon to solve the problem of the relations between naming and saying, holding over until tomorrow problems about the concepts of existence and non-existence. This is, I think, why at the present moment philosophers are far more inclined to liken their task to that of the cartographer than to that of the chemist or the detective. It is the foreign relations, not the domestic constitu-tions of sayables that engender logical troubles and demand logical arbitration.

9 PROPER NAMES

by John R. Searle

Do proper names have senses ? Frege [1] argues that they must have senses, for, he asks, how else can identity statements be other than trivially analytic. How, he asks, can a statement of the form a = b, if true, differ in cognitive value from a = a ? His answer is that though " a " and " b " have the same referent they have or may have different *senses*, in which case the statement is true, though not analytically so. But this solution seems more appropriate where " a " and " b " are both non-synonymous definite descriptions, or where one is a definite description and one is a proper name, than where both are proper names. Consider, for example, statements made with the following sentences :

(a) " Tully = Tully " is analytic.
But is
(b) " Tully = Cicero " synthetic ?
If so, then each name must have a different sense, which seems at first sight most implausible, for we do not ordinarily think of proper names as having a sense at all in the way that predicates do ; we do not, *e.g.* give definitions of proper names. But of course (b) gives us information not conveyed by (a). But is this information about words ? The statement is not about words.

For the moment let us consider the view that (b) is, like (a), analytic. A statement is analytic if and only if it is true in virtue of linguistic rules alone, without any recourse to empirical investigation. The linguistic rules for using the name " Cicero " and the linguistic rules for using the name " Tully " are such that both names refer to, without describing, the same identical object ; thus it seems the truth of the identity can be established solely by recourse to these rules and the statement is analytic. The sense in which the statement is informative is the sense in which any analytic statement is informative ; it illustrates or exemplifies certain contingent facts about words, though it does not of course describe these facts. On this account the difference between (a) and (b) above is not as great as might at first seem. Both are analytically true, and both illustrate contingent facts about our use of symbols. Some philosophers claim that (a) is

---

[1] *Translations from the Philosophical Writings of Gottlob Frege*, edited by Geach and Black, pp. 56 ff.

---

fundamentally different from (b) in that a statement using this form will be true for any arbitrary substitution of symbols replacing " Tully ".[1] This, I wish to argue, is not so. The fact that the same mark refers to the same object on two different occasions of its use is a convenient but contingent usage, and indeed we can easily imagine situations where this would not be the case. Suppose, *e.g.* we have a language in which the rules for using symbols are correlated not simply with a type-word, but with the order of its token appearances in the discourse. Some codes are like this. Suppose the first time an object is referred to in our discourse it is referred to by " x ", the second time by " y ", etc. For anyone who knows this code " x = y " is trivially analytic, but " x=x " is senseless. This example is designed to illustrate the similarity of (a) and (b) above ; both are analytic and both give us information, though each gives us different information, about the use of words. The truth of the statements that Tully = Tully and Tully = Cicero both follow from linguistic rules. But the fact that the words " Tully = Tully " are used to express this identity is just as contingent as, though more universally conventional in our language than, the fact that the words " Tully = Cicero " are used to express the identity of the same object.

This analysis enables us to see how both (a) and (b) could be used to make analytic statements and how in such circumstances we could acquire different information from them, without forcing us to follow either of Frege's proposed solutions, *i.e.* that the two propositions are in some sense about words (*Begriffsschrift*) or his revised solution, that the terms have the same reference but different senses (*Sinn und Bedeutung*). But though this analysis enables us to see how a sentence like (b) *could* be used to make an analytic statement it does not follow that it could not also be used to make a synthetic statement. And indeed some identity statements using two proper names are clearly synthetic ; people who argue that Shakespeare was Bacon are not advancing a thesis about language. In what follows I hope to examine the connection between proper names and their referents in such manner as to show how both kinds of identity statement are possible and in so doing to show in what sense a proper name has a sense.

I have so far considered the view that the rules governing use of a proper name are such that it is used to refer to and to describe a particular object, that it has reference but not sense. But now let us ask how it comes about that we are able to

---

[1] W. V. Quine, *From a Logical Point of View*, esp. chap. 2.

did not exist he might mean much more than simply that the name does not denote anyone.[1] If, for example, we challenged his statement by pointing out that a man named " Aristotle " lived in Hoboken in 1903, he would not regard this as a relevant countercharge. We say of Cerberus and Zeus that neither of them ever existed, without meaning that no object ever bore these names, but only that certain kinds (descriptions) of objects never existed and bore these names. So now it looks as though proper names do have a sense necessarily but have a reference only contingently. They begin to look more and more like shorthand and perhaps vague descriptions.

Let us summarise the two conflicting views under consideration : the first asserts that proper names have essentially a reference but not a sense—proper names denote but do not connote ; the second asserts that they have essentially a sense and only contingently a reference—they refer only on the condition that one and only one object satisfies their sense.

These two views are paths leading to divergent and hoary metaphysical systems. The first leads to ultimate objects of reference, the substances of the scholastics and the *Gegenstände* of the *Tractatus*. The second leads to the identity of indiscernibles, and variables of quantification as the only referential terms in the language. The subject-predicate structure of the language suggests that the first must be right, but the way we use and teach the use of proper names suggests that it cannot be right : a philosophical problem.

Let us begin by examining the second. If it is asserted that every proper name has a sense, it must be legitimate to demand of any name, " What is its sense ? " If it is asserted that a proper name is a kind of shorthand description then we ought to be able to present the description in place of the proper name. But how are we to proceed with this ? If we try to present a complete description of the object as the sense of a proper name, odd consequences would ensue, *e.g.* that any true statement about the object using the name as subject would be analytic, any false one self-contradictory, that the meaning of the name (and perhaps the identity of the object) would change every time there was any change at all in the object, that the name would have different meanings for different people, etc. So suppose we ask what are the necessary and sufficient conditions for applying a particular name to a particular object. Suppose for the sake of argument that we have independent means for locating an object ; then what are the conditions for applying a name to

[1] *Cf.* Wittgenstein, *Philosophical Investigations*, para. 79.

it ; what are the conditions for saying, *e.g.* " This is Aristotle "?
At first sight these conditions seem to be simply that the object
must be identical with an object originally christened by this
name, so the sense of the name would consist in a statement or
set of statements asserting the characteristics which constitute
this identity. The sense of " This is Aristotle " might be,
" This object is spatio-temporally continuous with an object
originally named ' Aristotle ' ". But this will not suffice, for,
as was already suggested, the force of " Aristotle " is greater than
the force of " identical with an object named ' Aristotle ' ", for
not just any object named " Aristotle " will do. " Aristotle "
here refers to a particular object named " Aristotle ", not to any.
" Named ' Aristotle ' " is a universal term, but " Aristotle ", is a
proper name, so "This is named 'Aristotle'" is at best a necessary
but not a sufficient condition for the truth of " This is Aristotle "?
Briefly and trivially, it is not the identity of this with any object
named " Aristotle ", but rather its identity with Aristotle that
constitutes the necessary and sufficient conditions for the truth
of " This is Aristotle ".

Perhaps we can resolve the conflict between the two views of
the nature of proper names by asking what is the unique function
of proper names in our language. To begin with, they mostly
refer or purport to refer to particular objects ; but of course
other expressions, definite descriptions and demonstratives,
perform this function as well. What then is the difference
between proper names and other singular referring expressions ?
Unlike demonstratives, a proper name refers without presupposing any stage settings or any special contextual conditions
surrounding the utterance of the expression. Unlike definite
descriptions, they do not in general *specify* any characteristics
at all of the objects to which they refer. " Scott " refers to the
same object as does " the author of *Waverley* ", but " Scott "
specifies none of its characteristics, whereas " the author of
Waverley " refers only in virtue of the fact that it does specify a
characteristic. Let us examine this difference more closely.
Following Strawson [1] we may say that referring uses of both
proper names and definite descriptions presuppose the existence
of one and only one object referred to. But as a proper name
does not in general specify any characteristics of the object
referred to, how then does it bring the reference off ? How is a
connection between name and object ever set up ? This, which
seems the crucial question, I want to answer by saying that
though proper names do not normally assert or specify any

---

[1] " On Referring ", MIND, 1950.

characteristics, their referring uses nonetheless presuppose that the object to which they purport to refer has certain characteristics. But which ones ? Suppose we ask the users of the name " Aristotle " to state what they regard as certain essential and established facts about him. Their answers would be a set of uniquely referring descriptive statements. Now what I am arguing is that the descriptive force of " This is Aristotle " is to assert that a sufficient but so far unspecified number of these statements are true of this object. Therefore, referring uses of " Aristotle " presuppose the existence of an object of whom a sufficient but so far unspecified number of these statements are true. To use a proper name referringly is to presuppose the truth of certain uniquely referring descriptive statements, but it is not ordinarily to assert these statements or even to indicate which exactly are presupposed. And herein lies most of the difficulty. The question of what constitutes the criteria for " Aristotle " is generally left open, indeed it seldom in fact arises, and when it does arise it is we, the users of the name, who decide more or less arbitrarily what these criteria shall be. If, for example, of the characteristics agreed to be true of Aristotle, half should be discovered to be true of one man and half true of another, which would we say was Aristotle ? Neither ? The question is not decided for us in advance.

But is this imprecision as to what characteristics exactly constitute the necessary and sufficient conditions for applying a proper name a mere accident, a product of linguistic slovenliness ? Or does it derive from the functions which proper names perform for us ? To ask for the criteria for applying the name " Aristotle " is to ask in the formal mode what Aristotle is ; it is to ask for a set of identity criteria for the object Aristotle. " What is Aristotle ? " and " What are the criteria for applying the name ' Aristotle ' ? " ask the same question, the former in the material mode, and the latter in the formal mode of speech. So if we came to agreement in advance of using the name on precisely what characteristics constituted the identity of Aristotle, our rules for using the name would be precise. But this precision would be achieved only at the cost of entailing some specific predicates by any referring use of the name. Indeed, the name itself would become superfluous for it would become logically equivalent to this set of descriptions. But if this were the case we would be in the position of only being able to refer to an object by describing it. Whereas in fact this is just what the institution of proper names enables us to avoid and what distinguishes proper names from descriptions. If the criteria for proper names were in all cases quite rigid and specific then a proper name would be nothing more than a shorthand for these criteria, a proper name would function exactly like an elaborate definite description.   But the uniqueness and immense pragmatic convenience of proper names in our language lie precisely in the fact that they enable us to refer publicly to objects without being forced to raise issues and come to agreement on what descriptive characteristics exactly constitute the identity of the object.   They function not as descriptions, but as pegs on which to hang descriptions.   Thus the looseness of the criteria for proper names is a necessary condition for isolating the referring function from the describing function of language.

To put the same point differently, suppose we ask, " Why do we have proper names at all ? "   Obviously, to refer to individuals.   " Yes, but descriptions could do that for us."   But only at the cost of specifying identity conditions every time reference is made : suppose we agree to drop " Aristotle " and use, say, " the teacher of Alexander ", then it is a necessary truth that the man referred to is Alexander's teacher—but it is a contingent fact that Aristotle ever went into pedagogy (though I am suggesting it is a necessary fact that Aristotle has the logical sum, inclusive disjunction, of properties commonly attributed to him : any individual not having at least some of these properties could not be Aristotle).

Of course it should not be thought that the only sort of looseness of identity criteria for individuals is that which I have described as peculiar to proper names.   Referring uses of definite descriptions may raise problems concerning identity of quite different sorts.   This is especially true of past tense definite descriptions.) " This is the man who taught Alexander " may be said to entail, e.g. that this object is spatio-temporally continuous with the man teaching Alexander at another point in space-time : but someone might also argue that this man's spatio-temporal continuity is a contingent characteristic and not an identity criterion.   And the logical nature of the connection of such characteristics with the man's identity may again be loose and undecided in advance of dispute.   But this is quite another dimension of looseness than that which I cited as the looseness of the criteria for applying proper names and does not affect the distinction in function between definite descriptions and proper names, viz. that definite descriptions refer only in virtue of the fact that the criteria are not loose in the original sense, for they refer by telling us what the object is.   But proper names refer without so far raising the issue of what the object is.

We are now in a position to explain how it is that " Aristotle " has a reference but does not describe, and yet the statement " Aristotle never existed " says more than that " Aristotle " was never used to refer to any object. The statement asserts that a sufficient number of the conventional presuppositions, descriptive statements, of referring uses of " Aristotle " are false. Precisely which statements are asserted to be false is not yet clear, for what precise conditions constitute the criteria for applying " Aristotle " is not yet laid down by the language.

We can now resolve our paradox : does a proper name have a sense ? If this asks whether or not proper names are used to describe or specify characteristics of objects, the answer is " no ". But if it asks whether or not proper names are logically connected with characteristics of the object to which they refer, the answer is " yes, in a loose sort of way ". (This shows in part the poverty of a rigid sense-reference, denotation-connotation approach to problems in the theory of meaning.)

We might clarify these points by comparing paradigmatic proper names with degenerate proper names like " The Bank of England ". For these latter, it seems the sense is given as straightforwardly as in a definite description ; the presuppositions, as it were, rise to the surface. And a proper name may acquire a rigid descriptive use without having the verbal form of a description : God is just, omnipotent, omniscient, etc., *by definition* for believers. Of course the form may mislead us ; the Holy Roman Empire was neither holy, nor Roman, etc., but it was nonetheless the Holy Roman Empire. Again it may be conventional to name only girls " Martha ", but if I name my son " Martha " I may mislead, but I do not lie.

Now reconsider our original identity, " Tully = Cicero ". A statement made using this sentence would, I suggest, be analytic for most people ; the same descriptive presuppositions are associated with each name. But of course if the descriptive presuppositions were different it might be used to make a synthetic statement ; it might even advance a historical discovery of the first importance.

10 ON REFERRING

by P. F. Strawson

WE very commonly use expressions of certain kinds to
mention or refer to some individual person or single object
or particular event or place or process, in the course of
doing what we should normally describe as making a statement about that person, object, place, event, or process. I
shall call this way of using expressions the 'uniquely referring use'. The classes of expressions which are most
commonly used in this way are: singular demonstrative
pronouns ('this' and 'that'); proper names (*e.g.* 'Venice',
'Napoleon', 'John'); singular personal and impersonal pronouns ('he', 'she', 'I', 'you', 'it'); and phrases beginning
with the definite article followed by a noun, qualified or
unqualified, in the singular (*e.g.* 'the table', 'the old man',
'the king of France'). Any expression of any of these classes
can occur as the subject of what would traditionally be
regarded as a singular subject-predicate sentence; and
would, so occurring, exemplify the use I wish to discuss.

I do not want to say that expressions belonging to these
classes never have any other use than the one I want to
discuss. On the contrary, it is obvious that they do. It is
obvious that anyone who uttered the sentence, 'The whale
is a mammal', would be using the expression 'the whale'
in a way quite different from the way it would be used by
anyone who had occasion seriously to utter the sentence,
'The whale struck the ship'. In the first sentence one is
obviously *not* mentioning, and in the second sentence one
obviously *is* mentioning, a particular whale. Again if I

said, 'Napoleon was the greatest French soldier', I should be using the word 'Napoleon' to mention a certain individual, but I should not be using the phrase, 'the greatest French soldier', to mention an individual, but to say something about an individual I had already mentioned. It would be natural to say that in using this sentence I was talking *about* Napoleon and that what I was *saying* about him was that he was the greatest French soldier. But of course I *could* use the expression, 'the greatest French soldier', to mention an individual; for example, by saying: 'The greatest French soldier died in exile'. So it is obvious that at least some expressions belonging to the classes I mentioned *can* have uses other than the use I am anxious to discuss. Another thing I do not want to say is that in any given sentence there is never more than one expression used in the way I propose to discuss. On the contrary, it is obvious that there may be more than one. For example, it would be natural to say that, in seriously using the sentence, 'The whale struck the ship', I was saying something about both a certain whale and a certain ship, that I was using each of the expressions 'the whale' and 'the ship' to mention a particular object; or, in other words, that I was using each of these expressions in the uniquely referring way. In general, however, I shall confine my attention to cases where an expression used in this way occurs as the grammatical subject of a sentence.

I think it is true to say that Russell's Theory of Descriptions, which is concerned with the last of the four classes of expressions I mentioned above (*i.e.* with expressions of the form 'the so-and-so'), is still widely accepted among logicians as giving a correct account of the use of such expressions in ordinary language. I want to show in the first place, that this theory, so regarded, embodies some fundamental mistakes.

What question or questions about phrases of the form 'the so-and-so' was the Theory of Descriptions designed to answer? I think that at least one of the questions may be illustrated as follows. Suppose someone were now to utter the sentence, 'The king of France is wise'. No one would say that the sentence which had been uttered was meaningless. Everyone would agree that it was significant. But everyone knows that there is not at present a king of France. One of the questions the Theory of Descriptions was designed to answer was the question: How can such a sentence as 'The king of France is wise' be significant even when there is nothing which answers to the description it contains, *i.e.*, in this case, nothing which answers to the description 'The king of France'? And one of the reasons why Russell thought it important to give a correct answer to this question was that he thought it important to show that another answer which might be given was wrong. The answer that he thought was wrong, and to which he was anxious to supply an alternative, might be exhibited as the conclusion of either of the following two fallacious arguments. Let us call the sentence 'The king of France is wise' the sentence S. Then the first argument is as follows:

(1) The phrase, 'the king of France', is the subject of the sentence S.

Therefore (2) if S is a significant sentence, S is a sentence *about* the king of France.

But (3) if there in no sense exists a king of France, the sentence is not about anything, and hence not about the king of France.

Therefore (4) since S is significant, there must in some sense (in some world) exist (or subsist) the king of France.

And the second argument is as follows:

(1) If S is significant, it is either true or false.

(2) S is true if the king of France is wise and false if the king of France is not wise.

(3) But the statement that the king of France is wise and the statement that the king of France is not wise are alike true only if there is (in some sense, in some world) something which is the king of France.

Hence (4) since S is significant, there follows the same conclusion as before.

These are fairly obviously bad arguments, and, as we should expect, Russell rejects them. The postulation of a world of strange entities, to which the king of France belongs, offends, he says, against 'that feeling for reality which ought to be preserved even in the most abstract studies'. The fact that Russell rejects these arguments is, however, less interesting than the extent to which, in rejecting their conclusion, he concedes the more important of their principles. Let me refer to the phrase, 'the king of France', as the phrase D. Then I think Russell's reasons for rejecting these two arguments can be summarized as follows. The mistake arises, he says, from thinking that D, which is certainly the *grammatical* subject of S, is also the *logical* subject of S. But D is not the logical subject of S. In fact S, although grammatically it has a singular subject and a predicate, is not logically a subject-predicate sentence at all. The proposition it expresses is a complex kind of *existential* proposition, part of which might be described as a 'uniquely existential' proposition. To exhibit the logical form of the proposition, we should re-write the sentence in a logically appropriate grammatical form ; in such a way that the deceptive similarity of S to a sentence expressing a subject-predicate proposition would disappear, and we should be safeguarded against arguments such as the bad ones I outlined above. Before recalling the details of Russell's analysis of S, let us notice what his answer, as I have so far given it, seems to imply. His answer seems to imply that in the case of a sentence which is similar to S in that (1) it is grammatically of the subject-predicate form and (2) its grammatical subject does not refer to anything, then the only alternative to its being meaningless is that it should not really (*i.e.* logically) be of the subject-predicate form at all, but of some quite different form. And this in its turn seems to imply that if there are any sentences which are genuinely of the subject-predicate form, then the very fact of their being significant, having a meaning, guarantees that there *is* something referred to by the logical (and grammatical) subject.   Moreover, Russell's answer seems to imply that there are such sentences.   For if it is true that one may be misled by the grammatical similarity of S to other sentences into thinking that it is logically of the subject-predicate form, then surely there must be other sentences grammatically similar to S, which *are* of the subject-predicate form.   To show not only that Russell's answer seems to imply these conclusions, but that he accepted at least the first two of them, it is enough to consider what he says about a class of expressions which he calls 'logically proper names' and contrasts with expressions, like D, which he calls 'definite descriptions'.   Of logically proper names Russell says or implies the following things:

(1) That they and they alone can occur as subjects of sentences which are genuinely of the subject-predicate form.

(2) That an expression intended to be a logically proper name is *meaningless* unless there is some single object for which it stands: for the *meaning* of such an expression just is the individual object which the expression designates.   To be a name at all, therefore, it *must* designate something.

It is easy to see that if anyone believes these two propositions, then the only way for him to save the significance of the sentence S is to deny that it is a logically subject-predicate sentence.   Generally, we may say that Russell recognizes only two ways in which sentences which seem, from their grammatical structure, to be about some particular person or individual object or event, can be significant:

(1) The first is that their grammatical form should be misleading as to their logical form, and that they should be analysable, like S, as a special kind of existential sentence.

(2) The second is that their grammatical subject should be a logically proper name, of which the meaning is the individual thing it designates.

I think that Russell is unquestionably wrong in this, and that sentences which are significant, and which begin with an expression used in the uniquely referring way, fall into neither of these two classes. Expressions used in the uniquely referring way are never either logically proper names or descriptions, if what is meant by calling them 'descriptions' is that they are to be analysed in accordance with the model provided by Russell's Theory of Descriptions.

There are no logically proper names and there are no descriptions (in this sense).

Let us now consider the details of Russell's analysis. According to Russell, anyone who asserted S would be asserting that:

(1) There is a king of France.

(2) There is not more than one king of France.

(3) There is nothing which is king of France and is not wise.

It is easy to see both how Russell arrived at this analysis, and how it enables him to answer the question with which we began, viz. the question: How can the sentence S be significant when there is no king of France? The way in which he arrived at the analysis was clearly by asking himself what would be the circumstances in which we would say that anyone who uttered the sentence S had made a true assertion. And it does seem pretty clear, and I have no wish to dispute, that the sentences (1)-(3) above do describe circumstances which are at least *necessary* conditions of anyone making a true assertion by uttering the sentence S. But, as I hope to show, to say this is not at all the same thing as to say that Russell has given a correct account of the use of the sentence S or even that he has given an account which, though incomplete, is correct as far as it goes; and is certainly not at all the same thing as to say that the model translation provided is a correct model for all (or for any) singular sentences beginning with a phrase of the form 'the so-and-so'.

It is also easy to see how this analysis enables Russell to answer the question of how the sentence S can be significant, even when there is no king of France. For, if this analysis is correct, anyone who utters the sentence S to-day would be jointly asserting three propositions, one of which (viz. that there is a king of France) would be false ; and since the conjunction of three propositions, of which one is false, is itself false, the assertion as a whole would be significant, but false. So neither of the bad arguments for subsistent entities would apply to such an assertion.

II

As a step towards showing that Russell's solution of his problem is mistaken, and towards providing the correct solution, I want now to draw certain distinctions. For this purpose I shall, for the remainder of this section, refer to an expression which has a uniquely referring use as 'an expression' for short ; and to a sentence beginning with such an expression as 'a sentence' for short. The distinctions I shall draw are rather rough and ready, and, no doubt, difficult cases could be produced which would call for their refinement. But I think they will serve my purpose. The distinctions are between :

(A1) a sentence,
(A2) a use of a sentence,
(A3) an utterance of a sentence,

and, correspondingly, between :

(B1) an expression,
(B2) a use of an expression,
(B3) an utterance of an expression.

Consider again the sentence, 'The king of France is wise'. It is easy to imagine that this sentence was uttered at various times from, say, the beginning of the seventeenth century onwards, during the reigns of each successive French monarch ; and easy to imagine that it was also uttered during the subsequent periods in which France was not a monarchy. Notice that it was natural for me to speak of 'the sentence' or 'this sentence' being uttered at various times during this period ; or, in other words, that it would be natural and correct to speak of *one and the same* sentence being uttered on all these various occasions. It is in the sense in which it would be correct to speak of one and the same sentence being uttered on all these various occasions that I want to use the expression (A·1) 'a sentence'. There are, however, obvious differences between different *occasions of the use* of this sentence. For instance, if one man uttered it in the reign of Louis XIV and another man uttered it in the reign of Louis XV, it would be natural to say (to assume) that they were respectively talking about different people ; and it might be held that the first man, in using the sentence, made a true assertion, while the second man, in using the same sentence, made a false assertion. If on the other hand two different men simultaneously uttered the sentence (*e.g.* if one wrote it and the other spoke it) during the reign of Louis XIV, it would be natural to say (assume) that they were both talking about the same person, and, in that case, in using the sentence, they *must* either both have made a true assertion or both have made a false assertion. And this illustrates what I mean by *a use* of a sentence. The two men who uttered the sentence, one in the reign of Louis XV and one in the reign of Louis XIV, each made a different use of the same sentence ; whereas the two men who uttered the sentence simultaneously in the reign of Louis XIV, made the same use [1] of the same sentence. Obviously in the case of this sentence, and equally obviously in the case of many others, we cannot talk of *the sentence* being true or false, but only of its being used to make a true or false assertion, or (if this is preferred) to express a true or a false proposition. And equally obviously we cannot talk of *the sentence* being *about* a particular person, for the same sentence may be used at different times to talk about

---

[1] This usage of 'use' is, of course, different from (*a*) the current usage in which 'use' (of a particular word, phrase, sentence)=(roughly) 'rules for using'=(roughly) 'meaning'; and from (*b*) my own usage in the phrase 'uniquely referring use of expressions' in which 'use'=(roughly) 'way of using'.

quite different particular persons, but only of *a use* of the sentence to talk about a particular person. Finally it will make sufficiently clear what I mean by an utterance of a sentence if I say that the two men who simultaneously uttered the sentence in the reign of Louis XIV made two different utterances of the same sentence, though they made the same *use* of the sentence.

If we now consider not the whole sentence, 'The king of France is wise', but that part of it which is the expression, 'the king of France', it is obvious that we can make analogous, though not identical distinctions between (1) the expression, (2) a use of the expression, and (3) an utterance of the expression. The distinctions will not be identical ; we obviously cannot correctly talk of the expression 'the king of France' being used to express a true or false proposition, since in general only sentences can be used truly or falsely ; and similarly it is only by using a sentence and not by using an expression alone, that you can talk about a particular person. Instead, we shall say in this case that you *use* the expression to *mention* or *refer to* a particular person in the course of using the sentence to talk about him. But obviously in this case, and a great many others, the *expression* (B1) cannot be said to mention, or refer to, anything, any more than the *sentence* can be said to be true or false. The same expression can have different mentioning-uses, as the same sentence can be used to make statements with different truth-values. 'Mentioning', or 'referring', is not something an expression does ; it is something that someone can use an expression to do. Mentioning, or referring to, something is a characteristic of *a use* of an expression, just as 'being about' something, and truth-or-falsity, are characteristics of *a use* of a sentence.

A very different example may help to make these distinctions clearer. Consider another case of an expression which has a uniquely referring use, viz. the expression 'I' ; and consider the sentence, 'I am hot'. Countless people may use this same sentence ; but it is logically impossible for two different people to make *the same use* of this sentence : or, if this is preferred, to use it to express the same proposition. The expression 'I' may correctly be used by (and only by) any one of innumerable people to refer to himself. To say this is to say something about the expression 'I' : it is, in a sense, to give its meaning. This is the sort of thing that can be said about *expressions*. But it makes no sense to say of the *expression* 'I' that it refers to a particular person. This is the sort of thing that can be said only of a particular use of the expression.

Let me use 'type' as an abbreviation for 'sentence or expression'. Then I am not saying that there are sentences and expressions (types), *and* uses of them, *and* utterances of them, as there are ships *and* shoes *and* sealing-wax. I am saying that we cannot say *the same things* about types, uses of types, and utterances of types. And the fact is that we do talk about types ; and that confusion is apt to result from the failure to notice the differences between what we can say about these and what we can say only about the *uses* of types. We are apt to fancy we are talking about sentences and expressions when we are talking about the uses of sentences and expressions.

This is what Russell does. Generally, as against Russell, I shall say this. Meaning (in at least one important sense) is a function of the sentence or expression ; mentioning and referring and truth or falsity, are functions of the use of the sentence or expression. To give the meaning of an expression (in the sense in which I am using the word) is to give *general directions* for its use to refer to or mention particular objects or persons ; to give the meaning of a sentence is to give *general directions* for its use in making true or false assertions. It is not to talk about any particular occasion of the use of the sentence or expression. The meaning of an expression cannot be identified with the object it is used, on a particular occasion, to refer to. The meaning of a sentence cannot be identified with the assertion it is used, on a particular occasion, to make. For to talk about the meaning of an expression or sentence is not to talk about its use on a particular occasion, but about the rules, habits, conventions governing its correct use, on all occasions, to refer or to assert. So the question of whether a sentence or expression *is significant or not* has nothing whatever to do with the question of whether the sentence, *uttered on a particular occasion*, is, on that occasion, being used to make a true-or-false assertion or not, or of whether the expression is, on that occasion, being used to refer to, or mention, anything at all.

The source of Russell's mistake was that he thought that referring or mentioning, if it occurred at all, must be meaning. He did not distinguish B1 from B2; he confused expressions with their use in a particular context; and so confused meaning with mentioning, with referring. If I talk about my handkerchief, I can, perhaps, produce the object I am referring to out of my pocket. I cannot produce the meaning of the expression, 'my handkerchief', out of my pocket. Because Russell confused meaning with mentioning, he thought that if there were any expressions having a uniquely **referring use**, which were what they seemed (*i.e.* logical sub**jects) and** not something else in disguise, their meaning must *be* the particular object which they were used to refer to. Hence the troublesome mythology of the logically proper name. But if someone asks me the meaning of the expression 'this' — once Russell's favourite candidate for this status — I do not hand him the object I have just used the expression to refer to, adding at the same time that the meaning of the word changes every time it is used. Nor do I hand him all the objects it ever has been, or might be, used to refer to. I explain and illustrate the conventions governing the use of the expression. This *is* giving the meaning of the expression. It is quite different from giving (in any sense of giving) the object to which it refers; for the expression itself does not refer to anything; though it can be used, on different occasion, to refer to innumerable things. Now as a matter of fact there is, in

English, a sense of the word 'mean' in which this word does approximate to 'indicate, mention or refer to'; *e.g.* when somebody (unpleasantly) says, 'I mean you'; or when I point and say, 'That's the one I mean'. But *the one I meant* is quite different from *the meaning of the expression* I used to talk of it. In this special sense of 'mean', it is people who mean, not expressions. People use expressions to refer to particular things. But the meaning of an expression is not the set of things or the single thing it may correctly be used to refer to: the meaning is the set of rules, habits, conventions for its use in referring.

It is the same with sentences: even more obviously so. Everyone knows that the sentence, 'The table is covered with books', is significant, and everyone knows what it means. But if I ask, 'What object is that sentence about?' I am asking an absurd question — a question which cannot be asked about the sentence, but only about some use of the sentence: and in this case the sentence has not been used to talk about something, it has only been taken as an example. In knowing what it means, you are knowing how it could correctly be used to talk about things: so knowing the meaning has nothing to do with knowing about any particular use of the sentence to talk about anything. Similarly, if I ask: 'Is the sentence true or false?' I am asking an absurd question, which becomes no less absurd if I add, 'It must be one or the other since it is significant'. The question is absurd, because the *sentence* is neither true nor false any more than it is *about* some object. Of course the fact that it is significant is the same as the fact that it *can* correctly be used to talk about something and that, in so using it, someone will be making a true or false assertion. And I will add that it will be used to make a true or false assertion *only* if the person using it *is* talking about something. If, when he utters it, he is not talking about anything, then his use is not a genuine one, but a spurious or pseudo-use: he is not making either a true or a false assertion, though he may think he is. And this points the way to the correct answer to the puzzle to which the Theory of Descriptions gives a fatally incorrect answer. The important point is that the question of whether the sentence is significant or not is quite independent of the question that can be raised about a particular use of it, viz. the question whether it is a genuine or a spurious use, whether it is being used to talk about something, or in make-believe, or as an example in philosophy. The question whether the sentence is significant or not is the question whether there exist such language habits, conventions or rules that the sentence logically could be used to talk about something; and is hence quite independent of the question whether it is being so used on a particular occasion.

III

Consider again the sentence, 'The king of France is wise', and the true and false things Russell says about it.

There are at least two true things which Russell would say about the sentence:

(1) The first is that it is significant; that if anyone were now to utter it, he would be uttering a significant sentence.

(2) The second is that anyone now uttering the sentence would be making a true assertion only if there in fact at present existed one and only one king of France, and if he were wise.

What are the false things which Russell would say about the sentence? They are:

(1) That anyone now uttering it would be making a true assertion or a false assertion;

(2) That part of what he would be asserting would be that there at present existed one and only one king of France.

I have already given some reasons for thinking that these two statements are incorrect. Now suppose someone were in fact to say to you with a perfectly serious air: 'The king of France is wise'. Would you say, 'That's untrue'? I think it is quite certain that you would not. But suppose he went on to *ask* you whether you thought that what he had just said was true, or was false ; whether you agreed or dis-agreed with what he had just said. I think you would be inclined, with some hesitation, to say that you did not do either ; that the question of whether his statement was true or false simply *did not arise*, because there was no such person as the king of France. You might, if he were obviously serious (had a dazed astray-in-the-centuries look), say something like : 'I'm afraid you must be under a mis-apprehension. France is not a monarchy. There is no king of France.' And this brings out the point that if a man seriously uttered the sentence, his uttering it would in some sense be *evidence* that he *believed* that there was a king of France. It would not be evidence for his believing this simply in the way in which a man's reaching for his raincoat is evidence for his believing that it is raining. But nor would it be evidence for his believing this in the way in which a man's saying, 'It's raining', is evidence for his be-lieving that it is raining. We might put it as follows. To say 'The king of France is wise' is, in some sense of 'imply', to *imply* that there is a king of France. But this is a very special and odd sense of 'imply'. 'Implies' in this sense is certainly not equivalent to 'entails' (or 'logically implies'). And this comes out from the fact that when, in response to his statement, we say (as we should) 'There is no king of France', we should certainly *not* say we were *contradicting* the statement that the king of France is wise. We are cer-tainly not saying that it is false. We are, rather, giving a reason for saying that the question of whether it is true or false simply does not arise.

And this is where the distinction I drew earlier can help us. The sentence, 'The king of France is wise', is certainly significant ; but this does not mean that any particular use of it is true or false. We use it truly or falsely when we use it to talk about someone ; when, in using the expression, 'The king of France', we are in fact mentioning someone.

The fact that the sentence and the expression, respectively, are significant just is the fact that the sentence *could* be used, in certain circumstances, to say something true or false, that the expression *could* be used, in certain circumstances, to mention a particular person; and to know their meaning is to know what sort of circumstances these are. So when we utter the sentence without in fact mentioning anybody by the use of the phrase, 'The king of France', the sentence does not cease to be significant: we simply *fail* to say anything true or false because we simply fail to mention anybody by this particular use of that perfectly significant phrase. It is, if you like, a spurious use of the sentence, and a spurious use of the expression; though we may (or may not) mistakenly think it a genuine use.

And such spurious uses [1] are very familiar. Sophisticated romancing, sophisticated fiction,[2] depend upon them. If I began, 'The king of France is wise', and went on, 'and he lives in a golden castle and has a hundred wives', and so on, a hearer would understand me perfectly well, without supposing *either* that I was talking about a particular person, *or* that I was making a false statement to the effect that there existed such a person as my words described. (It is worth adding that where the use of sentences and expressions is overtly fictional, the sense of the word 'about' may change. As Moore said, it is perfectly natural and correct to say that some of the statements in *Pickwick Papers* are *about* Mr. Pickwick. But where the use of sentences and expressions is not overtly fictional, this use of 'about' seems less correct; *i.e.* it would not *in general* be correct to say that a statement was about Mr. X or the so-and-so, unless there were such a person or thing. So it is where the romancing is in danger of being taken seriously that we might answer the question, 'Who is he talking about?' with 'He's not talking about anybody'; but, in saying this, we are not

---

[1] The choice of the word 'spurious' now seems to me unfortunate, at least for some non-standard uses. I should now prefer to call some of these 'secondary' uses.

[2] The unsophisticated kind begins: 'Once upon time there was . . .'

saying that what he is saying is either false or nonsense.)

Overtly fictional uses apart, however, I said just now that to use such an expression as 'The king of France' at the beginning of a sentence was, in some sense of 'imply', to imply that there was a king of France. When a man uses such an expression, he does not *assert*, nor does what he says *entail*, a uniquely existential proposition. But one of the conventional functions of the definite article is to act as a *signal* that a unique reference is being made — a signal, not a disguised assertion. When we begin a sentence with 'the such-and-such' the use of 'the' shows, but does not state, that we are, or intend to be, referring to one particular individual of the species 'such-and-such'. *Which* particular individual is a matter to be determined from context, time, place, and any other features of the situation of utterance. Now, whenever a man uses any expression, the presumption is that he thinks he is using it correctly : so when he uses the expression, 'the such-and-such', in a uniquely referring way, the presumption is that he thinks both that there is *some* individual of that species, and that the context of use will sufficiently determine which one he has in mind. To use the word 'the' in this way is then to imply (in the relevant sense of 'imply') that the existential conditions described by Russell are fulfilled. But to use 'the' in this way is not to *state* that those conditions are fulfilled. If I begin a sentence with an expression of the form, 'the so-and-so', and then am prevented from saying more, I have made no statement of any kind ; but I may have succeeded in mentioning some-one or something.

The uniquely existential assertion supposed by Russell to be part of any assertion in which a uniquely referring use is made of an expression of the form 'the so-and-so' is, he observes, a compound of two assertions. To say that there is a ϕ is to say something compatible with there being several ϕs ; to say there is not more than one ϕ is to say something compatible with there being none. To say there is one ϕ and one only is to compound these two assertions. I have so far been concerned mostly with the alleged assertion of existence and less with the alleged assertion of uniqueness. An example which throws the emphasis on to the latter will serve to bring out more clearly the sense of 'implied' in which a uniquely existential assertion is implied, but not entailed, by the use of expressions in the uniquely referring way. Consider, the sentence, 'The table is covered with books'. It is quite certain that in any normal use of this sentence, the expression 'the table' would be used to make a unique reference, *i.e.* to refer to some one table. It is a quite strict use of the definite article, in the sense in which Russell talks on p. 30 of *Principia Mathematica*, of using the article '*strictly*, so as to imply **unique**ness'. On the same page Russell says that a phrase of the form 'the so-and-so', used strictly, 'will only have an application in the event of there being one so-and-so and no more'. Now it is obviously quite false that the phrase 'the table' in the sentence 'the table is covered with books', used normally, will 'only have an application in the event of there being one table and no more'. It is indeed tautologically true that, in such a use, the phrase will have an application only in the event of there being one table and no more *which is being referred to*, and that it will be understood to have an application only in the event of there being one table and no more which it is understood as being used to refer to. To use the sentence is not to assert, but it is (in the special sense discussed) to imply, that there is only one thing which is *both* of the kind specified (*i.e.* a table) *and is being referred to* by the speaker. It is obviously not to assert this. To refer is not to say you are referring. To say there is *some table or other* to which you are referring is not the same as referring to a particular table. We should have no use for such phrases as 'the individual I referred to' unless there were something which counted as referring. (It would make no sense to say you had pointed if there were nothing which counted as pointing.) So once more I draw the conclusion that referring to or mentioning a particular thing cannot be dissolved into any kind of assertion. To refer is not to assert, though you refer in order to go on to assert.

Let me now take an example of the uniquely referring use of an expression not of the form, 'the so-and-so'. Suppose I advance my hands, cautiously cupped, towards someone, saying, as I do so, 'This is a fine red one'. He, looking into my hands and seeing nothing there, may say: 'What is ? What are you talking about ?' Or perhaps, 'But there's nothing in your hands'. Of course it would be absurd to say that, in saying 'But you've got nothing in your hands', he was *denying* or *contradicting* what I said. So 'this' is not a disguised description in Russell's sense. Nor is it a logically proper name. For one must know what the sentence means in order to react in that way to the utterance of it. It is precisely because the significance of the word 'this' is independent of any particular reference it may be used to make, though not independent of the way it may be used to refer, that I can, as in this example, use it to *pretend* to be referring to something.

The general moral of all this is that communication is much less a matter of explicit or disguised assertion than logicians used to suppose. The particular application of this general moral in which I am interested is its application to the case of making a unique reference. It is a part of the significance of expressions of the kind I am discussing that they can be used, in an immense variety of contexts, to make unique references. It is no part of their significance to assert that they are being so used or that the conditions of their being so used are fulfilled. So the wholly important distinction we are required to draw is between

(1) using an expression to make a unique reference; and
(2) asserting that there is one and only one individual which has certain characteristics (*e.g.* is of a certain kind, or stands in a certain relation to the speaker, or both).

This is, in other words, the distinction between

(1) sentences containing an expression used to indicate

or mention or refer to a particular person or thing ; and
(2) uniquely existential sentences.

What Russell does is progressively to assimilate more and more sentences of class (1) to sentences of class (2), and consequently to involve himself in insuperable difficulties about logical subjects, and about values for individual variables generally : difficulties which have led him finally to the logically disastrous theory of names developed in the *Enquiry into Meaning and Truth* and in *Human Knowledge*. That view of the meaning of logical-subject-expressions which provides the whole incentive to the Theory of Descriptions at the same time precludes the possibility of Russell's ever finding any satisfactory substitutes for those expressions which, beginning with substantival phrases, he progressively degrades from the status of logical subjects.[1] It is not simply, as is sometimes said, the fascination of the relation between a name and its bearer, that is the root of the trouble. Not even names come up to the impossible standard set. It is rather the combination of two more radical misconceptions : first, the failure to grasp the importance of the distinction (section II above) between what may be said of an expression and what may be said of a particular use of it ; second, a failure to recognize the uniquely referring use of expressions for the harmless, necessary thing it is, distinct from, but complementary to, the predicative or ascriptive use of expressions. The expressions which can in fact occur as singular logical subjects are expressions of the class I listed at the outset (demonstratives, substantival phrases, proper names, pronouns) : to say this is to say that these expressions, together with context (in the widest sense), are what one uses to make unique references. The point of the conventions governing the uses of such expressions is, along with the situation of utterance, to secure uniqueness of reference. But to do this, enough is enough. We do not, and we cannot, while referring, attain the point of complete

---

[1] And this in spite of the danger-signal of that phrase, '*misleading* grammatical form'.

explicitness at which the referring function is no longer performed.   The actual unique reference made, if any, is a
matter of the particular use in the particular context; the
significance of the expression used is the set of rules or conventions which permit such references to be made.   Hence
we can, using significant expressions, pretend to refer, in
make-believe or in fiction, or mistakenly think we are referring when we are not referring to anything.[1]

This shows the need for distinguishing two kinds (among
many others) of linguistic conventions or rules : rules for
referring, and rules for attributing and ascribing; and for
an investigation of the former.   If we recognize this distinction of use for what it is, we are on the way to solving a
number of ancient logical and metaphysical puzzles.

My last two sections are concerned, but only in the barest
outline, with these questions.

IV

One of the main purposes for which we use language is
the purpose of stating facts about things and persons and
events.   If we want to fulfil this purpose, we must have
some way of forestalling the question, 'What (who, which
one) are you talking about?' as well as the question, 'What
are you saying about it (him, her)?'   The task of forestalling
the first question is the referring (or identifying) task.   The
task of forestalling the second is the attributive (or descriptive
or classificatory or ascriptive) task.   In the conventional
English sentence which is used to state, or to claim to state,
a fact about an individual thing or person or event, the
performance of these two tasks can be roughly and approximately assigned to separable expressions.[2]   And in such a

[1] This sentence now seems to me objectionable in a number of ways, notably
because of an unexplicitly restrictive use of the word 'refer'.   It could be more
exactly phrased as follows : 'Hence we can, using significant expressions, refer
in secondary ways, as in make-believe or in fiction, or mistakenly think we are
referring to something in the primary way when we are not, in that way, referring
to anything'.]

[2] I neglect relational sentences; for these require, not a modification in
the principle of what I say, but a complication of the detail.

sentence, this assigning of expressions to their separate rôles corresponds to the conventional grammatical classification of subject and predicate. There is nothing sacrosanct about the employment of separable expressions for these two tasks. Other methods could be, and are, employed. There is, for instance, the method of uttering a single word or attributive phrase in the conspicuous presence of the object referred to; or that analogous method exemplified by, *e.g.*, the painting of the words 'unsafe for lorries' on a bridge, or the tying of a label reading 'first prize' on a vegetable marrow. Or one can imagine an elaborate game in which one never used an expression in the uniquely referring way at all, but uttered only uniquely existential sentences, trying to enable the hearer to identify what was being talked of by means of an accumulation of relative clauses. (This description of the purposes of the game shows in what sense it would be a game: this is not the normal use we make of existential sentences.) Two points require emphasis. The first is that the necessity of performing these two tasks in order to state particular facts requires no transcendental explanation: to call attention to it is partly to elucidate the meaning of the phrase, 'stating a fact'. The second is that even this elucidation is made in terms derivative from the grammar of the conventional singular sentence; that even the overtly functional, linguistic distinction between the identifying and attributive rôles that words may play in language is prompted by the fact that ordinary speech offers us separable expressions to which the different functions may be plausibly and approximately assigned. And this functional distinction has cast long philosophical shadows. The distinctions between particular and universal, between substance and quality, are such pseudo-material shadows, cast by the grammar of the conventional sentence, in which separable expressions play distinguishable rôles.[1]

To use a separate expression to perform the first of these

[1 What is said or implied in the last two sentences of this paragraph no longer seems to me true, unless considerably qualified.]

tasks is to use an expression in the uniquely referring way. I want now to say something in general about the conventions of use for expressions used in this way, and to contrast them with conventions of ascriptive use. I then proceed to the brief illustration of these general remarks and to some further applications of them.

What in general is required for making a unique reference is, obviously, some device, or devices, for showing both *that* a unique reference is intended and *what* unique reference it is; some device requiring and enabling the hearer or reader to identify what is being talked about. In securing this result, the context of utterance is of an importance which it is almost impossible to exaggerate; and by 'context' I mean, at least, the time, the place, the situation, the identity of the speaker, the subjects which form the immediate focus of interest, and the personal histories of both the speaker and those he is addressing. Besides context, there is, of course, convention; — linguistic convention. But, except in the case of genuine proper names, of which I shall have more to say later, the fulfilment of more or less precisely stateable contextual conditions is *conventionally* (or, in a wide sense of the word, *logically*) required for the correct referring use of expressions in a sense in which this is not true of correct ascriptive uses. The requirement for the correct application of an expression in its ascriptive use to a certain thing is simply that the thing should be of a certain kind, have certain characteristics. The requirement for the correct application of an expression in its referring use to a certain thing is something over and above any requirement derived from such ascriptive meaning as the expression may have; it is, namely, the requirement that the thing should be in a certain relation to the speaker and to the context of utterance. Let me call this the contextual requirement. Thus, for example, in the limiting case of the word 'I' the contextual requirement is that the thing should be identical with the speaker; but in the case of most expressions which have a referring use this requirement cannot be so precisely specified. A further, and perfectly general, difference between conventions for referring and conventions for describing is one we have already encountered, viz. that the fulfilment of the conditions for a correct ascriptive use of an expression is a part of what is stated by such a use ; but the fulfilment of the conditions for a correct referring use of an expression is never part of what is stated, though it is (in the relevant sense of 'implied') implied by such a use.

Conventions for referring have been neglected or misinterpreted by logicians. The reasons for this neglect are not hard to see, though they are hard to state briefly. Two of them are, roughly : (1) the preoccupation of most logicians with definitions ; (2) the preoccupation of some logicians with formal systems. (1) A definition, in the most familiar sense, is a specification of the conditions of the correct ascriptive or classificatory use of an expression. Definitions take no account of contextual requirements. So that in so far as the search for the meaning or the search for the analysis of an expression is conceived as the search for a definition, the neglect or misinterpretation of conventions other than ascriptive is inevitable. Perhaps it would be better to say (for I do not wish to legislate about 'meaning' or 'analysis') that logicians have failed to notice that problems of use are wider than problems of analysis and meaning. (2) The influence of the preoccupation with mathematics and formal logic is most clearly seen (to take no more recent examples) in the cases of Leibniz and Russell. The constructor of calculuses, not concerned or required to make factual statements, approaches applied logic with a prejudice. It is natural that he should assume that the types of convention with whose adequacy in one field he is familiar should be really adequate, if only one could see how, in a quite different field — that of statements of fact. Thus we have Leibniz striving desperately to make the uniqueness of unique references a matter of logic in the narrow sense, and Russell striving desperately to do the same thing, in a different way, both for the implication of uniqueness and for that of existence.

It should be clear that the distinction I am trying to draw is primarily one between different rôles or parts that expressions may play in language, and not primarily one between different groups of expressions; for some expressions may appear in either rôle. Some of the kinds of words I shall speak of have predominantly, if not exclusively, a referring rôle. This is most obviously true of pronouns and ordinary proper names. Some can occur as wholes or parts of expressions which have a predominantly referring use, and as wholes or parts of expressions which have a predominantly ascriptive or classificatory use. The obvious cases are common nouns; or common nouns preceded by adjectives, including participial adjectives; or, less obviously, adjectives or participial adjectives alone. Expressions capable of having a referring use also differ from one another in at least the three following, not mutually independent, ways:

(1) They differ in the extent to which the reference they are used to make is dependent on the context of their utterance. Words like 'I' and 'it' stand at one end of this scale — the end of maximum dependence — and phrases like 'the author of *Waverley*' and 'the eighteenth king of France' at the other.

(2) They differ in the degree of 'descriptive meaning' they possess: by 'descriptive meaning' I intend 'conventional limitation, in application, to things of a certain general kind, or possessing certain general characteristics'. At one end of this scale stand the proper names we most commonly use in ordinary discourse; men, dogs, and motor-bicycles may be called 'Horace'. The pure name has no descriptive meaning (except such as it may acquire *as a result of* some one of its uses as a name). A word like 'he' has minimal descriptive meaning, but has some. Substantival phrases like 'the round table' have the maximum descriptive meaning. An interesting intermediate position is occupied by 'impure' proper

names like 'The Round Table' — substantival phrases which have grown capital letters.

(3) Finally, they may be divided into the following two classes : (i) those of which the correct referring use is regulated by some *general* referring-cum-ascriptive conventions ; (ii) those of which the correct referring use is regulated by no general conventions, either of the contextual or the ascriptive kind, but by conventions which are *ad hoc* for each particular use (though not for each particular utterance). To the first class belong both pronouns (which have the least descriptive meaning) and substantival phrases (which have the most). To the second class belong, roughly speaking, the most familiar kind of proper names. Ignorance of a man's name is not ignorance of the language. This is why we do not speak of the meaning of proper names. (But it won't do to say they are meaningless.) Again an intermediate position is occupied by such phrases as 'The Old Pretender'. Only an old pretender may be so referred to ; but to know which old pretender is not to know a general, but an *ad hoc*, convention.

In the case of phrases of the form 'the so-and-so' used referringly, the use of 'the' together with the position of the phrase in the sentence (*i.e.* at the beginning, or following a transitive verb or preposition) acts as a signal *that* a unique reference is being made ; and the following noun, or noun and adjective, together with the context of utterance, shows *what* unique reference is being made. In general the functional difference between common nouns and adjectives is that the former are naturally and commonly used referringly, while the latter are not commonly, or so naturally, used in this way, except as qualifying nouns ; though they can be, and are, so used alone. And of course this functional difference is not independent of the descriptive force peculiar to each word. In general we should expect the descriptive force of nouns to be such that they are more efficient tools for the job of showing what unique reference is intended when such a reference is signalized; and we should also expect the descriptive force of the words we naturally and commonly use to make unique references to mirror our interest in the salient, relatively permanent and behavioural characteristics of things. These two expectations are not independent of one another; and, if we look at the differences between the commoner sort of common nouns and the commoner sort of adjectives, we find them both fulfilled. These are differences of the kind that Locke quaintly reports, when he speaks of our ideas of substances being *collections* of simple ideas; when he says that 'powers make up a great part of our ideas of substances'; and when he goes on to contrast the identity of real and nominal essence in the case of simple ideas with their lack of identity and the shiftingness of the nominal essence in the case of substances. 'Substance' itself is the troublesome tribute Locke pays to his dim awareness of the difference in predominant linguistic function that lingered even when the noun had been expanded into a more or less indefinite string of adjectives. Russell repeats Locke's mistake with a difference when, admitting the inference from syntax to reality to the extent of feeling that he can get rid of this metaphysical unknown only if he can purify language of the referring function altogether, he draws up his programme for 'abolishing particulars'; a programme, in fact, for abolishing the distinction of logical use which I am here at pains to emphasize.

The contextual requirement for the referring use of pronouns may be stated with the greatest precision in some cases (*e.g.* 'I' and 'you') and only with the greatest vagueness in others ('it' and 'this'). I propose to say nothing further about pronouns, except to point to an additional symptom of the failure to recognize the uniquely referring use for what it is; the fact, namely, that certain logicians have actually sought to elucidate the nature of a variable by offering such *sentences* as 'he is sick', 'it is green', as examples of something in ordinary speech like a *sentential function*. Now of course it is true that the word 'he' may be used on different occasions to refer to different people or different animals: so may the word 'John' and the phrase 'the cat'. What deters such logicians from treating these two expressions as quasi-variables is, in the first case, the lingering superstition that a name is logically tied to a single individual, and, in the second case, the descriptive meaning of the word 'cat'. But 'he', which has a wide range of applications and minimal descriptive force, only acquires a use as a referring word. It is this fact, together with the failure to accord to expressions, used referringly, the place in logic which belongs to them (the place held open for the mythical logically proper name), that accounts for the misleading attempt to elucidate the nature of the variable by reference to such words as 'he', 'she', 'it'.

Of ordinary proper names it is sometimes said that they are essentially words each of which is used to refer to just one individual. This is obviously false. Many ordinary personal names — names *par excellence* — are correctly used to refer to numbers of people. An ordinary personal name is, roughly, a word, used referringly, of which the use is *not* dictated by any descriptive meaning the word may have, and is *not* prescribed by any such general rule for use as a referring expression (or a part of a referring expression) as we find in the case of such words as 'I', 'this' and 'the', but is governed by *ad hoc* conventions for each particular set of applications of the word to a given person. The important point is that the correctness of such applications does not follow from any *general* rule or convention for the use of the word as such. (The limit of absurdity and obvious circularity is reached in the attempt to treat names as disguised description in Russell's sense; for what is in the special sense implied, but not entailed, by my now referring to someone by name is simply the existence of someone, *now being referred to*, who is *conventionally referred to* by that name) Even this feature of names, however, is only a symptom of the purpose for which they are employed. At present our choice of names is partly arbitrary, partly dependent on legal and social observances. It would be perfectly possible to have a thorough-going *system* of names, based *e.g.* on dates of birth, or on a minute classification of physiological and anatomical differences. But the success of any such system would depend entirely on the convenience of the resulting name-allotments for the purpose of making unique references; and this would depend on the multiplicity of the classifications used and the degree to which they cut haphazard across normal social groupings. Given a sufficient degree of both, the selectivity supplied by context would do the rest; just as is the case with our present naming habits. Had we such a system, we could use name-words descriptively (as we do at present, to a limited extent and in a different way, with some famous names) as well as referringly. But it is by criteria derived from consideration of the requirements of the referring task that we should assess the adequacy of any system of naming. From the naming point of view, no kind of classification would be better or worse than any other simply because of the kind of classification — natal or anatomical — that it was.

I have already mentioned the class of quasi-names, of substantival phrases which grow capital letters, and of which such phrases as 'the Glorious Revolution', 'the Great War', 'the Annunciation', 'the Round Table' are examples. While the descriptive meaning of the words which follow the definite article is still relevant to their referring rôle, the capital letters are a sign of that extra-logical selectivity in their referring use, which is characteristic of pure names. Such phrases are found in print or in writing when one member of some class of events or things is of quite outstanding interest in a certain society. These phrases are embryonic names. A phrase may, for obvious reasons, pass into, and out of, this class (*e.g.* 'the Great War').

V

I want to conclude by considering, all too briefly, three further problems about referring uses.

(a) *Indefinite references.* Not all referring uses of singular expressions forestall the question 'What (who, which one) are you talking about?' There are some which either invite this question, or disclaim the intention or ability to answer it. Examples are such sentence-beginnings as 'A man told me that . . .', 'Someone told me that . . .' The orthodox (Russellian) doctrine is that such sentences are existential, but not uniquely existential. This seems wrong in several ways. It is ludicrous to suggest that part of what is asserted is that the class of men or persons is not empty. Certainly this is *implied* in the by now familiar sense of implication; but the implication is also as much an implication of the *uniqueness* of the particular object of reference as when I begin a sentence with such a phrase as 'the table'. The difference between the use of the definite and indefinite articles is, very roughly, as follows. We use 'the' either when a previous reference has been made, and when 'the' signalizes that the same reference is being made; or when, in the absence of a previous indefinite reference, the context (including the hearer's assumed knowledge) is expected to enable the hearer to tell *what* reference is being made. We use 'a' either when these conditions are not fulfilled, or when, although a definite reference *could* be made, we wish to keep dark the identity of the individual to whom, or to which, we are referring. This is the *arch* use of such a phrase as 'a certain person' or 'someone'; where it could be expanded, not into 'someone, but you wouldn't (or I don't) know who' but into 'someone, but I'm not telling you who'.

(b) *Identification statements.* By this label I intend statements like the following:

(ia) That is the man who swam the channel twice on one day.

(ii*a*) Napoleon was the man who ordered the execution of the Duc d'Enghien.

The puzzle about these statements is that their grammatical predicates do not seem to be used in a straightforwardly ascriptive way as are the grammatical predicates of the statements :

(i*b*) That man swam the channel twice in one day.

(ii*b*) Napoleon ordered the execution of the Duc d'Enghien.

But if, in order to avoid blurring the difference between (i*a*) and (i*b*) and (ii*a*) and (ii*b*), one says that the phrases which form the grammatical complements of (i*a*) and (ii*a*) are being used referringly, one becomes puzzled about what is being said in these sentences. We seem then to be referring to the same person twice over and either saying nothing about him and thus making no statement, or identifying him with himself and thus producing a trivial identity.

The bogy of triviality can be dismissed. This only arises for those who think of the object referred to by the use of an expression as its meaning, and thus think of the subject and complement of these sentences as meaning the same because they could be used to refer to the same person.

I think the differences between sentences in the (*a*) group and sentences in the (*b*) group can best be understood by considering the differences between the circumstances in which you would say (i*a*) and the circumstances in which you would say (i*b*). You would say (i*a*) instead of (i*b*) if you knew or believed that your hearer knew or believed that *someone* had swum the channel twice in one day. You say (i*a*) when you take your hearer to be in the position of one who can ask : 'Who swam the channel twice in one day ?' (And in asking this, he is not saying that anyone did, though his asking it implies — in the relevant sense — that someone did.) Such sentences are like answers to such questions. They are better called 'identification-statements' than 'identities'. Sentence (i*a*) does not assert more or less than sentence (*ib*). It is just that you say (*ia*) to a man whom you take to know certain things that you take to be unknown to the man to whom you say (*ib*).

This is, in the barest essentials, the solution to Russell's puzzle about 'denoting phrases' joined by 'is'; one of the puzzles which he claims for the Theory of Descriptions the merit of solving.

(*c*) *The logic of subjects and predicates.* Much of what I have said of the uniquely referring use of expressions can be extended, with suitable modifications, to the non-uniquely referring use of expressions; *i.e.* to some uses of expressions consisting of 'the', 'all the', 'all', 'some', 'some of the', etc. followed by a noun, qualified or unqualified, in the *plural*; to some uses of 'they', 'them', 'those', 'these'; and to conjunctions of names. Expressions of the first kind have a special interest. Roughly speaking, orthodox modern criticism, inspired by mathematical logic, of such traditional doctrines as that of the Square of Opposition and of some of the forms of the syllogism traditionally recognized as valid, rests on the familiar failure to recognize the special sense in which existential assertions may be implied by the referring use of expressions. The universal propositions of the fourfold schedule, it is said, must *either* be given a negatively existential interpretation (*e.g.* for A, 'there are no Xs which are not Ys') *or* they must be interpreted as conjunctions of negatively and positively existential statements of, *e.g.*, the form (for A) 'there are no Xs which are not Ys, and there are Xs'. The I and O forms are normally given a positively existential interpretation. It is then seen that, whichever of the above alternatives is selected, some of the traditional laws have to be abandoned. The dilemma, however, is a bogus one. If we interpret the propositions of the schedule as neither positively, nor negatively, nor positively *and* negatively, existential, but as sentences such that *the question of whether they are being used to make true or false assertions does not arise except when the existential condition is fulfilled for the subject term*, then all the traditional laws hold good together.   And this interpretation is far closer to the most common uses of expressions beginning with 'all' and 'some' than is any Russellian alternative.   For these expressions are most commonly used in the referring way.   A literal-minded and childless man asked whether all his children are asleep will certainly not answer 'Yes' on the ground that he has none; but nor will he answer 'No' on this ground. Since he has no children, the question does not arise.   To say this is not to say that I may not use the sentence, 'All my children are asleep', with the intention of letting someone know that I have children, or of deceiving him into thinking that I have.   Nor is it any weakening of my thesis to concede that singular phrases of the form 'the so-and-so' may sometimes be used with a similar purpose.   Neither Aristotelian nor Russellian rules give the exact logic of any expression of ordinary language; for ordinary language has no exact logic.

11 ON DESCRIBING

by S. E. Toulmin and K. Baier

DESCRIPTIONS can be as emotive as you please, and are never 'true or false'.

If this truism appears paradoxical, that shows only how far the terms 'describe', 'description', 'descriptive' and the like have been distorted in recent philosophical discussions.

Unfortunately, philosophers have made these changes unwittingly, and have as a result been driven into defending untenable positions. Indeed, the whole programme, in connection with which these words have acquired their recent philosophical currency, is ill-conceived. For the aim has been to throw light on the status of controversial types of utterance, such as moral ones, by drawing a single, sharp distinction; this has been marked by such pairs of words as 'descriptive' and 'emotive', 'descriptive' and 'normative', 'description' and 'prescription', and 'description' and 'decision'; and has frequently been identified with the distinction between the classes of statement to which the epithets 'true' and 'false' can and cannot be applied. Such a programme, it will be argued, rests on a misunderstanding of the ways in which we classify our utterances, and on an over-simplification of the process by which language is made to serve our purposes.

I

In this first section, we shall consider briefly some of the conditions which have to be fulfilled if we are to make proper use of the verb 'describe'.

The reasons for concentrating on the verb 'describe', rather than the noun 'description' or the adjective and adverb 'descriptive' and 'descriptively', will become clear as we go along. It may be said at once, however, that these different parts of speech can generally be used equivalently, so that the conditions for the use of one will, *mutatis mutandis*, apply equally to the others. Thus we can say, alternatively:

"In the first part of his paper, Rutherford describes his apparatus"; "The first part of Rutherford's paper describes his apparatus"; "The first part of Rutherford's paper is a description of his apparatus"; or, less elegantly, "The first part of Rutherford's paper is descriptive of his apparatus"; and each of these ordinarily entails that the first part of Rutherford's paper is a description or is descriptive. Notice particularly that, when we say of a chapter, paragraph or passage that *it* describes so-and-so, we are imputing no activity to the passage itself; for to say this is equivalent to saying that, in the chapter, paragraph or passage, *the author* describes so-and-so. This point is none the less important for seeming obvious and trivial. For people have sometimes tried to explain on what conditions a passage can properly be said to describe so-and-so by reference to the form of the passage, the sorts of words used in it, etc. *alone* : as we shall see, however, it is necessary to pay attention rather to the circumstances in which the author wrote or published the passage. And the same applies to the associated words ' description ' and ' descriptive '.

The sense of the word ' describe ' with which we are concerned is an unusually precise one. Indeed, the compilers of the *Shorter Oxford Dictionary* go out of their way to label it as ' the ordinary current sense '. They mention otherwise only such non-linguistic senses as that in which the figure of a gladiator can be said to be described upon marble, or a triangle upon a line, and that in which the sun describes a circle in the heavens. There are, nevertheless, two markedly different uses to which the word is put, which it will be necessary to keep distinct.

For our purposes, the more important use of the word is that in which John Doe can only be said to describe anything if what he writes or says consists of one or more complete sentences, mentioning *inter alia* a number of characteristics of the thing concerned. This use is also the one which most closely fits the *Shorter Oxford* definition : ' to set forth in words by reference to characteristics ; to give a detailed or graphic account of '. We may compare " John Doe described so-and-so to Richard Roe " with " John Doe reported on such-and-such to Richard Roe ", which also implies the use of at least one complete sentence; and we can oppose it to " John Doe welcomed Richard Roe " and " John Doe is teaching Richard Roe the alphabet ", which ordinarily imply the use of speech, but not necessarily of complete sentences.

On occasion, however, we use the word ' describe ', in the form of words ' describe . . . as . . . ', in a way which implies rather the use of a noun or noun-phrase. Thus, *Pravda* might be said to describe Marshal Tito as ' the servile lackey of the

Imperialist West ', a letter to the *Times* describe television as ' a menace to the mental health of the younger generation ', and a sophisticated tramp describe himself as ' a wayfarer '. This use is a very weak use, having little of the precision of the primary use. At its weakest, " John Doe *described* so-and-so *as* such-and-such " means only " John Doe *called* so-and-so ' such-and-such ' ", or " John Doe *said that* so-and-so *was* such-and-such ". It is accordingly important to keep these two uses distinct. We shall find later that, from the beginning of the recent philosophical discussion of ' descriptions ', these very different uses have been telescoped.[1]

The corresponding senses of the noun ' description ' can easily be distinguished. The primary sense is used to refer to passages or utterances consisting of one or more sentences, and calls for such epithets as ' detailed ' and ' graphic ' : the weaker sense is used to refer to a noun or noun-phrase, and calls rather for such epithets as ' apt ', ' appropriate ' and ' grotesque '. To see just how different these senses are, notice that we might even have occasion to ask how far to use a particular description (noun-phrase) would be to describe its object, *i.e.* whether the description was at all descriptive ; and it might very well be held not to be at all so. For the question is : if the ' description ' (noun-phrase) is reformulated as a sentence or series of sentences and offered as a description (primary sense), how far will it be acceptable as one ? Suppose, for instance, that the noun-phrase ' the servile lackey of the Imperialist West ' is replaced by the sentence, " Marshal Tito's chief characteristic is servility, and his behaviour towards the Imperialist West is that of a lackey " : then we can always ask, how far this could be accepted as a description of Marshal Tito, in the primary sense of the word. And it is this primary sense on which we shall concentrate for the rest of this section.

Suppose, therefore, that John Doe has written or uttered some string of words : in what circumstances will it be appropriate to say that he was *describing* something ? Several different types of condition must commonly be fulfilled. These are concerned, respectively, with John Doe's audience, the topic or subject of his utterance, his position *vis-à-vis* his audience and subject, the purpose which the utterance is designed to serve, and the extent to which it does in fact serve this purpose. Let us consider these in turn.

---

[1] *Punch* exploited this distinction some years ago (Jan.–June 1934, p. 374): *Policeman,* to man with black eye, "Can you describe your assailant ? " *Man,* "That's what 'e 'it me for, describing 'im ! "

Audience.—To say of John Doe that he is describing something implies that he has an audience. John Doe describes so-and-so *to Richard Roe.*

Consider what we say if this condition is not fulfilled. Suppose, for instance, that John Doe is alone on a mountain-top, and utters a string of sentences—either " Monte Generoso is 1700 metres in height and commands a magnificent view of the Alps : there is a funicular railway up the Swiss side, but easy tracks lead to the summit from both sides . . . ", or else " Here the elements struggle for mastery against a backcloth of rock and snow. How the knife-edge of the wind catches at our throats as we crest the lonely summit, while the dark caterpillar of the train crawls off round the shoulder. . . . " Are we to say in such a case that he is describing the mountain ? If not, how are we to classify his utterance ?

What we shall say depends upon a number of things. If he simply murmurs the words to himself, without any intention of presenting them to an audience—and especially if he makes no attempt to record them or commit them to memory—we shall say that he is soliloquizing, talking to himself about the mountain. If he says them over to himself slowly and several times, gradually improving or adding to them, intending later on to write them down and publish them, or to utter them to some friend down at the hotel, or to his club back home, we may speak of him as composing a possible description of the mountain. If he first jots them down and then declaims them to see how they sound, we may say that he is rehearsing his description of the mountain. One can think of many different cases.

Notice, however, that in none of the cases does one say that he *is* describing the mountain, for to do that immediately gives rise to the question, " To whom ? " Certainly in many of them one can speak of his words as constituting a (possible) description of the mountain, but to do so is to look forward to the time when the sentences he is composing or rehearsing or jotting down *will* be published, or uttered to an audience. In reporting the one case in which no question of later publication arises, one can hardly say more than that his soliloquy took the form of a description of the mountain—*i.e.* that in other circumstances it might have done duty as one. The words which he uttered to himself may be *the very words* in which he later describes the mountain to Richard Roe ; their *meaning* may be exactly the same in both cases ; nevertheless, when he first uttered them he was not describing the mountain. To describe a mountain to someone, is to do one thing ; to rehearse a description of it, for later delivery to someone, is to do another ; to soliloquize about it for your own private ear alone, in words taking the form of a description, is to do a third.

Topic.—If we are to use the word ' describe ' to report what John Doe said to Richard Roe, it must make sense to ask *what* John Doe described, what was the topic or subject of his description. John Doe describes *so-and-so* to Richard Roe. The verb ' describe ', in other words, must have an object ; and a number of points arise about this object.

(i) Not anything and everything can be the topic of a description. We can describe persons and things, such as Mr. Gladstone, New College garden, a chair or a dress ; events and incidents, such as the Opening of Parliament or a car accident ; processes and techniques, such as Bessemer's method of steel production or how to make almond fingers ; and much besides. But a fact, which is sometimes spoken of as though it were the topic *par excellence*, cannot be described : it can only be stated. Further, a statement of fact about something may sometimes constitute the beginning of description of that thing, as in " Their Christmas tree was decorated only with candles ". But very often it will not : " Hurry up ! Mother is waiting ", or " It is ten past four ". This is one indication of the differences between a description and a statement of fact. ' Description ' is not a word parallel to the phrase ' statement of fact ' : it refers rather to a *type of use* to which a sentence may be put.

(ii) The thing described must be what it is held out as being. One cannot say in general what this means, but some illustrations will help to make the point clear. If the utterance purports to describe a certain material object, such as a house, chair, or dress, then this object must exist at the time the description refers to ; if an event, happening, incident or episode, then this must have occurred at the material time ; if a figure in a novel, a fairy-tale or a mythology, then there must really be such a figure in that novel, fairy-tale or mythology ; if some process, method or technique, then there must really be such a process, method or technique. If John Doe describes Mr. Pickwick to Richard Roe on the understanding that he is telling him about a character in a novel, well and good ; but if he lets it be thought that he is talking about his best friend, and so a real person, Roe may complain that Doe was only ' pretending to describe ' someone. There is no King of France, no Greek god called Venizelos, no famous heroine called Francesca Pepper, no technique of intuiting ; hence there can be no description of the King of France, etc. Someone who, thinking that there was, claimed to be describing one of them, would merely think that he was. In fact, he would either, and unwittingly, be describing something else which he had taken for the King of France, say, or else not be describing anything at all—however much what he said might take the form of, and purport to be, a description. Again, if John Doe empties his safe, ties himself to his chair, and rings for the police, the story he tells them about masked men stealing the firm's ready cash cannot be called a description of a robbery, for there has been no robbery. What he tells them is all made up.

(iii) At some point it must be specified what *sort* of thing is being described : characteristics alone do not ordinarily suffice. Unless either John Doe or Richard Roe has already indicated what is being, or is to be, described, John Doe's words must, *inter alia*, do so : " What I have lost is a six-week-old, tabby *kitten*, with a white waistcoat. . . . " If this is not done, John Doe's words will be understood, not as a description, but perhaps as a riddle : " It walks on four legs in the morning, two at midday, three in the evening. (What is it ?) "—though notice once again that a riddle, like a soliloquy or a false report, may take the form of a description.

Relative position of speaker and audience.—If John Doe is to be said to be describing something to Richard Roe, he must be in a better position than Roe to speak about it. One special case is important : we should not usually talk of Doe describing to Roe something which was there in front for both of them to see. We happily speak of a radio commentator as describing a football match to his unseeing audience, but are less happy to use the word of a television commentator, who follows the play for viewers, for the viewers can see what is going on. Yet the words used by the two men may be the same.

Thus, John Doe can describe the view from M. Generoso to Richard Roe, provided Roe has never been up the mountain, or never in such good conditions. But if they are together on the summit we could speak of Doe describing the view to Roe only if Roe were, say, blind, and so unable to see for himself. Again suppose that, after both seeing the view, they go home, and Doe writes a description of it, *e.g.* for delivery to his Rotary Club : if Doe reads this over to Roe, we can still not say that he is describing the view to him, for Roe knows the view quite as well as Doe. Rather we shall have to say some such thing as, that he is trying out his description on him.

Two apparent exceptions to this : (i) Even if they were both on the top of M. Generoso, with Monte Rosa clearly visible, one might yet in certain circumstances speak of John Doe as describing M. Rosa to Richard Roe. But this would be, perhaps, because Roe did not know which of the many mountains he could see was M. Rosa; and John Doe would describe it for him so as to enable him to pick it out : " It's the one at the left-hand end of the chain, with a row of spiky peaks like a comb ". We can, that is, speak of Doe ' describing ' something to Roe, either if they both know what exactly is being described but Doe is or has been in a better position to observe it than Roe, or if both are equally well placed, but the auditor needs a description in order to identify that to which his attention is being drawn.

(ii) We learn at school about such things as ' the llama ' and ' Bessemer's method of making steel ', and may have to repeat to the teacher or examiner the descriptions from which we learnt about them. Accordingly the examination paper may, for brevity, read, " 5. Describe the llama ". But there remains something paradoxical about saying, " Johnny is describing the llama to his natural history master ", when the master knows so much more about the animal than he does. Only if Johnny had come from South America or Whipsnade, or had worked in a steel-works, could he, in the full sense of the phrase, describe the llama or Bessemer's method to the teacher.

One rather complicated example—Suppose John Doe and Richard Roe have both seen the same incident, but separately and unknown to each other ; then Doe may talk about it to Roe afterwards, and say of himself that he is describing the incident to Roe. Roe, however, may not be happy about calling Doe's words a description, feeling that Doe is in no position to describe to him an incident about which he knows quite as much, if not more. He might prefer to say, for instance, that John Doe was giving him his account of the incident. Here again, there need be no quarrel between them as to the exact *words* Doe used : the decision to apply or withhold the word ' description ' is made on other grounds.

Function.—Roughly speaking, we say that John Doe is describing something to Richard Roe only if the purpose of his utterance is of a kind which a picture might serve. Many of the foregoing points arise out of this fact.

(i) The purpose of a description, and equally of a picture, is in many cases to act as an aid to recognition. Thus a police notice, or a notice about a missing animal, will consist largely of a description of the wanted man or the lost dog. And it will be a better description in proportion as it helps the reader to recognize the man or the dog. Very often, indeed, a police notice will include a photograph of the wanted man. And further, the better the picture, the less need there is of a description. If, to take an extreme case, a coloured and moving waxwork, uttering typical remarks in the appropriate accent, were sent round to police stations instead of a ' Wanted ' notice, it need hardly be accompanied by any description at all.

In the case of descriptions of events and techniques, the same sort of thing often holds.   Thus the eye-witnesses of a car accident may be called on by the police to describe the accident as they saw it ; their descriptions will be the better, the more nearly they will do duty for a suitably-taken ciné film of the accident ; and if such a film of the accident were in fact available, the descriptions would hardly be needed.   Again, a speaker on the wireless may describe a method of making Dundee cake ; the description will be the better, the more nearly it will do instead of a demonstration ; and, given a demonstration, one hardly needs a description.

It is the purpose of such descriptions that explains why their typical merits and demerits are what they are—namely : exactness, minuteness, accuracy, detail, fullness, sketchiness, misleadingness and so on.   And the justice of the comparison of descriptions with pictures will be seen if one notices how many of the corresponding epithets, ' exact ', ' minute ', etc., could be used equally of a drawing.

(ii) In other cases, a picture is drawn or painted in such a way that likeness is wholly or partly sacrificed for the sake of something else. The picture is then a success if it is ' vivid ', ' graphic ', ' colourful ', ' stirring ', ' atmospheric ', ' evocative ', or ' moving '. It serves its purpose, that is, not in the way that a passport photograph, or the picture in a ' Wanted ' notice does, but in some other way.

The same is true of descriptions. The primary merit of a description is not always that it is exact or detailed : at other times, and for other purposes, we may value a description for being colourful or vivid, for taking one in imagination to the place described, for being a stirring description of a battle, or for being moving, perhaps like Dickens' description of the death of Little Nell.

In consequence, there is no more one and only one description of anything than there is one and only one picture of it. For, whatever we are talking about, we may want to do a number of things involving it, any of which a picture or a description can forward.   The things which Baedeker chooses to record about Florence in his description of it will accordingly differ from those which a student of architecture and still more a poet would include—just as a photograph of the Ponte Vecchio would differ from an architectural drawing of it, and that again from an Impressionist painting of it.

(iii) It is helpful to contrast those things which we do call descriptions (*i.e.* verbal substitutes for pictures, films and demonstrations) with other uses of language which, by themselves, we do not call descriptions. Thus to say of what sort a thing is is not necessarily to describe it ; to say where it is is not to describe it ; to tell someone the way from Oxford to Cheltenham is not to describe the road between those towns ; to say what happened is not necessarily to describe an event ; to say how you did something is not necessarily to describe your method of doing it.

(*a*) John Doe tells Richard Roe that he has lost his pet animal. Roe : " What sort of animal ? " Doe : " A zebra ". Roe finds a zebra straying half a mile down the road, secures it, and telephones Doe : " I've found what must be your zebra ". Here Doe has only told Roe of what sort his missing pet is ; he has not described it to him ; and correspondingly Roe cannot say, after encountering it, that he recognized it as Doe's zebra. To describe the zebra, Doe must mention salient and special characteristics for Roe to look out for, such as two pink stripes on the withers and a lop ear ; and only if he is told such things as these can Roe later say, " I recognized it as yours from your description ".

Where no classification is available (or known to the speaker), a description may be used *faute de mieux*. Doe : " I don't know of what breed my dog is, but let me describe it to you. It has the head of a spaniel, but the hindquarters of a sealyham. . . ." This use of ' description ' begins only where classification dries up. For to classify something, to say what it is, is to tell in what pigeonhole it belongs : to describe it, to say what it is like, is to say only what are the nearest pigeonholes, when there is no particular (known) one to specify. The commoner use of ' description ', by contrast, is to tell how a particular thing may be distinguished from, or recognized from among, others belonging in the same pigeonhole, or passing under the same common noun.

(*b*) John Doe invites Richard Roe to go and look at his pet zebra. Roe : " Where is it ? " Doe : " You'll find it in the paddock." Given this information, Roe will be able to locate Doe's zebra, and so, unless he finds several of them there, to identify it ; but once again he cannot claim to have recognized it, for Doe has only told him where it is, and has not described it.

(*c*) To tell someone the way from Oxford to Cheltenham is one thing, to describe to him the road from Oxford to Cheltenham is another. An itinerary may be full of facts about the route, yet we distinguish between this and a description of the route. The latter will give one not so much instructions for getting from the one place to the other, as a pre-view of the route. It will tell one, for instance, that the road is winding and hilly, but with a good surface, that it runs through wooded valleys to begin with, changing later to bare uplands, that it passes this striking church and that beauty spot, and so on.

(d) To tell someone what happened is one thing, to describe an event to him is another. "A bomb hit the house" tells him what happened. To describe the event one might say, "We had been lying underneath the staircase all evening. Mother was just saying to Father, ' I wonder whether we should go upstairs : I think I heard the All-Clear ', when there was a terrific crash, Father was thrown against the wall. . . ." Similarly, to say how you did something may require only the words, "I used Bessemer's method" or "I followed Mrs. Beeton's recipe"; whereas to describe your method of doing it would be a far longer task.

The success of a description.—In order to describe something, we must ordinarily mention a number of things about it. One brush-stroke does not make a picture. Grammatically speaking, therefore, a description is normally a complex affair. Accordingly, we may ask whether the individual statements composing a description are true or false, but we never ask of the description as a whole, whether it is true or false. The questions which arise in practice are always whether enough information has been given for the purpose in hand, that is, whether the description is sufficiently full ; whether it is accurate or accurate so far as it goes ; whether it has been appropriately selected and presented, that is, whether it is balanced, one-sided, or misleading, and so on. The ways in which a description can be improved are, correspondingly, by giving more information, correcting some of the component statements, going into more detail on some points, removing misunderstandings about others, and so on—and this is quite different from (and a more complicated business than) correcting a single statement. Where descriptions are concerned, there is no place for the simple black-and-white distinction between ' true ' and ' false ', so it is no wonder that in practice we never apply these epithets to them.

What we frequently do instead is to use the words ' describe ' and ' description ' in a way which implies success. To speak of John Doe as having described so-and-so to Richard Roe then implies, not only that his utterance satisfied the conditions we have already noticed, but also that it was sufficiently full, fair, accurate and well-balanced. If we feel that this is not the case, we can challenge his words by saying that he has misdescribed the thing—that what he said was a misdescription, never that it was a false description. This is a fairly general charge, and may preface a number of different sorts of criticism (the answers to the question " In what respect ? ") ; and it is also a fairly serious one, which we reserve for cases in which we can point to many or big inaccuracies, a misleadingly one-sided selection, etc. The charge that an utterance is a ' misdescription ' must, of course, not be confused with the statement that it is ' not a description at all ' : the one finds fault with what is said, the other with a suggested classification of the utterance.

There is, nevertheless, one use we do make of the phrase ' a true description '. When making a formal statement (*e.g.* to the police) we may have to sign a declaration to the effect that the facts stated constitute a ' full and true description ' of an event, say. But this is manifestly a declaratory use of the word : by signing, one certifies the description, and thereby commits oneself in various ways, laying oneself open to penalties if the information turns out to have been incorrect. There is no room in such a case for true to be opposed to false. To write out a description of something and sign under it the declaration, " The above is a false description of . . .", would be self-stultifying and lead to paradox in the way in which it would, if one were to use formulae like " I dishonestly assure you that . . ." or " I insincerely promise to . . ." One cannot give a description and challenge it, at the same time and in the same words. And notice: even if one challenges a description which someone else declares to be true, one will not have occasion to use the simple word ' false ', but rather such phrases as ' inadequate and misleading ', ' riddled with inconsistencies ', and ' a tissue of falsehoods '. Notice the metaphors : the description is a cloth made up of individual statements which are threads, or a shield, which is vulnerable, in so far as the individual statements composing it are false.

When checking individual items of information in the description, we may use the words ' correct ' and ' incorrect '. Thus, in John Doe's description of Monte Generoso, the mountain may be ' incorrectly stated to be, or described as ' 2,000 metres high. But it is the individual statements which are correct or incorrect, not the description as a whole : this we speak of rather as accurate or inaccurate. It is sometimes tempting to talk as though one could extend the use of ' correct ' and ' incorrect ' to the description itself, and accordingly to look for *the* one and only 'correct' description. But there are no correct or incorrect descriptions except in the 'describe . . . as . . .' sense, the noun-phrase sense, in which to describe Princess Elizabeth as 'the heir-apparent to the throne of England' is obviously to give a correct description of her. And notice that, when we use the phrase 'describe. . . as . . .' and the corresponding sense of 'description', we do not imply anything about the truth, accuracy or correctness of what has been said : we do not, in this sense, oppose 'describing' to 'misdescribing'. Whatever the height of Monte Generoso, John Doe can properly be said to 'describe it as 2,000 m. high '.

Our use of the phrase 'complete description' must also be noticed. In the case of such things as inventories, verbatim reports and balance-sheets, there is a use for the pair of terms 'complete '/' incomplete' quite distinct from that of the pair of terms 'finished '/' unfinished ', for we have a standard, an ideal, which such things must attain in order to be called 'complete ' : every item or word or asset and liability must be included. In the case of descriptions, this is not so : there is no end to the number of things we might put into a description of anything. So we ordinarily contrast a complete description with an uncompleted, interrupted, unfinished one. Sometimes, it is true, we may be asked, "Have you completed your description ? " or "Is this a complete description ? " meaning not "Have you finished saying what you intend to say ? " but "Have you included all the relevant information you know ? " or " Have you mentioned everything required by the authorities ? " But it always makes sense to talk of adding to a description, making it fuller than it is : the ideal of a complete description as one which enumerates *all* the qualities of the thing described is accordingly an illusion.

II

To give an exhaustive account of the notion of a description would be a very large task : it is enough for our purposes to show in outline what sorts of job the word 'describe' and its derivatives have. And one thing comes out even from a cursory examination : namely, that the words 'describe ', 'description ', and 'descriptive' mark off, not a particular class of sentences or words, still less a particular kind of subject-matter, or a type of effect that an utterance may produce, but rather a particular kind of way in which we *use* sentences and words.

The counterparts of the word 'describe', that is to say, are such words as 'declare', 'tell', 'record', 'report', 'account for', 'explain', 'predict', 'interrogate', 'reprimand', 'soliloquize', 'harangue', 'inform' and 'pray'. Each of these words marks off a particular sort of linguistic activity or performance, in the course of which sentences and words of *all* kinds may be used, so that the same sentence may well appear at one time in a description, and at another time in a report or a soliloquy. And, just as the same sentence is not confined to a single role on all occasions, so also it may have more than one role on a particular occasion of use : a report on the state of a mine may contain a description of the mine, and one can sometimes reprimand someone simply by describing to him how his behaviour appeared to others. Different kinds of linguistic performance are, therefore, not necessarily exclusive one of another. At the same time not all of them are compatible with one another : a soliloquy, as we have seen, can never be a description, however much it may take the form of one.

Among the sorts of classification in which the words 'describe', 'description' and 'descriptive' do *not* belong are the following : *grammatical* classification, as indicative, imperative, adjectival, interrogative ; *stylistic* classification, as poetic, slang, technical, flowery ; classification by *subject*, as geological, anatomical, scientific, legal, sporting, diplomatic, moral, economic ; and classification by *effect*, as boring, ineffective, discouraging, moving, stirring, heart-rending, blood-curdling. Nor do we say anything about the *meaning* of a passage by calling it a description.

There seems no reason to suppose that the categories in any two of these systems of classification need coincide : accordingly, for all that logic can show, it is possible to perform any linguistic activity, using passages containing each grammatical type of word and sentence, in any style, on any subject, with any effect. Certainly some combinations are incongruous, for practical reasons : one would rarely have occasion to soliloquize in geological terms, and it would be an ineffective harangue which consisted entirely of rhetorical questions expressed in sporting slang. Still, any of these things might be done, and several common and familiar possibilities are of philosophical importance.

A description, for instance, need not consist entirely of sentences in the indicative. One learns at school to interlard one's indicatives with imperatives, interrogatives and so on, so as to vary the style. This can produce a tiresome effect if badly managed, but few descriptions of any merit stick resolutely to the indicative throughout. In any case, one does not say that a passage or utterance which contains a sentence in a mood other than the indicative is *ipso facto* any less of a description, any less descriptive : the things that lead us to speak of it as a description are things about the circumstances in which it was uttered or published, not things about its grammar.

Again, a description may appear in a work on any subject, and be expressed in any kind of terms : there is no list of words which are allowed to appear in descriptions, or of words which are barred from them. The reverse is also true : thus a paper on physics will usually consist, partly of a description of an experimental apparatus, partly of a report on the results of an experiment made using the apparatus, and partly of a theoretical discussion of the significance of these results. One can have geological, anatomical, legal and sporting passages and utterances which are descriptions, and others which are not. One can have a geological description of the Galapagos Islands, a geological report on their mineral resources, or a geological explanation of the peculiar rock-formations there. Moral terms, likewise, are not, as one might suppose from what some philosophers have written, confined to harangues, reprimands, instructions, condemnations and the like : indeed, descriptions of character demand to be expressed in moral terms—" He is a saintly, courageous, kindly, and conscientious old man, to whom duty is a pleasure ", or " He is an unprincipled rascal, with an eye for the main chance alone ". And conversely, there are plenty of commands, reprimands and so on which are expressed in other than moral terms, and turn on other than moral considerations : instructions for the use of a coal-cutter, an adverse report on a brand of face-powder, and the like.

A description need be none the less a description for being emotive. Not all descriptions are bald and factual, any more than all pictures are photographic ; and some, like Dickens' description of Little Nell's death-bed are designedly moving. The effect which an utterance has on the reader or hearer is one thing, the kind of linguistic performance it represents is another, and a description no less than a story can be either boring or blood-curdling.

Two passages meaning exactly the same may one of them constitute a description, the other not ; and the same words may, without alteration of meaning, constitute a description on one occasion of use or to one hearer, but on another occasion or to another hearer not. This was brought out earlier, when we noticed that the same words might constitute first a soliloquy, and later a description, or first the rehearsal of a description, and later the description itself. Notice that, when we say that a particular soliloquy took the form of a description, we imply, not that it was a description, but rather that in other circumstances the same words could have served as a description.

'Descriptive' is an adjective neither of grammar, of style, of effect, nor of meaning: in the same way, a classification by subject is distinct from one by effect or style or meaning. A geological report may be depressing or heartening, and a moral defence may be vehement and winning or dispassionate and convincing. And there is something paradoxical about Stevenson's suggestion that one can identify the meaning of an utterance with its effect, even on suitably-conditioned hearers.

If we consider the wide use, 'describe . . . as . . .', and the corresponding 'noun-phrase' sense of the word 'description', the situation remains materially the same. If John Doe describes something as such-and-such, his description can be expressed in any terms, in any style, produce any effect and have any meaning. It may be appropriate or inappropriate, correct or incorrect, flattering, neutral or insulting, and designed to anger or appease or to do neither. We can describe something either as an unsuccessful attempt or as a praiseworthy effort, and someone either as a 68-year-old recidivist or as a villainous old rascal. Descriptions, in the noun-phrase sense of the word, are as often commendatory and condemnatory as descriptions in the primary sense.

To sum up: there are several different ways in which words and sentences, passages and utterances, can be classified. These cut across one another. One may classify a passage on grammatical and stylistic grounds, by subject, effect and meaning, and still leave open the question what kind of linguistic performance it constitutes; whether it was a description or not. The converse is also true. One can even interrogate someone without using interrogatives: "I put it to you that you then struck him with the hammer—deny that if you can!" And we all know those heart-rending descriptions full of sentences in the Dickensian imperative: "Struggle on, game heart, to sustain the last embers of life in the little frame!" And all this is independent of the further question, what sorts of passage and utterance it does, and what sorts it does not make sense to criticise as false, or to defend as true.

III

It has already been seen that the term ' description ' applies ordinarily, not to sentences as such, but to one of the uses to which sentences can be put. Mr. Strawson [1] and Mr. Warnock [2] have already drawn attention to this distinction in the cases of the terms ' refer ' and ' point ', and have shown how serious can be the consequences of ignoring it. And further, it should be clear by now that the distinction between describing and other types of linguistic performance and activity is a fairly subtle one.

In recent analytical philosophy, however, it has often been taken for granted that the terms ' describe ', ' description ' and ' descriptive ' are so simple as hardly to need examination, that they can be reserved for some class of words and sentences, as such, as opposed to a class of uses to which we can put any words and sentences in appropriate situations, and that they can be used at the same time to mark distinctions of grammar, of logic, of subject-matter, of psychological effect and of meaning.

In order to see how this has come about, we must go back a little into recent history, and see how the technical use of the term ' description ' has developed.

Some features of this technical use of the term spring originally from the work of Kirchhoff, Mach and Pearson [3] who applied it to scientific statements, laws and theories. Their point in so doing was to contrast scientific explanations with metaphysical ones, and to rebut the view that the task of science is to find hidden causes, and to reveal ' necessities in nature ' : Pearson in particular stresses the contrast between scientific laws, which are ' descriptive ', and civil laws which are ' prescriptive '. It was certainly not their aim to identify the terms ' scientific ' and ' descriptive ', or to suggest that they could be used interchangeably, as I. A. Richards later came to do. Nor could they consistently have done so, for they all agreed in regarding predictions as scientifically respectable pronouncements ; and predictions are not necessarily, and are perhaps never, descriptions. Nevertheless, one does find in their work the first, harmless deviations from our familiar idea of a description. Sometimes they treat the term as equivalent to ' simile ' or   model .

---

[1] " On Referring ", MIND, July, 1950.

[2] " Empirical Propositions and Hypothetical Statements ", MIND, January, 1951.

[3] *Cf.* E. Mach, *Popular Scientific Lectures*, pp. 190-225, and K. Pearson, *The Grammar of Science*, esp. ch. 3.

Sometimes they use it more as we do the term ' record ' ; and this last use leads naturally on to Carnap's use of the term ' *Protokol* ' for the fundamental type of descriptive statement.

Another influential use of the term was that made by Russell in his famous Theory of Descriptions. Russell called phrases such as ' the author of *Waverley* ', ' the highest mountain in Nebraska ', and ' the present King of France ' by the name of ' definite descriptions '. He had first called them denoting phrases, but abandoned this name because one of his main points was that such phrases may denote nothing ; and the phrase ' definite description ' seems to have struck him as more appropriate. He probably did not consider, or care very much, whether his use of this phrase was in line with our ordinary use or not. Nevertheless, he certainly tried to give the impression that it was. Consider the example he makes use of in his *Introduction to Mathematical Philosophy*, p. 167—" ' Who did you meet ? ' ' I met a man.' ' That is a very indefinite description.' " This is clearly intended to be understood in the ordinary, non-technical way. But the question asked, " Who did you meet ? " is not a request for a description. Nor is the reply, which properly answers the question, a description, but a very general and uninformative classification of the person met. One might, of course, if asked to describe the person you met, say in reply, " All I can tell you is that, to judge by the clothes, it was a man " —but this would amount to an admission that you could not comply with the request. Again, Russell seems to be following ordinary usage when he says (p. 140), " There are innumerable correct descriptions of any given object ". But at this point he shifts from the stricter sense of ' description ', which applies to a passage consisting of at least one complete sentence, to the very wide ' noun-phrase ' sense of the word, derived from the form ' describe . . . as . . .' : " Socrates ", he writes, " can be *described as* ' the master of Plato ', or as ' the philosopher who drank the hemlock ', or as ' the husband of Xantippe '." (Our italics.) And thereafter he uses ' description ' for *any phrase* that could ever be used to classify, describe, identify, refer to . . . something or someone, rather than for the use of such a phrase to describe it, or him. As a result, the conditions we examined in section I of this paper are all ignored : ' describe ' comes to be used, in the way ' describe . . . as . . .' is more commonly used, as equivalent to ' make a statement, whether true or false, about . . .' This foreshadows the technical use of ' description ', now common, to cover any sentence which can be spoken of as true or false.

Quite as important as Russell's use of the term 'description'
is the model of 'describing' introduced by Moore about the same
time. Consider the following quotation from his essay, "The
Conception of Intrinsic Value" (written before 1917, and published
in *Philosophical Studies*, 1922):

> "I can only vaguely express the kind of difference I feel there to
> be [between 'intrinsic properties' and 'value predicates'] by saying
> that intrinsic *properties* seem to describe the intrinsic nature of what
> *possesses* them in a sense in which predicates of value never do.
> if you could *enumerate* all the intrinsic properties a given thing
> possessed, you would have given a *complete description* of it, and would
> not need to mention any predicates of value it possessed ; whereas
> no description of a given thing could be complete which omitted any
> intrinsic property." (Our italics.)

Notice two things :

(a) Moore says (or implies) that, if asked to describe something, one would not use value predicates alone in one's reply.
This is true. One would not say, for instance, " It is good,
beautiful and priceless ". And if one did, one could not be said
to have given much of a description of the thing in question.

(b) It is a different matter, however, to suggest that value
predicates have no place at all in descriptions of things. One
would not use value predicates alone, certainly : but one would
not use size predicates or odour predicates alone either—predicates of several kinds would generally be needed.

Notice, therefore, that he also says (*The Philosophy of G. E.
Moore*, p. 590), that " in ascribing to a thing a property which is
not a natural intrinsic property [*e.g.* intrinsically good], you are
not describing it *at all*, whereas, if you ascribe to a thing a natural
intrinsic property, you always are describing it to some extent,
though, of course, the description may be very vague and very
far from complete." Here he implies that to describe something
is simply to ascribe to it certain kinds of property, *i.e.* to apply
certain classes of adjective to it. And this explains the italicized
words in his earlier paper ; for Moore's model of describing can
now be recognized. A description is an 'inventory of the intrinsic properties possessed by the thing described', and a
'complete' description one which 'enumerates all these properties '. This model of Moore's drops many of our normal
requirements about descriptions, but introduces a fresh one, for
in this inventory only certain kinds of property are to be listed :
namely, those which are 'intrinsically possessed by' the thing.
From this it is a short step to saying that certain kinds of adjective
are out of place in a description.

This next step was taken, a year after the publication of Moore's *Philosophical Studies*, in Ogden and Richards' *The Meaning of Meaning* (1923) : they conclude that certain words, *i.e.* those which 'stand for natural intrinsic properties', should be taken as peculiarly descriptive, and others, such as moral and aesthetic words, as peculiarly non-descriptive. Thus on pp. 124-25 they say :

> " Amongst these [very subtle dangers] is the occurrence, in hitherto quite unsuspected numbers, of words which have been erroneously regarded without question as symbolic in function. The word 'good' may be taken as an example . . . The word stands for nothing whatever [*i.e.* corresponds to no item in Moore's 'inventory'], and has no symbolic function. . . . It serves only as an emotive sign expressing our attitude . . ., and perhaps evoking similar attitudes in other persons, or inciting them to actions of one kind or another."

The authors do not say whether certain words are descriptive entirely and others emotive entirely, or whether all words are both descriptive and emotive, but in different proportions. They do, however, say quite plainly that, in certain uses, certain words are purely emotive, *e.g.* 'good' and 'beautiful'.

With this step, the technical use of the terms 'descriptive', 'description' etc. assumes its present form. At its most extreme, this use rests on the following doctrine. There are two large classes into which sentences, and the words which figure in them, can be divided. On the one hand, there are those sentences, to be dignified by the title of 'statements', which express propositions ; which are the concern of the sciences, and of those everyday activities which are like the sciences in having to do with facts and the stating of facts ; which express beliefs ; which are properly couched in the indicative mood ; and whose meaning consists in the cognitive or rational effect which their utterance has on a suitably-conditioned hearer's beliefs. These, and these alone, can be spoken of as true or false, according as the propositions which they express do or do not correspond with the facts. On the other hand, there are those sentences, to which it is advisable to deny the title of statements, which do not express propositions ; which are the concern of, for instance, ethics, aesthetics, poetry and cognate activities ; which express or evince attitudes ; which are only misleadingly couched in the indicative mood ; and whose meaning consists in the affective or persuasive effect which their utterance has on a hearer's attitudes. Since these sentences do not express propositions, there is no question of their being true or false. It is to the sentences in the first of these two large divisions and to the words which can appear in them, that the words 'descriptive' and 'description' have recently come to be applied. They have been spoken of and written about as 'descriptive statements and words', and contrasted with the 'emotive (normative, persuasive, prescriptive, imperatival, performatory) expressions' of the second group. Alternatively, they have been labelled as 'descriptions', and contrasted with the 'decisions', 'exclamations', 'ejaculations', 'prescriptions', 'proposals', 'formulae', etc. of the second group.

IV

The divergence between the ordinary uses of the words 'describe', 'description', 'descriptive', etc. examined in section I, and their technical use, whose development was sketched in the last section, is so great that it does not need to be underlined. But three things are worth emphasizing.   First, the divergence seems as a matter of history to have developed gradually, so that the writers responsible for each fresh departure probably made it unwittingly.   Secondly, from the beginning of this development the wide use, 'describe . . . as . . .', and the precise use have been telescoped.   Thirdly, the very paradigms of a 'description', in the technical sense—"this is red" and "this is a table", said when the thing concerned is currently under observation— would, in the ordinary sense, qualify for the title only in exceptional circumstances and then only by courtesy, since the hearer would have to be blind, or otherwise prevented from seeing the thing, and the words would have to be but the beginning of a longer utterance.   And perhaps it is worth repeating, yet again, that the technical use makes the use of the term dependent on the sort of words used ; whereas in the ordinary sense any words can in appropriate circumstances figure in a description.

"No doubt", someone may reply, "this is all very true, and even interesting.   Perhaps the terms are indeed used as you have argued.   And perhaps there are divergences between the ordinary and the philosophical uses.   But that does not mean that the philosophical use is a farthing the worse.   The most it shows is that philosophers have tumbled on rather an unhappy word to mark the distinction they are interested in.   So all that you can ask is that they replace the terms 'descriptive' and 'description' by others : 'informative' or 'fact-stating', and 'assertion' or 'statement' would do as well instead."

To this suggestion there is a two-fold reply.   To begin with, let any words be chosen to take the places of 'descriptive' and 'description', the situation remains as bad as ever ; for the distinction which they are required to mark is itself illegitimate. And in the second place, to drop the words ' descriptive ' and ' description ' for others would actually only make matters worse ; for all that serves to hide the illegitimacy of the distinction is the veil provided by the ordinary associations of these words.

These points must be explained. The philosophical distinction between descriptive statements and other sentences is illegitimate in an interesting way. For no one could say that there was no distinction here to be drawn. On the contrary, there are nine or ten, *viz.*

(i) the distinction of subject ; between the natural sciences, the social sciences, ethics, poetry, aesthetics, etc. ;

(ii) that of grammar ; between sentences couched in the indicative mood and other moods ;

(iii) that between sentences with different meanings :

(iv) that between describing and other types of linguistic performance and activity ;

(v) that of manner, style or mode of expression ; between the dry, flowery, technical, emotive, etc. ;

(vi) that between arguments relying for a great or small part of their weight on logical and careful reasoning ; between the reasoned and the merely persuasive ;

(vii) that of effect, between the boring, blood-curdling, etc., or, in the jargon of psychology, between the cognitive and the affective ;

(viii) that between beliefs, feelings, attitudes, etc. ;

(ix) that between the sorts of sentence and passage of which one can use the words ' true ' and ' false ', and others ;

(x) that between contexts in which one can use such phrases as ' a matter of fact ', ' that's a fact ', etc., and those in which one cannot.

These distinctions themselves probably need sub-dividing ; and we have not listed the further, technical distinctions between sentences which ' express propositions '/' correspond to facts '/ can be called ' statements ', and other sentences—for they serve only to enshrine the doctrine to which we object.

The trouble is, that these distinctions cut across one another. They are distinctions of different kinds, are drawn on different grounds, and in consequence cannot be expected to cut along the same line. There may be a few occasions on which we utter a sentence or argument which falls in every respect on one side or the other of the Great Divide. But this is certainly not always so, as the examples produced in section II indicate. When faced with a controversial class of utterances, which falls across the Divide, such as moral, aesthetic, mathematical, judicial, or ritual utterances, philosophers have too often reacted by consolidating some or all of these distinctions, and arguing as though they cut along the same line. But the result of welding these nine or ten different distinctions, or a selection of them, into a single, monolithic distinction is not to clear away the philosophical fog surrounding such utterances : it only thickens it.

Further, the arguments used to justify the division of all utterances into descriptive and others commonly involve appeals to the ordinary senses of the words. And only in this way are the paradoxical conclusions drawn from it given an appearance of inevitability. Thus Ayer, in the course of a paper on " The Analysis of Moral Judgments ",[1] writes : " A valuation is not a description of something very peculiar ; it is not a description at all." And this reads very plausibly, for of course, as we ordinarily use the words, a valuation is indeed one thing, a description another. Valuing (as a professional valuer does it) is indeed a different activity from describing, although a typical valuation does contain descriptions of the objects valued. Even if we understand ' valuation ', not in its everyday sense, but as meaning ' calling something " beautiful ", " good ", " right ", etc. ', the appeal is still plausible ; for the conditions on which something can count as a valuation, in this sense, are more stringent than those on which it can count as a description, in the ordinary sense. It must now be expressed in a special vocabulary, that is, in moral or aesthetic terms.

It is only when the word ' description ' is consciously taken in its technical sense that the claim, that ' a valuation is not a description at all ', becomes clearly questionable. For in the technical sense of the term, to agree to this commits us to some fair proportion of the following views : that moral terms are necessarily out of place in descriptions, that moral utterances are all normative, that one should not use the terms ' belief ', ' fact ', ' true ' or ' false ' in connection with moral utterances, that they are not really statements, and that they are only misleadingly couched in the indicative. But these are the very paradoxes which the appeal to our common-sense views about descriptions were intended to justify. The argument is, in other words, of the familiar form : ' Such-and-such does not constitute a description, in the ordinary sense ; only descriptions, in the technical sense, have the feature so-and-so (e.g. can be spoken of as true or false) ; ergo such-and-such has not got the feature so-and-so '

[1] *Horizon*, Sept. 1949, p. 179.

This can be confirmed if we consider the suggestion that the words ' description ' and ' descriptive ', in their technical sense, should be replaced by some other words. For if we try to use, in their place, any of the words which it is natural to suggest as alternatives—' informative ', ' fact-stating ', ' assertion ' or ' statement '—appeals to the ordinary uses of these words no longer carry the same weight ; they are ordinarily far from equivalent to ' description ' and ' descriptive '. Whereas it is plausible enough to say, " A valuation is not a description of something very peculiar ; it is not a description at all ", it is far less obvious that a valuation " does not give one information at all, not even information of a very peculiar kind ", that it " tells one no facts ", or that it " is not an assertion ". So the fact that philosophers have used the terms ' description ' and ' descriptive ' to mark their Great Divide is not just an unhappy accident : it is, rather, the one thing which gives the Divide some appearance of respectability.

Nor is the resemblance between Ayer's view that " A valuation is not a description at all " and Moore's view that, in calling something ' intrinsically good ', " you are not describing it *at all* " an accident either. For both conclusions are the result of thinking about adjectives as the names of properties, not just in a manner of speaking, but so strictly that you regard them as ascribing to objects properties which reside in them, and which could, in principle, be enumerated in an inventory or complete description. The pity is that, when Ogden and Richards pointed out the error of regarding ' good ', ' beautiful ' and the like as ' symbolic in function ', they did not recognize that it was quite as much of an error to regard ' red ', ' big ' and the like as ' symbolic in function '. That would have spared us many tears.

V

Many analytical philosophers to-day would refuse to subscribe to some part at least of the Great Divide. Nevertheless, it has left its mark, even on those who would reject the more paradoxical conclusions drawn with its aid. For one can see, easily enough, the impossibility of drawing, at a single stroke, all the ten or more distinctions which are concertina'ed in the extreme form of the doctrine ; but it is not so easy to disentangle completely the many things which it entangles. One pair of distinctions, in particular, remains obstinately glued together ; that between describing and other linguistic activities and performances, and that between utterances of which we can and cannot use the words 'true' and 'false'. (This is probably the effect of the secondary form, 'describe . . . as . . .', acting *via* Russell's 'theory of descriptions'.)

Thus Mr. Hart, in writing about judicial decisions, says : [1]

> "Since the judge is literally deciding that on the facts before him a contract does or does not exist, and to do this is neither to describe the facts nor to make inductive or deductive inferences from the statement of facts, what he does may be either a *right* or a *wrong* decision or a *good* or *bad* judgment and can be either *affirmed* or *reversed* and (where he has no jurisdiction to decide the question) may be *quashed* or *discharged*. What cannot be said of it is that it is either *true* or *false*, logically necessary or absurd."

And again he writes,[2] of the statement "Smith hit her", that

> "If, on investigating the facts, it appears that we should have said 'Smith hit her accidentally', our first judgment has to be qualified. But it is important to notice that it is not withdrawn as a false statement of fact. . . . Our ascription of responsibility is no longer justified in the light of the new circumstances of which we have notice. So we must judge again : *not describe again*."

In both these passages, it is assumed that only when we describe the facts can the things we say be true or false, and that to deliver a verdict or ascribe responsibility is incompatible with deciding the facts. In each case this assumption leads to paradox. For if Smith accidentally strikes Mrs. Jones, and Jones later comes and says to him "You hit her", Smith will certainly feel entitled to reply, "that's not true : it was an accident", and to insist that Jones has been misinformed as to the facts. This is not to deny that, as Mr. Hart illuminatingly remarks, to say "Smith hit her" is to ascribe responsibility to him, in a way in which to say "Smith hit her accidentally" is not. In the case of many judicial decisions, the paradox is still more marked. For, whatever may hold in contract cases, if in a murder trial the foreman delivers the verdict, "We find the prisoner *Guilty*", the prisoner may protest, "It's not true ! I didn't do it !", with perfect logical propriety. One may, of course, consider a verdict 'simply *qua* verdict', *i.e.* ask whether it was properly arrived at, and so restrict oneself to the question whether it was good or bad, whether it should be affirmed or reversed, accepted or appealed against. But it is in the nature of the law that verdicts should often imply things about what happened at the material time : so considered, they can very naturally be criticised as false (or should it be 'not true' ?).

[1] "The Ascription of Responsibility and Rights", *Proc. Arist. Soc.*, 1948-49, p. 182 (reprinted in Flew, *Essays on Logic and Language*, p. 155).
[2] *Op. cit.*, p. 193 (Flew, p. 165).

Only so long as one supposes that different types of linguistic performance are necessarily *exclusive* of one another can one conclude that a verdict, being, as it were, a performatory utterance, is thereby disqualified from being true or false.

It is true, as Mr. Hart says, that the Judge is not required " to make deductive or inductive inferences from the statement of facts ". But he is none-the-less required to make the *appropriate* kind of inferences : and, as with all inferences, we can ask two kinds of question about the conclusion, " Is it true ? " and " Does it follow ? ". Only by confining our attention to the latter question can we keep the word ' true ' out of the picture. But of course it *makes sense*, however improbable it may be, to say of the best and most carefully-drawn of judgments that it was a miscarriage of justice.

Mr. Austin, too, wishes to restrict ' true ' and ' false ' to descriptive statements, and opposes these to performatory utterances, value-judgments and the rest. Thus he writes : [1]

> " Recently it has come to be realized that many utterances which have been taken to be statements (merely because they are not, on grounds of grammatical form, to be classed as commands, questions, etc.) are not in fact descriptive, nor susceptible of being true or false. When is a statement not a statement ? When it is a formula in a calculus : when it is a performatory utterance : when it is a value-judgment : when it is a definition : when it is part of a work of fiction—there are many such suggested answers . . . It is a matter for decision how far we should continue to call such masqueraders ' statements ' at all, and how widely we should be prepared to extend the uses of ' true ' and ' false ' in ' different senses '. My own feeling is that it is better, when once a masquerader has been unmasked, *not* to call it a statement and *not* to say it is true or false."

And, to make no mistake, he has gone out of his way to call ' performatory ' utterances, like the words " I do " as used in the marriage service, by the name of ' non-descriptions '.[2]

Here again the last traces of the Great Divide can be seen. To begin with, grammatical form is accepted as a *prima facie* ground for regarding an utterance as being descriptive ; as being susceptible of being true or false ; and as being genuinely a statement. When these four independent distinctions are found not to cut cleanly along the same line, the offending utterances are accused of masquerading and thrust into outer darkness. But it is not the countless different ways in which we ordinarily classify utterances that are open to criticism : what is misconceived is, rather, the attempt to run them together.

---

[1] *Arist Soc. Supp. Vol.* xxiv, 1950, p. 125.
[2] The title of a paper read to the Cambridge University Moral Sciences Club, 1947.

As well might a man confound the distinction between cabbages and lettuces with the distinction between cabbage lettuces and cos lettuces ; insist on calling lettuces ' non-cabbages ' ; and dismiss the term ' cabbage lettuces ' as a misnomer.

Forms of words and vegetables alike, poor things, are incapable of masquerading.   But we who classify them, for our own purposes, may be confused about our own classifications. Just how our different distinctions are drawn, is something that no one has ever clearly stated.   The first thing is to recognize this fact : then we can begin on the laborious but indispensable task of coming to understand our own linguistic techniques.

12 PARENTHETICAL VERBS

by J. O. Urmson

I N this paper I intend to examine a group of verbs which are not usually considered as a group. Many of these verbs, including such important ones as *know, believe,* and *deduce,* are frequently misconstrued by philosophers, and their consideration as a group may help to get them into better perspective. None of these verbs is here examined exhaustively; in general only that which can be said of all is said of each. For convenience this group is here called the group of parenthetical verbs; no great significance should be attached to this title. Such significance as it has can more conveniently be explained later.

Delimitation of the group of parenthetical verbs. In prose the verb *to read* is used in the present continuous form 'I am reading' to report a contemporary happening; the present perfect form 'I read' is used only to report what one often, or habitually, does. This is true of most of the verbs in the language. It has been observed in recent years, but only, even by philologists, in recent years, that some verbs do not conform to this pattern, since they either have no present continuous tense, or, when they have, it is only so in one out of two easily distinguishable uses. Thus the verb *to prefer* has no present continuous tense, we never say 'I am preferring'; the verb *to wish* can have a present continuous form, as in 'I wish whenever I pass a wishing-well', 'I am wishing at a wishing-well', but has not when we say 'I wish that you would make up your mind'. Here in the third example the use of 'I wish' is similar to the use neither of 'I wish' nor of 'I am wishing' in the first two examples. It is clear, then, that these verbs are not simply defective of a present continuous tense, having only a normal present perfect tense ; for 'I prefer' and 'I wish' (as used in the third example) are not used in the way that 'I read' and 'I play' are used.

Some of these anomalous verbs are used normally with a direct object ; examples are *love, like, hate, prefer* : some are used normally with a subjunctive or other non-indicative clause ; examples are *wish, command, beg, beseech*. These verbs do not fall within the group of parenthetical verbs, and are not further discussed in this paper, though they are well worth discussing as groups. I intend to discuss only a special set of verbs which lack a present continuous tense, which must now be distinguished from the others.

Let us start with an example. Taking the verb *to suppose*, we may note that in the first person present we can idiomatically say any of the following :

> I suppose that your house is very old.
> Your house is, I suppose, very old.
> Your house is very old, I suppose.

A verb which, in the first person present, can be used, as in the example above, followed by 'that' and an indicative clause, or else can be inserted at the middle or end of the indicative sentence, is a parenthetical verb. Note that this is a grammatical distinction, and that these verbs are called parenthetical because of this grammatical feature of their use. 'Parenthetical' is sometimes used of a piece of information slipped into another context, but I do not wish to imply that these verbs are parenthetical in any sense except that they are sometimes used parenthetically in a purely grammatical sense ; beyond that 'parenthetical' is merely a convenient label. In some contexts it will be virtually indifferent, on all but stylistic grounds, whether the verb occurs at the beginning, middle, or end of the indicative sentence with which it is conjoined ; this will not always be so, but when it is the verb will be said to be used purely parenthetically. Thus in most contexts 'I suppose that your house is very old' would be used purely parenthetically, for it would mean virtually the same as either 'Your house is very old, I suppose' or 'Your house is, I suppose, very old'; if one person says 'I suppose that your house is quite new' and another says 'Well, I suppose that it is very old', then in the latter statement the verb *to suppose* is not being used purely parenthetically. We shall study parenthetical verbs in their more or less pure parenthetical use for the sake of simplicity; on other occasions most of what we have to say will remain true, but will be more or less far from being the full story. It would be perhaps more accurate to say that the features of parenthetical verbs to which I shall draw attention are one aspect of their use which is relatively more important on the occasions on which we shall concentrate than on others, but it is convenient to talk of a parenthetical use; purists may substitute *aspect* for *use* throughout.

Another preliminary point must be made before we get down to philosophical business. Part of what I design to show is how differently these verbs are used in the first person present and in other persons and tenses. Therefore we shall at first confine our attention to their pure parenthetical use in the first person present. It will be no accident therefore that all examples will be in this person and tense, nor will it be an objection to my thesis that what I say will not be true if examples in other persons or tenses are substituted for the ones given; it will in fact be a partial confirmation of my thesis.

A random and incomplete list of parenthetical verbs might be helpful at this stage: *Know, believe, deduce, rejoice, regret, conclude, suppose, guess, expect, admit, predict.* A few minutes' reflection will enable anyone to treble this list. Some of these verbs, like *conclude*, are always parenthetical, though of course not always used purely parenthetically. Others, like *rejoice*, may be non-parenthetical and have a present continuous tense; we shall only be concerned with these verbs when they are parenthetical. We shall find easy tests to distinguish their different uses.

Parenthetical verbs are not psychological descriptions. Let us take for comparison three sentences:

(1) I rejoice whenever my sailor brother comes home.

(2) I am rejoicing because my sailor brother is home.

(3) I rejoice that you have returned home at last.

In sentences (1) and (2) *rejoice* is not a parenthetical verb. In (1) the main verb reports the periodic recurrence of a psychological condition, the occasions of which are given in the subordinate clause ; in (2) the main verb reports that something is going on now, and the subordinate clause states the cause.   No such explanation can be given of (3), where *rejoice* is a parenthetical verb though not used purely parenthetically.   The point becomes even clearer if we contrast a purely parenthetical use with a clearly descriptive verb :

(A) He is, I regret, unwell.

(B) I am miserable because he is unwell.

Note that it would be absurd to say :

(A′) He is, I am miserable, unwell.

(B′) I regret because he is unwell.

'I am miserable' does, 'I regret' does not, describe a psychological condition.   In (B), 'because he is unwell' gives the cause of a mental state.   (B′) is absurd because a cause is given where nothing has been described needing a causal explanation.   It should surely be obvious that though we are, in some sense, dealing with psychological or mental verbs, they are not parts of psychological histories as are verbs like *ponder* or *be miserable*.   Nor, so far as I can see, is it any more plausible to say that they report dispositions to behave in certain ways.   This has, however, not seemed obvious in the case of some parenthetical verbs to some philosophers.   For while the difficulty of regarding 'I know' and 'I believe' as if they reported contemporary events (as if we said 'I am knowing' and 'I am believing') has been appreciated, many philosophers tend to treat *know* and *believe* as though they were simply defective of a present continuous tense.   Thus 'I know' and 'I believe' have been construed as ordinary present perfects implying, not the frequent truth of 'I am knowing' and 'I am believing', but of 'I am doing this thing and the other thing'. It is an alternative to this mistaken view that will shortly be given.

Implied claims to truth. Whenever anyone utters a sentence which could be used to convey truth or falsehood there is an implied claim to truth by that person, unless the situation shows that this is not so (he is acting or reciting or incredulously echoing the remark of another). This needs an explanation. Suppose that someone utters the sentence 'It will rain to-morrow' in ordinary circumstances. This act carries with it the claim that it is true that it will rain to-morrow. By this is meant that just as it is understood that no one will give orders unless he is entitled to give orders, so it is understood that no one will utter a sentence of a kind which can be used to make a statement unless he is willing to claim that that statement is true, and hence one would be acting in a misleading manner if one uttered the sentence if he was not willing to make that claim. The word 'implies' is being used in such a way that if there is a convention that X will only be done in circumstances Y, a man implies that situation Y holds if he does X.

This point has often been made before, though not always in these terms, and it is, I believe, in substance uncontroversial. I now wish to make the point that when a speaker uses a parenthetical verb of himself with an indicative sentence p, there is not merely an implied claim that the whole statement is true but also that p is true. This is surely obvious in some cases — 'I believe it will rain', 'He is, I regret, too old', 'You intend, I gather, to refuse'. But I think that a little thought shows that it is also true in the case of, say, 'I hear that he is ill in bed', or 'He is, I hear, ill in bed'. We should not and would not say these things if we did not accept the reports on which our statements were based, and by saying them we imply a claim to their truth. The claim to truth need not be very strong, we shall indeed find that the whole point of some parenthetical verbs is to modify or to weaken the claim to truth which would be implied by a simple assertion p; but even if we say 'He is, I suppose, at home', or 'I guess that the penny will come down heads', we imply, with however little reason, that this is what we accept as true.

Positive examination of parenthetical verbs. We make our statements in contexts, social as well as logical. For example, we often have an emotional attitude to the fact we state, or it is likely to arouse emotion in our hearers. To some extent, both by accident and by design, our manner, intonation, and choice of words betray our attitude and prepares our hearers. But this is imprecise and uncertain, and, in writing, is difficult to get right for all but the great stylist. Again, content and manner give some clue to the hearer or reader of how he is to understand the statement in relation to its logical context, but not infallibly. Further, we make our statements sometimes with good, sometimes with moderate, sometimes with poor, evidence; which of these situations we are in need not be obvious to the hearer, and it would be cumbersome always to say explicitly. It is my contention that parenthetical verbs are one of the sets of devices that we use in order to deal with these matters, though not the only set. By them we prime the hearer to see the emotional significance, the logical relevance, and the reliability of our statements. This we do not by telling him how we are moved or how he should be moved by them, nor by telling him how our statement fits into the context, nor by describing the evidential situation, but by the use of warning, priming or orientating signals; we show rather than state. This is the contention which will now be somewhat elaborated.

Suppose that I go to a mother in wartime as a messenger to inform her of the death of her son. I can, no doubt, merely say 'Madam, your son is dead'. But this would be abrupt and harsh, and I would more probably say 'Madam, I regret that your son is dead'. For anyone other than a great actor it is easier to steer a course between callousness and false sentiment as a stranger bearing news by the use of a parenthetical verb in this way than by means of intonation. Clearly

I am mainly bearing news, and the addition of 'I regret' (not necessarily at the beginning of the sentence) shows without it being actually said that it is being offered, and will be received as, sad news.   I am not being a hypocrite, even within the excusable, conventional, limits of hypocrisy, if I personally have no feelings on the matter at all — messengers of that sort can rarely have much feeling in wartime about each case.   If, for the moment, we turn to a less purely parenthetical use of the same verb, we shall find that the essential point remains the same.   If, as a friend of the family, I go to the mother when the death is well known and say 'I much regret that your son is dead, he was a dear friend' then, no doubt, I am no longer mainly bearing news.   But I am still not describing my feelings; it is rather that the signal is being made for its own sake as an act of sympathy, the indicative clause giving the occasion of my sympathy.   *Regret* and *rejoice* are two of the most obvious examples of verbs which give emotional orientation when used parenthetically.

Another set of these verbs is used to signal how the statement is to be taken as fitting logically into the discussion. 'I admit that he is able' assigns the statement that he is able to the logical position of being support for the opposed position, or a part of the opposed position which will not be assailed — one shows while saying that he is able that this is to be treated as an admission.   One is forestalling a possible misapprehension — 'But don't you see, that is part of my point' — one is not reporting the occurrence of a bit of admitting, whatever that may be supposed to be.   The parenthetical verb in 'Jones was, I conclude, the murderer' assigns to the statement the status of following from what has been said before, preventing it from being taken as, say, an additional fact to be taken into account.   There is no specific activity of concluding.   Other verbs which fulfil approximately similar tasks are *deduce, infer, presume, presuppose, confess, concede, maintain* and *assume*.

Another rough group is constituted by such verbs as *know, believe, guess, suppose, suspect, estimate*, and, in a metaphorical use, *feel*. This group is probably more controversial than the previous ones, and will require more explanation.   This is the group which is used to indicate the evidential situation in which the statement is made (though not to **describe** that situation), and hence to signal what degree of reliability is claimed for, and should be accorded to, the statement to which they are conjoined. Thus 'I guess that this is the right road to take' is a way of saying that this is the right road, while indicating that one is just plumping and has no information, so that the statement will be received with the right amount of caution; 'I know' shows that there is all the evidence one could need ; and so on. Some of these verbs can clearly be arranged in a scale showing the reliability of the conjoined statement according to the wealth of evidence — *know, believe, suspect, guess*, for example ; and adverbs can make the situation even plainer — 'I strongly believe', 'I rather suspect' and so on.   We are, in fact, in a position where we can either make our statements 'neat', and leave it to the context and the general probabilities to show to the hearer how much credence he should give to the statement ; or, in addition to making the statement we can actually describe the evidential situation in more or less detail ; or give a warning such as, 'Don't rely on this too implicitly, but . . .' ; or I can employ the warning device of a parenthetical verb 'I believe it will rain'.   If this is insufficient for any reason (perhaps it is an important matter), then the hearer can ask why and get the description of the evidential situation.   More will have to be said about these verbs, but it will be convenient first to introduce another topic.

Adverbs corresponding to parenthetical verbs. I mentioned earlier that parenthetical verbs were not the only device that we have for warning the hearer how our statements are to be taken while making it ; it will perhaps make it clearer how parenthetical verbs are used if one of these other devices is briefly outlined.   We were taught at school that an adverb modifies a verb ; but this is inaccurate, for some adverbs are quite as loosely attached to sentences as are parenthetical verbs. Examples are : *luckily, happily, unfortunately, consequently, presumably, admittedly, certainly, undoubtedly, probably*, and *possibly*. Note that the position of these adverbs is variable in relation to the sentence as in the case of parenthetical verbs ; we can say 'Unfortunately he is ill,' or 'He is, unfortunately, ill'. If the word 'modify' is to be used these adverbs can perhaps be said to modify the **whole** statement to which they are attached. But how do they modify them ? Surely by giving a warning how they are to be understood. *Luckily, happily* and *unfortunately* indicate the appropriate attitude to the statement, for example ; *admittedly, consequently* and *presumably*, among others, indicate how to take the statement in regard to the context ; *certainly, probably* and *possibly*, among others, show how much reliability is to be ascribed to the statement. Perhaps it is worth saying, though the matter should be sufficiently obvious, that no importance should be attached to the grouping of verbs and adverbs into three sets which has been adopted. It has been done purely for convenience in an outline exposition. There are differences between the members of each of my groups and the groups are not sharply divided ; it is easy to think of verbs which might with equal reason be placed in either of two groups. Once again it must be said that our aim is to lay down general lines for the interpretation of parenthetical verbs, not to do full justice to any of them.

Comparison of these adverbs and parenthetical verbs. Provided that it is not construed as a list of synonyms, we can couple these adverbs with parenthetical verbs as follows : happily — I rejoice ; unfortunately — I regret ; consequently — I infer (deduce) ; presumably — I presume ; admittedly — I admit ; certainly — I know ; probably — I believe. This is not, I repeat, a list of synonyms ; apart from questions of nuance of meaning the adverbs are more impersonal — *admittedly* suggests that what is said would be regarded by anyone as an admission whereas *I admit* shows only the way that the statement is to be regarded here. Also it is not possible to say that every adverb has a verb corresponding to it which has more or less the same import, or *vice versa*. But it does seem that these adverbs and parenthetical verbs play much the same rôle and have much the same grammatical relation to the statements which they accompany, and that, therefore, the comparison is illuminating in both directions.

But now I must meet an objection which will certainly be made by some philosophers to this comparison ; and I intend to meet it by a fairly detailed examination of the example which they themselves would most likely choose. In doing this we shall further explain the use of parenthetical verbs.

Probably and I believe. To say that something is probable, my imaginary objector will say, is to imply that it is reasonable to believe, that the evidence justifies a guarded claim for the truth of the statement ; but to say that someone believes something does not imply that it is reasonable for him to believe it, nor that the evidence justifies the guarded claim to truth which he makes. Therefore, the objector will continue, the difference between the use of the word 'believe' and the word 'probably' is not, as we have suggested, merely one of nuance and degree of impersonality, for in one case reasonableness is implied and in the other not. This objection can be met, but to do so we must first make a more general point.

Implied claims to reasonableness. Earlier it was said that there was an implied claim to truth whenever a sentence is uttered in a standard context, and the meaning of this was explained. Now we must add that whenever we make a statement in a standard context there is an implied claim to reasonableness, and this contention must be explained. Unless we are acting or story-telling, or preface our remarks with some such phrase as 'I know I'm being silly, but . . .' or, 'I admit it is unreasonable, but . . .' it is, I think, a presupposition of communication that people will not make statements, thereby implying their truth, unless they have some ground, however tenuous, for those statements. To say, 'The King is visiting Oxford to-morrow', and then, when asked why, to answer 'Oh, for no reason at all', would be to sin against the basic conventions governing the use of discourse. Therefore, I think, there is an implied claim to reasonableness which goes with all our statements, *i.e.* there is a convention that we will not make statements unless we are prepared to claim and defend their reasonableness. With this prolegomenon we can return to the question of the relation of belief and probability.

Defence of our account of belief and probability. We can now say, with less risk of being misunderstood, that when a man says, 'I believe that he is at home' or 'He is, I believe, at home', he both implies a (guarded) claim of the truth, and also implies a claim of the reasonableness of the statement that he is at home. Thus, if our objector points out that 'probably he is at home' implies, in the view of the speaker, the reasonableness and justifiability of the statement, we may answer that this is equally true of 'believe' in the first person present, in such a form as 'I believe that he is at home'. What our objector has failed to do is to notice the vast array of situations in which the verb 'believe' is used. We will now single out some, but only some, of these uses.

(A) Jones says, 'X is, I believe, at home'. Here Jones makes an implied guarded claim (that is the effect of adding 'I believe') to the truth and also an implied claim to the reasonableness, of the statement 'X is at home'. This is the case already examined.

(B) Smith, reporting Jones, says 'X is, Jones believes, at home'. This is *oratio obliqua*, reporting Jones' parenthetical use of the verb. Smith, by uttering the sentence, implies the truth and reasonableness of the statement that Jones has made the statement that X is at home (Jones thereby implying its truth and reasonableness with the conventional warning signal about the evidential situation).

(C) Smith, who has discovered that there has been a sudden railway stoppage, sees Jones making his habitual morning dash to the station, and says, 'Jones believes that the trains are working'. This is a new, and, however important, derivative, use of the verb 'believe'. Note that in this context Smith could not say, 'The trains, Jones believes, are working'. Jones, who has probably not considered the matter at all, is behaving in the way that someone who was prepared to say either 'The trains are running' or 'I believe that the trains are running' would behave (no doubt he would be prepared to say one or other of these things if he considered the matter). We thus, in a perfectly intelligible way, extend our use of the verb 'to believe' to those situations in which a person behaves as a person who has considered the evidence and was willing to say 'I believe' would consistently behave. In this case, but in this case alone, there is some point in saying that the verb is used dispositionally; but note that it is so used with reference to another use of 'believe'. It is also noteworthy that the verb cannot be so used in the first person present. To say 'I believe' in this sense is no more possible than to say 'I am under the delusion that'. 'I believe' is always used parenthetically, though not always purely so. If one recognizes that a belief that one has held is unreasonable, one either gives it up or is driven to saying 'I can't help believing'. This is psychological history, and carries with it no claim to truth or reasonableness.

Thus we see that 'Jones believes p' does not imply the reasonableness of p any more than 'It *seems* probable to Jones that p' does. On the other hand, both 'Probably p' and 'I believe that p' do imply the reasonableness of p. Thus, so far at least as we are concerned with the well-known objection about reasonableness, the parallel between 'probably' and 'I believe' has stood the test without difficulty.

At the risk of digression we may pause to comment on the history of the analysis of belief. Of old, philosophers tried to find a primary occurrent use of 'believe' as a psychological description; but in recent times the impossibility of this has been amply demonstrated, and philosophers have resorted to the so-called dispositional analysis, assuming that if the verb does not describe an occurrence it must describe a tendency to occurrences. There is, as we have seen, some point in the traditionalist reply to this that belief is here analysed as being the behaviour, if any, which would consistently accompany itself. A recognition that in the analysis of belief the non-descriptive parenthetical use is primary seems to me to illuminate and resolve this dispute.

This is all that can here be said about belief. It far from exhausts even all the relevant considerations, but our aim is not to examine any one parenthetical verb exhaustively; rather it is to shed new light on them all by presenting them as a group. I want to say the main things which may be said about a set of verbs which are not normally considered together as an aid to the thorough examination of each which I do not undertake. Individually, none of these verbs can be exhaustively treated in their capacity as parenthetical verbs and I must not be taken as suggesting that they can.

Further consideration of the third group. 'I guess' has nowadays a colloquial use in which its significance is, at the best, very indeterminate. But in a stricter use it serves to warn that what is being said is a guess. Suppose that one is asked 'Do you know who called this afternoon?' one may answer 'No, but I guess that it was Mrs. Jones'. Even here one is making an implied claim that it was Mr. Jones who called and that this is a reasonable thing to say; if one had said 'I guess that it was Mr. Stalin' one would have been making a clumsy joke and not really guessing at all. It seems to me to be quite impossible that anyone should think that here 'I guess' reports any mental events or any tendency to behave in any special way. It is put in to show that one is making one's statement without any specific evidence, that it is, in fact, a guess. What makes it a guess is not a mental act nor a disposition to behave in any way, but, if it is a genuine guess, its being said without any specific evidence, and its being potentially silly or lucky, not well-based or ill-supported. I cannot see that there is any essential difference between *guess* on the one hand and *know*, *opine*, and *suspect*, for example, on the other. The epistemological situation is more complicated in the latter set of cases, and some of them have special quirks in their use, *know* being a notorious example, but that is all. They are essentially the same sort of verb.

It might be worth while to compare this view of knowledge with what Professor Austin said in his valuable paper on 'Other Minds'.[1] Among other, less immediately relevant, things, Austin there distinguishes a class of performatory verbs and compares our use of *know* with our use of these verbs. In particular, he compares it with *guarantee*. But Austin is careful not to say that *know* is a performatory verb. He also points out important differences between the two verbs. I agree that the comparison which he makes between *know* and performatory verbs is just and illuminating. Parenthetical and performatory verbs have much in common as against ordinary descriptive verbs. I am not therefore disagreeing with Austin, but trying to locate the verb *to know* in a class which it was not his purpose to consider.

Relation of the parenthetical use of parenthetical verbs to their other uses. We have now distinguished a set of parenthetical verbs and have made the following main points about their parenthetical use in the first person of the present tense :

(i) They occur in the present perfect, not the continuous tense, though their use is different from that of the present perfect tense of verbs which have a present continuous tense.

(ii) Though, in a wide sense, psychological verbs, they are not psychologically descriptive.

(iii) They function rather like a certain class of adverbs to orient the hearer aright towards the statements with which they are associated. The ways in which they do this may be roughly indicated as being aids to placing the statements aright against the emotional, social, logical, and evidential background.

(iv) There is, as when the conjoined statements are used alone, an implied claim for the truth and reasonableness of these associated statements.

[1] *P.A.S.* Supp. Vol. XX (reprinted in L. L., II). Much of my approach was suggested by this paper.

But parenthetical verbs are not always used parenthetically in the first person present, to which use we have so far confined practically all our attention. We must now say something about their other uses. First, we may consider the positive analogy. In connexion with point (1) above, there is a positive analogy, though not a very tidy one. The analogy seems to hold completely in the case of some verbs; one cannot say, 'I was believing', 'he is believing', 'I was knowing', 'he was knowing', 'I was suspecting' or 'he was suspecting'. In the case of some other parenthetical verbs, we find a rare and anomalous imperfect tense. For example, we can say that you were admitting something if you were interrupted in the middle of a statement which you were making as an admission; or again, we can say that someone is deducing the consequences of a set of premisses, while he is stating a succession of things as deductions. But these are not genuine exceptions. In the case of another set of these verbs an imperfect is not so strange. At the end of an argument which I have put forth someone might say, for example, 'All the while you were assuming (presupposing, accepting) that so and so'. But this is not like the imperfect tense of ordinary verbs which report the continuance throughout a period of some occurrence. I was not throughout the period continuously doing an act of assumption which I carefully refrained from mentioning. Rather I was arguing as a man would reasonably argue who was prepared to say, 'I assume that so-and-so'; that is to say, I was arguing in a way that required so and so as a premiss if the argument was to be valid. I ought, therefore, to be willing to state so-and-so as a premiss. Thus here, too, the other use has to be understood in the light of the parenthetical use.

We must also note that, in general, these verbs can throughout be used in parenthesis; we can say 'Jones was, Smith admitted, able'. This seems to be so whenever the use is either definite *oratio obliqua* or, at any rate, a fair paraphrase. Some verbs, such as *deduce* and *admit*, seem always to be used in this way. But others, including, as we have already seen, *assume, presuppose,* and *believe,* are sometimes used, not of a man who has said, 'I assume (believe, presuppose)', or words to that effect, but of a man who behaves as a man reasonably would who was prepared to say that. In such a use, which is a genuine descriptive use, the parenthetical insertion (in a grammatical sense) of the verb seems to be impossible.

Continuing with the positive analogy, it seems to follow from the above that, except in some derivative uses, parenthetical verbs are not used as psychological descriptions in other parts of their conjugation any more than in the first person present. And even in these derivative uses, they seem to describe general behaviour rather than to be specifically mental.

The obvious negative analogy is, first, that the adverbs can only be used to correspond to the first person present (see point (iii) above). But this negative analogy is only so in a very limited way. If the adverbs did correspond exactly to the whole conjugation of the verb, then the conjugation would appear to be otiose. But the adverbs can be systematically correlated with the whole conjugation of the parenthetical verbs with the aid of the verb *to seem.* This point is illustrated by these two groups of four sentences : I regret that it is too late — Unfortunately it is too late ; He regretted that it was too late — it seemed to him to be unfortunately too late ; believe that it is lost — It is probably lost ; He believed that it was lost — It seemed to him to be probably lost.

The second obvious negative analogy is that in connexion with point (iv) what is said to be supposed, regretted, believed, etc., by others, or by oneself in the past, is not in general implied to be true or reasonable by the speaker (there are exceptions to this, in each case with a special reason, *know* being an obvious example). But here, again, this is exactly what is to be expected ; while 'He believed that it was lost', if said by me, does not imply a modified truth claim to reasonableness by me for the statement that it is lost, it does allege exactly that of the man to whom I refer. The same would be true of 'He suggested', 'He concluded', and so on. The point of these verbs remains as a kind of orientating signal, but when not in the first person present they report the statement-cum-signal rather than making it.

Beyond this I do not see my way to a general account of the relation of other uses of these verbs to their parenthetical use in the first person present. Such relation is in detail different and more or less close in the case of different verbs. Sometimes the parenthetical use seems to be the basic use and to be requisite for an understanding of the others; in other cases the illumination is of much lower candle-power. I have already indicated, for example, that I regard the parenthetical use as basic in the case of 'believe', and how I regard some other standard uses as being related to it. If the point of 'I know' is, roughly, to signal complete trust-worthiness for a statement made in the best evidential con-ditions, then the point of other uses of the verb may be said with reasonable accuracy to be the assertion that somebody else, or oneself at another time, was in a position in which he was entitled to say 'I know'. This is a different, though equally close, connexion, from that which we found in the case of belief. *Know* is a rather special case, but many parenthetical verbs are very similar to *believe* in this respect. Thus, if to say 'I presuppose that *p*' is to assert *p* with an indication that it is to be fitted into the logical context as an unproved premiss, so to say 'He presupposed that *p*' is either to say that he said *p* in that way, or, at one remove, to say that he put forward *p* as one would reasonably do if he were making a presupposition. This last use corresponds to the use of 'he believes that *p*' to indicate that someone is acting as he would reasonably act if he believed in the sense that he was willing to say 'I believe that *p*'. *Assume* is the same in this respect. *Deduce, conclude* and *guess* seem to be different again. We would never say that someone deduced *p* unless we believed that he had seen that *p* followed, even though it was a possible deduction and he appeared to accept *p*, which is a difference from the case of belief. On the other hand we can say that someone deduced p, where we are not ourselves prepared to treat p as a legitimate deduction, which is a difference from the case of knowledge. In the case of still other verbs which have a parenthetical use in the first person present this use does not seem to be at all central, a key to the understanding of other uses, as in the case of the verbs above mentioned. Examples of such verbs are *hear, rejoice, expect*; it is among these verbs that possible exceptions to some of our generalizations are to be sought.

It is perhaps worth mentioning a fact which will make it especially clear that too much generalization about the relation of other uses to the first person present is not possible. It is possible to manufacture parenthetical uses of verbs which are not normally parenthetical, even in the first person present, by the addition of the infinitive *to say*. Thus the verb 'I am sorry that' is normally a formula of apology or of self-reproach; but we can convert it into a parenthetical verb by the addition of *to say*: 'He is, I am sorry to say, unwell'. 'I am glad' can be treated in the same way, and so can other verbs. It thus becomes abundantly clear that we must not always try to see the parenthetical use as central. It might also be interesting to note at this point that we can use the device of the infinitive to get two parenthetical verbs into association with one sentence. Thus 'I regret to hear that p' combines 'I regret' and 'I hear', thereby orientating the hearer in two different ways at the same time. Compare 'I am sorry to conclude'. These points should make it clear that one cannot generalize too much about the relation of parenthetical to other uses of verbs.

Before attempting to draw the threads together, we will anticipate a possible criticism. It may be said that the grammatical feature of being used sometimes in parenthesis, in the grammatical sense, is not a sufficient test of a verb's parenthetical character in my sense. *Guarantee*, it may be said, is a performatory verb, since to say 'I guarantee' is to guarantee, not to orientate the hearer. Similarly to say 'I bet' is to bet, and to say 'I warrant' is to warrant. But we can put these verbs into parenthesis. My answer is that we do not put these verbs into parentheses when we are using them in a performatory way; to treat 'He'll come to a bad end, I guarantee' as a guarantee, or to ask for the odds or to cry 'Taken!' when someone says 'He'll forget to come, I bet' would be, as Aristotle would say, the mark of an uneducated man. We have here another case of the borrowing of another sort of verb for parenthetical uses. But it must, of course, be acknowledged that grammatical form is likely to be, here as elsewhere, but a fallible guide to the logical nature of a statement. In the end, the feature of being capable of occurring in parentheses is only a heuristic device for picking out a certain class of verbs, which is certainly different from, say, performatory verbs. A little more is said below about the relation of my philosophical thesis to the grammatical fact to which I draw attention.

Another objection which should be anticipated will be made on different grounds. It may be said that I have often given the appearance of conducting a grammatical rather than a philosophical investigation, and that, for example, the point about the lack of a present continuous tense could not be made in many languages. It is true that I have been using the grammatical features of English as a clue to philosophical points; but one can find similar, if different, grammatical clues in other languages. The actual point about parenthesis seems to apply to French; and one should try to explain why in French one says 'Je regrette de vous informer que votre fils est mort' and 'Je suis désolé du fait que votre fils est mort'. It would surely be out of the question to say 'Je regrette du fait que . . .'. Similarly, I am informed by those with a better command of German than I have that my point about the similar use of parenthetical verbs and some adverbs is reinforced by the fact that in German the verb would often be most naturally translated by an adverb, e.g. 'I regret' would often be translated most naturally by 'leider'. The fact that one makes use of the clues given by one's own language does not make the thesis inapplicable to other languages which have the same devices. There is, of course, no reason to hold dogmatically that every language has devices closely similar to the use of parenthetical verbs in English.

We may now sum up, and reiterate the point of what has been said in this paper. It must be admitted that there are verbs which may be said to describe a mental process, however mental processes have in the end to be analysed. Examples are *meditate, ponder, worry, imagine,* and *work out.* In the case of all these verbs one uses the present continuous tense to say what is happening now. Other verbs such as *wish, command, implore,* or *like, hate, approve, love* are interestingly different from the above and need discussion, but are not discussed here. But there is another class of verbs, different from any of the above, whose peculiarity is that they can be used either parenthetically in the normal grammatical sense, or else followed by *that*, in either case with an indicative clause. Further, they are so used in the present perfect tense, though not with the same dispositional force as are the general run of verbs. These verbs are the ones for which I have invented the technical name of parenthetical verbs. They are important because they include such philosophical war-horses as *know, believe,* and *deduce.* I have tried to show

(i) that when these verbs are used in the first person of the present tense, as is very clear when they occur grammatically in parenthesis, the assertion proper is contained in the indicative clause with which they are associated, which is implied to be both true and reasonable. They themselves have not, in such a use, any descriptive sense but rather function as signals guiding the hearer to a proper appreciation of the statement in its context, social, logical, or evidential. They are not part of the statement made, nor additional statements, but function with regard to a statement made rather as 'READ WITH CARE' functions in relation to a subjoined notice, or as the foot stamping and saluting can function in the Army to make clear that one is making an official report. Perhaps they can be compared to such stage-directions as 'said in a mournful (confident) tone' with reference to the lines of the play. They help the understanding and assessment of what is said rather than being a part of what is said.

(ii) I have further wished to show that in the case of many important verbs an understanding of this use of the verb is basic for a philosophical understanding of them; other uses of the verbs must be explained in terms of it.

(iii) It must, however, be clearly understood that there is a great deal which importantly needs saying about these verbs which has not been said here. I have not attempted to say all that there is to say about *know*, for instance, but only to bring out certain peculiarities which it has in common with a number of other verbs alongside of which it is not normally considered. But we must not be too modest; we have exposed such views as that these verbs report occurrences or tendencies to behave in certain ways. Most philosophers have been obsessed with the idea that verbs always describe some goings on — if not a simple event, then a complicated set of events. I have tried to pick out one class of verbs which do not report any goings on or even patterns of goings on at all. That the present discussion of them has been lucid and accurate, let alone final, may very well be doubted; that the set of characteristics which these parenthetical verbs share is significant and important is, however, something of which I feel very much more confident.

BIBLIOGRAPHY

Included here are some of the anthologies, books, and articles of ordinary-language (and some other) philosophers which have to do, at least in part, with language. An asterisk (*) indicates a bibliography. The following abbreviations are used: *Phil.* for *Philosophical, PAS* for *Proceedings of the Aristotelian Society,* sup. for supplementary volume (of the *PAS*), and U.P. for University Press. Anthologies are referred to by their editors' names (as Ayer for *Logical Positivism,* ed. A. J. Ayer) and Flew I, Flew II, and Flew III refer respectively to the First and Second Series of *Logic and Language,* and to *Essays in Conceptual Analysis,* all edited by Antony Flew.

Books and Anthologies

Austin, J. L.: *Philosophical Papers,* ed. J. O. Urmson and G. J. Warnock, Oxford: Clarendon Press, 1961.
————: *Sense and Sensibilia,* reconstructed by G. J. Warnock, Oxford: Clarendon Press, 1962.
————: *How to Do Things with Words,* ed. J. O. Urmson, Oxford: Clarendon Press, 1962.
*Ayer, A. J., ed.: *Logical Positivism,* Glencoe, Ill.: Free Press, 1959.
Black, Max: *Language and Philosophy,* Ithaca, N.Y.: Cornell U.P., 1949.
*————, ed.: *Philosophical Analysis,* Ithaca, N.Y.: Cornell U.P., 1950.
————: *Problems of Analysis,* Ithaca, N.Y.: Cornell U.P., 1954.
————: *Models and Metaphors,* Ithaca, N.Y.: Cornell U.P., 1962.
Butler, R. J., ed.: *Analytical Philosophy,* Oxford: Blackwell, 1963.
*Chappell, V. C., ed.: *The Philosophy of Mind,* Englewood Cliffs, N.J.: Prentice-Hall, 1962.
Flew, Antony, ed.: *Logic and Language,* First Series, Oxford: Blackwell, 1951.
————, ed.: *Logic and Language,* Second Series, Oxford: Blackwell, 1953.
————, ed.: *Essays in Conceptual Analysis,* London: Macmillan, 1956.
*Fodor, J., and Katz, J., eds.: *The Structure of Language,* Englewood Cliffs, N.J.: Prentice-Hall, 1964.
Hampshire, Stuart: *Thought and Action,* London: Chatto & Windus, 1959.

Holloway, John: *Language and Intelligence,* London: Macmillan, 1951.

Lewis, H. D., ed.: *Contemporary British Philosophy,* Third Series, London: George Allen & Unwin, 1956.

*Linsky, Leonard, ed.: *Semantics and the Philosophy of Language,* Urbana: University of Illinois Press, 1952.

Macdonald, Margaret, ed.: *Philosophy and Analysis,* Oxford: Blackwell, 1954.

Mace, C. A., ed.: *British Philosophy in the Mid-Century,* London: George Allen & Unwin, 1957.

Moore, G. E.: *Philosophical Papers,* London: George Allen & Unwin, 1959.

Nowell-Smith, P. H.: *Ethics,* Harmondsworth, Middlesex: Penguin, 1954.

*Passmore, John: *A Hundred Years of Philosophy,* London: Duckworth, 1957.

La Philosophie Analytique, Paris: Editions de Minuit, 1962.

Ryle, Gilbert: *Philosophical Arguments,* an inaugural lecture, Oxford: Clarendon Press, 1946; reprinted in Ayer.

————: *The Concept of Mind,* London: Hutchinson, 1949.

————: *Dilemmas,* Cambridge: Cambridge U.P., 1954.

Strawson, P. F.: *Introduction to Logical Theory,* London: Methuen, 1952.

————: *Individuals,* London: Methuen, 1959.

Toulmin, S. E.: *The Uses of Argument,* Cambridge: Cambridge U.P., 1958.

Urmson, J. O.: *Philosophical Analysis,* Oxford: Clarendon Press, 1956.

*Warnock, G. J.: *English Philosophy Since 1900,* London: Oxford U.P., 1958.

Wisdom, John: *Other Minds,* Oxford: Blackwell, 1952.

————: *Philosophy and Psychoanalysis,* Oxford: Blackwell, 1953.

Wittgenstein, Ludwig: *Philosophical Investigations,* tr. G. E. M. Anscombe, Oxford: Blackwell, 1953; 2nd ed., 1958.

————: *Remarks on the Foundations of Mathematics,* ed. G. H. von Wright, R. Rhees, and G. E. M. Anscombe, tr. G. E. M. Anscombe, Oxford: Blackwell, 1956.

————: *The Blue and Brown Books,* Oxford: Blackwell, 1958; 2nd ed., 1960.

Ziff, Paul: *Semantic Analysis,* Ithaca, N.Y.: Cornell U.P., 1960.

Articles

Arner, D.: "On Knowing," *Phil. Review,* LXVIII (1959), 84-92.

Austin, J. L.: "Other Minds," *PAS,* sup. XX (1946), 148-187; reprinted in Flew II and in *Phil. Papers.*

————: "Truth," *PAS,* sup. XXIV (1950), 111-128; reprinted in *Phil. Papers.*

Austin, J. L.: "How to Talk," *PAS,* LIII (1953), 227-246; reprinted in *Phil. Papers.*
———: "A Plea for Excuses," *PAS,* LVII (1957), 1-30; reprinted in *Phil. Papers.*
———: "Unfair to Facts," in *Phil. Papers.*
———: "Performative Utterances," in *Phil. Papers.*
Baier, K.: "The Ordinary Use of Words," *PAS,* LII (1952), 47-70.
———: "Contradiction and Absurdity," *Analysis,* 15 (1954), 31-40.
Baker, A. J.: "Presupposition and Types of Clause," *Mind,* LXV (1956), 368-378.
Berlin, I.: "Logical Translation," *PAS,* L (1950), 157-188.
———: "Empirical Propositions and Hypothetical Statements," *Mind,* LIX (1950), 289-312.
Black, Max: "The Semantic Definition of Truth," *Analysis,* 8 (1948), 49-63; reprinted in *Language and Philosophy.*
———: "Definition, Presupposition, and Assertion," *Phil. Review,* LXI (1952), 532-550; reprinted in *Problems of Analysis.*
———: "Saying and Disbelieving," *Analysis,* 13 (1952), 25-33; reprinted in *Problems of Analysis* and in Macdonald.
———: "Presupposition and Implication," in *A Way to the Philosophy of Science,* ed. Seizi Uyeda, Tokyo: Waseda U.P., 1958; reprinted in *Models and Metaphors.*
———: "Notes on the Meaning of 'Rule'," *Theoria,* XXIV (1958), 107-136 and 139-161; reprinted in *Models and Metaphors* as "The Analysis of Rules."
———: "Necessary Statements and Rules," *Phil. Review,* LXVII (1958), 313-341; reprinted in *Models and Metaphors.*
Cavell, S.: "Must We Mean What We Say?", *Inquiry,* I (1958), 172-212.
Chisholm, R.: "Intentionality and the Theory of Signs," *Phil. Studies,* III (1952), 56-63.
Duncan-Jones, Austin: "Further Questions About 'Know' and 'Think'," *Analysis,* 5 (1938), 74-83; reprinted in Macdonald.
Ebersole, F. B.: "The Definition of 'Pragmatic Paradox'," *Mind,* LXII (1953), 80-85.
Evans, J. L.: "On Meaning and Verification," *Mind,* LXII (1953), 1-19.
Feyerabend, P. K.: "Wittgenstein's *Phil. Investigations,*" *Phil. Review,* LXIV (1955), 449-483.
Fleming, B. N.: "On Avowals," *Phil. Review,* LXIV (1955), 614-625.
Fodor, J.: "What Do You Mean?", *Journal of Philosophy,* LVII (1960), 499-506.
———: "Of Words and Uses," *Inquiry,* IV (1961), 190-208.
———, and Katz, J.: "What's Wrong with the Philosophy of Language," *Inquiry,* V (1962), 197-237; reprinted in part in Fodor and Katz.
Geach, P. T.: "Subject and Predicate," *Mind,* LIX (1950), 461-482.
———: "Russell's Theory of Descriptions," *Analysis,* 10 (1950), 84-88.

Goddard, L.: "Counting," *Australasian Journal of Philosophy,* 39 (1961), 223-240.

Grant, C. K.: "Pragmatic Implication," *Philosophy,* XXXIII (1958), 303-324.

Grice, H. P.: "Meaning," *Phil. Review,* LXVI (1957), 377-388.

———: "The Causal Theory of Perception," *PAS,* sup. XXXV (1961), 121-152.

———, and Strawson, P. F.: "Defence of a Dogma," *Phil. Review,* LXV (1956), 141-158.

Hall, R.: "Assuming: One Set of Positing Words," *Phil. Review,* LXVII (1958), 52-75.

———: "Presuming," *Phil. Quarterly,* 11 (1961), 10-21.

Hamblin, C. L.: "Questions," *Australasian Journal of Philosophy,* 36 (1958), 159-168.

Hampshire, Stuart: "On Referring and Intending," *Phil. Review,* LXV (1956), 1-13.

———: "Identification and Existence," in Mace.

———, and Hart, H. L. A.: "Decision, Intention and Certainty," *Mind,* LXVII (1958), 1-12.

Hare, R. M.: "Freedom of the Will," *PAS,* sup. XXV (1951), 201-216.

———: "Philosophical Discoveries," *Mind,* LXIX (1960), 145-162.

Hart, H. L. A.: "The Ascription of Responsibility and Rights," *PAS,* XLIX (1949), 171-194; reprinted in Flew I.

———: "A Logician's Fairy Tale," *Phil. Review,* LX (1951), 198-212.

Hungerland, Isabel C.: "Contextual Implication," *Inquiry,* III (1960), 211-258.

Lemmon, E. J.: "On Sentences Verifiable by Their Use," *Analysis,* 22 (1962), 86-89.

MacIver, A. M.: "Some Questions About 'Know' and 'Think'," *Analysis,* 5 (1938), 43-50; reprinted in Macdonald.

Malcolm, Norman: "Certainty and Empirical Statements," *Mind,* LI (1942), 18-46.

———: "Defending Common Sense," *Phil. Review,* LVIII (1949), 201-220.

———: "Philosophy for Philosophers," *Phil. Review,* LX (1951), 329-340.

———: "Knowledge and Belief," *Mind,* LXI (1952), 178-189.

———: "Discussion: Wittgenstein's *Phil. Investigations,*" *Phil. Review,* LXIII (1954), 530-559; reprinted in Chappell.

———: "Knowledge of Other Minds," *Journal of Philosophy,* LV (1958), 969-978; reprinted in Chappell.

Mayo, Bernard: " 'Rules' of Language," *Phil. Studies,* II (1951), 1-7.

Midgley, G. C. J.: "Linguistic Rules and Language Habits," *PAS,* sup. XXIX (1955), 185-212.

Moore, G. E.: "Is Existence a Predicate?", *PAS,* sup. XV (1936), 175-188; reprinted in Flew II and in *Phil. Papers.*

Nowell-Smith, P. H.: "Contextual Implication and Ethical Theory," *PAS,* sup. XXXVI (1962), 1-18.

O'Connor, D. J.: "Pragmatic Paradoxes," *Mind,* LVII (1948), 358-359.

Passmore, John: "Professor Ryle's Use of 'Use' and 'Usage'," *Phil. Review,* LXIII (1954), 58-64.

Ryle, Gilbert: "Categories," *PAS,* XXXVIII (1938), 189-206; reprinted in Flew II.

————: "Discussion: Meaning and Necessity," *Philosophy,* XXIV (1949), 69-76.

————: " 'If', 'So', and 'Because'," in Black.

————: "Heterologicality," *Analysis,* 11 (1951), 61-69; reprinted in Macdonald.

Searle, John R.: "Meaning and Speech Acts," *Phil. Review,* LXXI (1962), 423-432.

Shwayder, D. S.: "Self-Defeating Pronouncements," *Analysis,* 16 (1956), 74-85.

————: "Uses of Language and Uses of Words," *Theoria,* XXVI (1960), 31-43.

Strawson, P. F.: "Truth," *Analysis,* 9 (1949), 83-97; reprinted in Macdonald.

————: "Truth," *PAS,* sup. XXIV (1950), 129-156.

————: "Critical Notice: Wittgenstein's *Phil. Investigations,*" *Mind,* LXIII (1954), 70-99.

————: "A Reply to Mr. Sellars," *Phil. Review,* LXIII (1954), 216-231.

Toulmin, S. E.: "Probability," *PAS,* sup. XXIV (1950), 27-62; reprinted in Flew III.

————: "Critical Notice: R. Carnap's *Logical Foundations of Probability,*" *Mind,* LXII (1953), 86-98.

Urmson, J. O.: "On Grading," *Mind,* LIX (1950), 145-169; reprinted in Flew II.

————: "Some Questions Concerning Validity," *Revue Internationale de Philosophie,* 7 (1953), 217-229.

Vendler, Zeno: "Verbs and Times," *Phil. Review,* LXVI (1957), 143-160.

————: "Each and Every, Any and All," *Mind,* LXXI (1962), 145-160.

Waismann, Friedrich: "Verifiability," *PAS,* sup. XIX (1945), 119-150; reprinted in Flew I.

————: "Analytic-Synthetic," in installments in *Analysis*: I: 10 (1949), 25-40; II: 11 (1950), 25-38; III: 11 (1951), 49-61; IV: 11 (1951), 115-124; V: 13 (1952), 1-14; VI: 13 (1953), 73-89. V is reprinted in *The Importance of Language,* ed. Max Black, Englewood Cliffs, N.J.: Prentice-Hall, 1962.

————: "Language Strata," in Flew II.

Warnock, G. J.: "Verification and the Use of Language," *Revue Internationale de Philosophie,* 5 (1951), 307-322.

————: "Discussion: Empirical Propositions and Hypothetical Statements," *Mind,* LX (1951), 90-94.

Weitz, Morris: "Oxford Philosophy," *Phil. Review,* LXII (1953), 187-233.

Wheatley, J. M. O.: "Deliberative Questions," *Analysis,* 15 (1955), 49-60.

White, A. R.: "Synonymous Expressions," *Phil. Quarterly,* 8 (1958), 193-207.

Wisdom, John: "Philosophical Perplexity," *PAS,* XXXVII (1937), 71-88; reprinted in *Philosophy and Psychoanalysis.*

————: "Metaphysics and Verification," *Mind,* XLVII (1938), 452-498; reprinted in *Philosophy and Psychoanalysis.*

Wolterstorff, Nicholas: "Referring and Existing," *Phil. Quarterly,* 11 (1961), 335-349.

Wood, O. P.: "The Force of Linguistic Rules," *PAS,* LI (1951), 313-328.

Yard ring about it; it contrasts well with such expressions as 'spec-ulation', 'hypothesis', 'system-building' and even 'preaching' and 'writing poetry'. On the other hand it is a hopelessly misleading word in some important respects. It falsely suggests, for one thing, that any sort of careful elucidation of any sorts of complex or subtle ideas will be a piece of philosophizing; as if the judge, in explaining to the members of the jury the differences between man-slaughter and murder, was helping them out of a philosophical quandary. But, even worse, it suggests that philosophical pro-blems are like the chemist's or the detective's problems in this respect, namely that they can and should be tackled piecemeal. Finish problem A this morning, file the answer, and go on to pro-blem B this afternoon. This suggestion does violence to the vital fact that philosophical problems inevitably interlock in all sorts of ways. It would be patently absurd to tell someone to finish the problem of the nature of truth this morning, file the answer and go on this afternoon to solve the problem of the relations between naming and saying, holding over until tomorrow problems about the concepts of existence and non-existence. This is, I think, why at the present moment philosophers are far more inclined to liken their task to that of the cartographer than to that of the chemist or the detective. It is the foreign relations, not the domestic constitu-tions of sayables that engender logical troubles and demand logical arbitration.

9 PROPER NAMES

by John R. Searle

Do proper names have senses ? Frege[1] argues that they must have senses, for, he asks, how else can identity statements be other than trivially analytic. How, he asks, can a statement of the form a = b, if true, differ in cognitive value from a = a ? His answer is that though " a " and " b " have the same referent they have or may have different *senses*, in which case the statement is true, though not analytically so. But this solution seems more appropriate where " a " and " b " are both non-synonymous definite descriptions, or where one is a definite description and one is a proper name, than where both are proper names. Consider, for example, statements made with the following sentences :

(*a*) " Tully = Tully " is analytic.

But is

(*b*) " Tully = Cicero " synthetic ?

If so, then each name must have a different sense, which seems at first sight most implausible, for we do not ordinarily think of proper names as having a sense at all in the way that predicates do ; we do not, *e.g.* give definitions of proper names. But of course (*b*) gives us information not conveyed by (*a*). But is this information about words ? The statement is not about words.

For the moment let us consider the view that (*b*) is, like (*a*), analytic. A statement is analytic if and only if it is true in virtue of linguistic rules alone, without any recourse to empirical investigation. The linguistic rules for using the name " Cicero " and the linguistic rules for using the name " Tully " are such that both names refer to, without describing, the same identical object ; thus it seems the truth of the identity can be established solely by recourse to these rules and the statement is analytic. The sense in which the statement is informative is the sense in which any analytic statement is informative ; it illustrates or exemplifies certain contingent facts about words, though it does not of course describe these facts. On this account the difference between (*a*) and (*b*) above is not as great as might at first seem. Both are analytically true, and both illustrate contingent facts about our use of symbols. Some philosophers claim that (*a*) is

[1] *Translations from the Philosophical Writings of Gottlob Frege*, edited by Geach and Black, pp. 56 ff.

fundamentally different from (*b*) in that a statement using this form will be true for any arbitrary substitution of symbols replacing " Tully ".[1] This, I wish to argue, is not so. The fact that the same mark refers to the same object on two different occasions of its use is a convenient but contingent usage, and indeed we can easily imagine situations where this would not be the case. Suppose, *e.g.* we have a language in which the rules for using symbols are correlated not simply with a type-word, but with the order of its token appearances in the discourse. Some codes are like this. Suppose the first time an object is referred to in our discourse it is referred to by " x ", the second time by " y ", etc. For anyone who knows this code " x = y " is trivially analytic, but " x=x " is senseless. This example is designed to illustrate the similarity of (*a*) and (*b*) above ; both are analytic and both give us information, though each gives us different information, about the use of words. The truth of the statements that Tully = Tully and Tully = Cicero both follow from linguistic rules. But the fact that the words " Tully = Tully " are used to express this identity is just as contingent as, though more universally conventional in our language than, the fact that the words " Tully = Cicero " are used to express the identity of the same object.

This analysis enables us to see how both (*a*) and (*b*) could be used to make analytic statements and how in such circumstances we could acquire different information from them, without forcing us to follow either of Frege's proposed solutions, *i.e.* that the two propositions are in some sense about words (*Begriffsschrift*) or his revised solution, that the terms have the same reference but different senses (*Sinn und Bedeutung*). But though this analysis enables us to see how a sentence like (*b*) *could* be used to make an analytic statement it does not follow that it could not also be used to make a synthetic statement. And indeed some identity statements using two proper names are clearly synthetic ; people who argue that Shakespeare was Bacon are not advancing a thesis about language. In what follows I hope to examine the connection between proper names and their referents in such a manner as to show how both kinds of identity statement are possible and in so doing to show in what sense a proper name has a sense.

I have so far considered the view that the rules governing the use of a proper name are such that it is used to refer to and not to describe a particular object, that it has reference but not sense. But now let us ask how it comes about that we are able to refer

[1] W. V. Quine, *From a Logical Point of View*, esp. chap. 2.

to a particular object by using its name.   How, for example, do
we learn and teach the use of proper names ?   This seems quite
simple—we identify the object, and, assuming that our student
understands the general conventions governing proper names,
we explain that this word is the name of that object.   But unless
our student already knows another proper name of the object,
we can only *identify* the object (the necessary preliminary to
teaching the name) by ostension or description ; and, in both
cases, we identify the object in virtue of certain of its characteristics.   So now it seems as if the rules for a proper name must
somehow be logically tied to particular characteristics of the
object in such a way that the name has a sense as well as a
reference ; indeed, it seems it could not have a reference unless it
did have a sense, for how, unless the name has a sense, is it to be
correlated with the object ?

Suppose someone answers this argument as follows : " The
characteristics located in teaching the name are not the rules for
using the proper name : they are simply pedagogic devices
employed in teaching the name to someone who does not know
how to use it.   Once our student has identified the object to
which the name applies he can forget or ignore these various
descriptions by means of which he identified the object, for they
are not part of the sense of the name ; the name does not have a
sense.   Suppose, for example, that we teach the name ' Aristotle '
by explaining that it refers to a Greek philosopher born in
Stagira, and suppose that our student continues to use the name
correctly, that he gathers more information about Aristotle,
and so on.   Let us suppose it is discovered later on that Aristotle
was not born in Stagira at all, but in Thebes.   We will not now
say that the meaning of the name has changed, or that Aristotle
did not really exist at all.   In short, explaining the use of a name
by citing characteristics of the object is not giving the rules
for the name, for the rules contain no descriptive content at all.
They simply correlate the name to the object independently of
any descriptions of it."

But is the argument convincing ?   Suppose most or even all
of our present factual knowledge of Aristotle proved to be true
of no one at all, or of several people living in scattered countries
and in different centuries ?   Would we not say for this reason
that Aristotle did not exist after all, and that the name, though
it has a conventional sense, refers to no one at all ?   On the above
account, if anyone said that Aristotle did not exist, this must
simply be another way of saying that " Aristotle " denoted no
objects, and nothing more ; but if anyone did say that Aristotle